HARMONIAN MAN

SELECTED WRITINGS OF CHARLES FOURIER

MARK POSTER is an Assistant Professor of History at the University of California, Irvine. He received his M.A. and Ph.D. in History at New York University, working with Professor Frank E. Manuel. His book *The Utopian Thought of Restif de la Bretonne* appeared recently. Among the articles he has written is "Fourier's Concept of the Group." He is currently at work on a study of French thought since World War II which will treat the relationship of Marxism to Existentialism.

SUSAN ANN HANSON received degrees in French from San Diego State College and the University of California at Irvine. She has also studied in France at the University of Grenoble and at the Sorbonne in Paris.

HARMONIAN MAN

SELECTED WRITINGS OF CHARLES FOURIER

EDITED WITH AN INTRODUCTION BY MARK POSTER

—WITH NEW TRANSLATIONS BY SUSAN HANSON—

ANCHOR BOOKS

DOUBLEDAY & COMPANY, INC., GARDEN CITY, NEW YORK

1971

The Anchor Books edition is the first publication of
HARMONIAN MAN: SELECTED WRITINGS OF CHARLES FOURIER
Anchor Books edition: 1971

Library of Congress Catalog Card Number 70–150868
Copyright © 1971 by Mark Poster
Printed in the United States of America

For Marianne and Winifred

CONTENTS

ABBREVIATIONS AND NOTE
ON THE TRANSLATION

OC for *Oeuvres complètes de Charles Fourier* (Paris: Duverger, 1841–70) 6 vols.

NMA for *Le nouveau monde amoureux*, ed. S. Debout-Oleszkiewicz (Paris: Editions Anthropos, 1967).

AP for *L'attraction passionnée*, ed. René Scherer (Paris: Pauvert, 1967).

PHS for *Passions of the Human Soul*, trans. John R. Morell (London: Hippolyte Bailliere, 1851).

TSO for *The Theory of Social Organization*, ed. A. Brisbane (New York: Somerby, 1876).

About one half of the selections are reprinted from nineteenth-century translations. In the case of the single selection from *Passions of the Human Soul* this was done because the French is still in manuscript form in Paris and these manuscripts were not available to me. For the rest, I chose to use the old translation from Brisbane's edition rather than do a new one because the nineteenth-century style is close to Fourier's and could not be done as well today. Our translation has attempted to preserve the spirit of Fourier's exceedingly difficult prose. I have also used parts of *The Theory of Social Organization* because the book is rare, being available only in a few libraries. However, to simply reprint the book in its entirety would falsify the reader's impression of Fourier's thought, because Brisbane, and even Fourier's French disciples, systematically repressed their master's criticisms of the bourgeois family and bourgeois patterns of love and sexuality. They limited themselves to his critiques of the bourgeois economic system and the educational system. Furthermore, no representative collection of Fourier's writings can exclude *Le nouveau monde amoureux,* which is as important in a re-evaluation of Fourier as the *Economic and Philosophic Manuscripts* are to Marx. Thus, I have reprinted Brisbane's translation on the topics of capitalism and education and used new translations on the ideas of love, the group, and the family. At the end of each selection I have indicated its source; all those from OC, NMA, and AP were translated by Miss Hanson for this collection.

The missing words in NMA are explained by S. Debout-Oleszkiewicz on p. o [*sic*] as follows "All blanks in this text, indicated by my empty brackets, correspond to words skipped by Fourier. . . ." Fourier never went back to fill in the words; the words that do appear in brackets in this book are my own interpolations.

MP

THE WRITINGS OF CHARLES FOURIER

INTRODUCTION

CHARLES FOURIER AND FRENCH SOCIETY

Fourier's literary career spanned the Napoleonic Empire, the Restoration regimes of Louis XVIII and Charles X, and the "Bourgeois Monarchy" of Louis Philippe. His thought reflects the dramatic contrasts of these regimes: the promise of vast social reorganization of Napoleon, the futile attempts to undo 1789 by the Restoration, and the unspectacular denouement of cynicism and corruption in government after 1830. Having witnessed the upheavals of the 1790s, the abrupt uprooting of a traditional social order which, though much of its strengths had already been eroded, still presented a façade of impervious solidity, Fourier and many of his contemporaries yearned for the establishment of a new order. Napoleon only served to exacerbate this hope since he seemed quite capable of reforming society into new and more humane structures.

Fourier's social thought, mirroring these sharply contrasting promises, sought to establish a new social world which would end forever the disturbing and tragic upheavals he had experienced. In mapping out his projects of reform Fourier wandered along new channels well outside the markers reached by the philosophes of the eighteenth century toward a new horizon of socialism.

The place reserved for Fourier in the history of socialism by Engels,[1] has made it difficult for historians to read Fourier with-

---

[1] F. Engels, "Socialism: Utopian and Scientific," in *Marx and Engels, Basic Writings on Politics and Philosophy*, ed. by L. Feuer (New York: Anchor, 1959) 76.

out bias. Stamped as a utopian by the pope of socialist ortho-
doxy, it has been Fourier's misfortune to be misunderstood by
generation after generation of scholars. Seen in his own terms, in
the context of his own intellectual problematic, Fourier emerges
as a brilliant pioneer of questions that have not been fully examined until the twentieth century. The fate of the passions in
bourgeois society, the limitations of the nuclear family, the prospects of communal education, the types of love relations in industrial society, the possibility of attractive labor, the nature of
groups and the role of sex in the formation of groups, the de-
humanization of market relations, the effects of psychic frustration, the possibility of a non-repressive society—all of these questions, which were dropped by the socialist tradition and never
even raised by liberalism have only recently been resurrected
from the oblivion fated for all questions relating merely to the
"superstructure," by Wilhelm Reich, N. O. Brown, Herbert
Marcuse, and the imaginative irreverence of the Youth Culture.
With a thoroughgoing re-examination of the meaning of human
liberation now fully under way, students of the history of ideas
may belatedly assess the thought of Charles Fourier with the
requisite undaunted imagination. The recent republication of
Fourier's works,[2] including the appearance for the first time of
Le Nouveau monde amoureux, lightens the task of reassessment.
This present volume of selections is intended to introduce the
English-reading public to Fourier,[3] giving the reader the full

[2] *Oeuvres complètes de Charles Fourier* (Paris: Editions anthropos,
1967) 12 Vols.
[3] Previous English translations are careless and inadequate. The
best is a translation by Hugh Doherty of manuscripts entitled
Passions of the Human Soul (London: Bailliere, 1851) 2 Vols. and
reprinted by Augustus Kelly (New York, 1968). A poor selection
from the first six volumes of *Oeuvres complètes*, which neglects to
indicate where the excerpts were taken, is *Theory of Social Organization* (New York: Somerly, 1876) with an introduction by Albert
Brisbane, a New York journalist who proselytized for Fourier in the
United States. Finally, there is a short book, *Selections from the
Works of Fourier*, trans. by J. Franklin (London: Sonnenschein,
1901) with a translated introduction of Charles Gide's essay. Gide
was a prominent French economist. This book's drawback is that the

range of Fourier's central concepts and withholding nothing of the boldness of his mind.

FOURIER'S LIFE

What immediately strikes the reader of Fourier is the contrast between the pettiness of his life, his cramped writing style, his compulsive personality, his monkish bachelorhood and lonely ways, on the one hand, and his effusive, fecund, sensual imagination on the other. Born in Besançon in 1772 to a cloth merchant of moderate means, Fourier was raised in the trivial atmosphere of the provincial petite bourgeoisie. After only a spotty education, his parents sought to quickly get the boy, Charles, earning his own keep. At an early age Charles was initiated into the world of commerce, and his immediate response was rebellious. "I am a child of the marketplace, born and brought up in mercantile establishments. I have witnessed the infamies of commerce with my own eyes, and I shall not describe them from hearsay as our moralists do."[4] Charles was outraged by the general deceptiveness of human relations in the marketplace and he made it his life task to expose and help transform these conditions. The flagrant contradictions between Christian moral homilies and bourgeois practices were a favorite target of Fourier's venom.

From that time on I noted the contrast which prevails between commerce and truth. I was taught in the catechism and at school that one must never lie; then I was taken to the store to be trained from an early age in the noble occupation of lying, that is, in *the art of selling*. Shocked by the chicanery and the fraud which I saw, I proceeded to take aside the merchants who were the victims and to reveal the deception to them. One of them in his complaint mala-

---

selections are exclusively about Fourier's ideas on commerce and industry.

[4] Cited in Frank E. Manuel, *Prophets of Paris* (New York: Harper and Row, 1965), 200.

droitly gave me away, which cost me a thorough spanking.
My parents, seeing that I had a taste for truth, cried out
in a voice of reprobation: "This child will never be worth
anything in commerce." In fact I conceived a secret aversion for commerce, and at the age of seven I swore the
oath which Hannibal had sworn against Rome: I swore
an eternal hatred of commerce.[5]

Because Fourier rarely wrote about himself it would be difficult to make firm psychological judgments about him, but from
the evidence of this passage, one might speculate that his rebellion against society was bound up with his rebellion against his
parents. His avowed "eternal hatred of commerce" expressed as
well his hatred of his parents. Fourier's struggle with his father
and with the world of commerce continued after his father's
death as the inheritance went to Fourier only if he managed the
family store. Fourier *père* was unrelenting in his efforts to force
his son into the role of a merchant.

When Fourier became an independent entrepreneur he entered the larger stage of social affairs as a counterrevolutionary
backing the Lyons uprising against the Republic in 1793, an
event which cost Fourier all his wealth in destroyed inventories.
After this misfortune Fourier was never to recoup his losses, and
his career in commerce shifted from entrepreneur to employee.
Living in shabby apartments, frequenting run-down cafes, working in a variety of lowly positions in the drabber corners of the
new industrial world, Fourier endured an unexciting existence
with periods of grim poverty.

After several articles in Lyons journals, Fourier published
Théorie des quatre mouvements et des destinées générales in
1808, the first major statement of his total vision. Fourteen years
later came *Traité de l'association domestique-agricole*, subse-
quently called *Théorie de l'unité universelle*. Without adding
much new material, Fourier continued his battle against capitalism with *Le Nouveau monde industriel et sociétaire, ou in-*

[5] Cited in N. Riasanovsky, *The Teachings of Charles Fourier*
(Berkeley: University of California Press, 1969), 3.

vention du procédé d'industrie attrayante et naturelle, distribuée en séries passionnées in 1829. His last major published work, appearing only shortly before his death and indicating the undiminished intensity of his energies, was *La Fausse industrie morcelée, répugnante, mensongère et l'antidote, l'industrie naturelle, combinée, attrayante, véridique, donant quadruple produit et perfection extrème en toutes qualités. Mosaique des faux progrès, des ridicules et circles vicieux de la Civilization. Parallèle des deux mondes industriels, l'ordre morcelé et l'ordre combiné,* a title which, if read carefully, reveals much of Fourier's thought. Between *Théorie des quatre mouvements* (1808) and *Théorie de l'unité universelle* (1822), Fourier worked on a manuscript entitled *Le Nouveau monde amoureux* which has only been in print since 1967[6] and which demonstrates the centrality of a sexual revolution in his socialism.

One of the most remarkable features of the thought of the early-nineteenth-century socialists was its sanguinary expectation of the imminent enactment of far-reaching social change. Reason to them was easily transmutable into practice. Henri de Saint-Simon, for example, wrote letters to Napoleon offering advice on the reform of European institutions, apparently confident that the Emperor would see the wisdom of his suggestions and carry them out. The English socialist Robert Owen also anticipated quick results when he made a report to Parliament on his radical social experiments. England's rulers having paid no heed to him, Owen invited Europe's most prominent leaders to witness New Lanark (an experimental community based on socialist principles) to experience firsthand the transformation of a ragged pack of ne'er-do-wells, drunkards, thieves, and prostitutes, into a respectable working-class community through the implementation of a few simple principles of social engineering, and to take back with them to the Continent what they learned and to act upon it.

Fourier was himself also deluded into thinking that communism, being the only rational principle of human organization,

[6] (Paris: Editions anthropos).

would be adopted by the aristocratic-bourgeois ruling class as a matter of course. Lacking only adequate financing for the first Phalanstery which would be so attractive a model community that it would spread quickly throughout France, Europe, and the world, Fourier waited, during the last years of his life, in his apartment every day at noon for a philanthropist to appear offering to begin the final phase of human emancipation. Although no one came, no one, that is, with enough capital, Fourier attracted quite a following: from the United States, where scores of Fourierist communes were begun in the desperate years of the 1840s, to Rumania, of all places, where a nobleman converted his estate into a Phalanstery only to have it burned to the ground by self-righteous, neighboring peasants who were so obtuse as to see joyous free love as obscene debauchery. In intellectual circles too Fourier's doctrines scored a rapid success only to be dampened by the pessimistic mood that engulfed Europe after the failures of the Revolutions of 1848. In Paris, the center of radical intellectual ferment in the 1830s and 1840s, Fourier and his disciples did battle with the opposing total vision of the Saint-Simonians. As far away as Russia, in the Petrachevsky circle, a young socialist named Fyodor Dostoyevsky argued with his companions whether Fourier or Saint-Simon had found the key to history and the solution to all human woes. After 1848 more hard-bitten doctrines of world transformation gained wide acceptance, and Fourierism was not considered again until André Breton and his Surrealist friends rediscovered the relationship of sex and socialism in the twentieth century. The eccentric salesman who waited for a knock at his door would undoubtedly have had a wry smile on his face if he had seen this belated caller. The strange doctrines of Charles Fourier have received an appropriately strange fate.

L'Écart Absolu AND THE IDEA OF GOD

For the utopian socialist the modern world lacked coherence both spiritually and materially, in its values and ideas and in its social and economic structures. Given this perception of contemporary reality—a perception shared by most creative intellectuals of the early nineteenth century—Fourier set out to create a total system of thought that would serve as a basis for reconstituting European society. Indeed, Fourier's writings do embody a comprehensive re-evaluation of man's condition, but unevenly. For some of the questions he faced, Fourier's answers were sharp, novel, and provocative; others were bizarre, inane, and uninspired. Among his more fantastic notions were those about metaphysics, cosmogony, and history.

The stance Fourier took toward previous philosophy was one that he termed *l'écart absolu,* the total rejection of the corpus of European thought. Of the 400,000 books he estimated were devoted to questions about man and nature, scarcely one was worthy of reading. Indeed, Fourier did not bother with them very much. Only Newton was consistently praised in his pages for having discovered the mechanics of nature. Now Charles Fourier would expand Newton's work to the mechanics of society and the passions. What made it possible for Fourier to dismiss so cavalierly the work of earlier intellectual giants was his sense that they had not escaped the limitations of their times in their investigations of moral questions. Moralists had condemned three-fourths of man's passions, his actions and desires, banishing them from human possibility without realizing that there was nothing inherently evil in the passions, but rather it was the way they were expressed in society that made them seem injurious and dangerous. Fourier sensed what Marcuse has called "surplus repression" which could be accounted for by improper social organization.[7] Since previous philosophers always justified the unnecessary repression of the passions, Fourier refused to consider their ideas. Thus, *l'écart absolu* stemmed from the sense of the irrationality of moral restrictions and the vast possibilities of liberation implied in abolishing them.

Starting with *l'écart absolu,* Fourier proceeded to raise the question of the nature of God. The fact of God's existence was all Fourier needed to prove the perfectibility of man; God was

[7] *Eros and Civilization* (New York: Vintage, 1962).

good, the universe was created on a wise plan, and it was man's task to realize this plan. This deist or pantheist God had created the universe which consisted in essence of passion, which, in turn, moved according to mathematical principles. Fourier demonstrated the mathematical organization of the passions on the principle of analogy. Certainly the idea of mathematical passions is no more than a myth, but one which Fourier consistently held. The best way of understanding Fourier's concept of God is to think of the passions as a substructure of reality, for Fourier often spoke of God as a source of the passions or as identical with them.

COSMOGONY AND HISTORY

If Fourier's concept of God is arbitrary and even gratuitous, his cosmogony is weird and fantastic. The galaxy was a vast field of copulation with planets engaging in sexual relations which affected the tone and degree of the passions throughout the universe.[8] All matter was permeated by the stuff of life, the passions, rendering the galaxy fundamentally biological. In the Romantic imagination of the lonely salesman from Bescançon, the universe lost its dead, mechanical image acquired since the intellectual triumph of the Newtonian world-machine, and became organic, pulsating with life throughout. Biological more than physical in nature, the universe evolved and its history had a pattern that was marked by the varying movements of the passions. In short, the universe had a life of its own, and history was characterized by the cycle of its birth, childhood, maturity, and eventual death. The history of mankind was but a small chapter in the longer history of the passions. The evolution of the cosmos was a cycle taking eighty thousand years to complete, composed of forty thousand years of "ascending vibrations" and an equal period of "descending vibrations." The first half of the cycle was divided into epochs of chaos, for five thousand years,

8 Helène Tuzet, "Deux types de cosmogonies vitalistes: 2. Charles Fourier, hygieniste du cosmos," *Revue des sciences humaines*, 1961, N. Sér. F., 101, 37–47.

and harmony, for thirty-five thousand years. Contemporary Europe approached the final years of "ascending chaos." The ages of savagery, patriarchy, and barbarism preceded the age of civilization, and the last did not differ fundamentally from the earlier epochs. Fourier intended his philosophy of history to place bourgeois civilization in close proximity to primitive society because both were repressive social systems. Judged by the norm of passionate fulfillment, European society was backward and underdeveloped. Fourier suggested that the degree of liberty women had was another sound standard of social progress, and patriarchal Europe again scored poorly.

Still, Fourier was optimistic, seeing in man's future thirty-five thousand years of radically expanded levels of passionate gratification. Following his idiosyncratic astrological readings, he prophesied a beneficial increase in the passionate intensity of the Earth which would gradually transform the briny seas into a tangy lemonade flavor, the neutral smelling atmosphere into a perfumed mist, and the pests of man, fleas, rats, crocodiles, and lions, into far more pleasant species, anti-fleas, anti-rats, anti-crocodiles, and anti-lions. However ludicrous these prophesies may be, they nevertheless emphasized what was central to Fourier's social thought: man had far greater capacities, especially emotional, than he now experienced. With proper changes in social organization the limits of man's happiness as they were presently perceived would vanish, and glorious new delights would appear to the man of the future as the normal condition. This expansive ideal of human potentials was typical of contemporary Romantic thought.

THE PASSIONS

Starting with these strange notions of God, cosmogony, and history, Fourier earned Engels' high praise by uncovering the ways in which man's passions were distorted and unfulfilled in commercial and industrial society. While elaborating his criticism of contemporary bourgeois capitalism, Fourier revealed European society as wasteful of human potentials and psychologi-

cally repressive. Man's passions, he declared, were nothing less
than "hungers," ignored or frustrated only with great hurt to
man's constitution. The passions of the human soul were irre-
pressible needs which, when repressed, were distorted. Fourier's
notion of the transformations passions undergo was a clear antic-
ipation of Freud. More significantly, his idea that the passions
had a "need" for direct expression was a denial of the bourgeois
image of man as an "empty cabinet," a tabula rasa, a machine
for the processing of sensations that had been so compelling to
Locke, Helvetius, d'Holbach, Bentham, and the Enlightenment
traditions in France and England in their struggles against the
pessimistic Christian image of man. Fourier found a content to
human nature, the passions, that limited the environmentalism
of sensationalist psychology and utilitarian moral theories, fixed
a boundary to the malleability of man, and directed legislators
to shape their statutes to allow the full expression of man's
needs. His attack on bourgeois forms of moral theory and psychology began with an appreciation of the need to establish
social institutions that were psychologically gratifying.

Over and over again Fourier denounced the hallmarks of
eighteenth-century thought: man could not be viewed as an
abstraction, men were not equal, men were not at bottom isolated individuals but interdependent parts of a social whole. To
combat the bourgeois image of man Fourier elaborated a complex notion of the passions that refuted the assumptions that
men were uniform and the same in their essential natures. Looking to the passions as the essence of man, rather than to reason
where there were more grounds for stressing human homogene-
ity, Fourier noted the diversity and multiplicity of human types.
There were, he claimed, no fewer than 810 fundamentally different varieties of men and the same number for women. Society
was perfected only through the fulfillment of each type interact-
ing with all other types. Hence the ideal community numbered
about 1600 and no more. The anarchic implosion of people into
cities guided only by the capitalist principles of the labor market
and private property caused social chaos. Men had to have control over their social relations and decide what size community

was most suitable and overcome the undeliberate social relations determined only by the impersonal laws of the marketplace.

The full variety of human passions was achieved through the combination of twelve more basic passions: the five senses each had a corresponding passion; there were four spiritual or affective passions, ambition, friendship, love, and family feeling; and finally, the three co-ordinating passions that led men into passionally ordered groups, the "cabalist" desire for intrigue, the "butterfly" desire for diversity, and the "composite" desire for the simultaneous experience of many passions, a qualitatively novel passion based on a quantitative accumulation of satisfactions. Fourier bemoaned civilized morality which repressed totally the three co-ordinating passions even though they influenced human happiness so much. A separate passion of "unityism" represented the perfect realization of all twelve, the complete fulfillment of the individual. The degree to which men experienced the satisfaction of the passions depended upon the moment in the cosmological cycle which, in turn, was reflected in the extent to which social institutions were harmonious with the passions. Bourgeois civilization was "disordered," "fragmented," "chaotic," and "delusive" with respect to the gratification of the passions. Consequently, the passions were "choked" or "suffocated" and therefore were expressed as sadism, aggression, and hostility. If men appeared to be unloving brutes, this was only for lack of proper social organization and not in the nature of things. The closer social institutions and relations matched passionate needs, the less "evil" man would be. In fact morality was only the attempt to stifle man's passions after they had been perverted by poor social organization. Morality was a futile, misdirected battle against the passions whose arbitrary and irrational nature was manifest in the changing codes of good behavior from century to century and place to place.

The loss of human gratification was greater than simple unfulfillment or repression of the passions. Because the passions were suffocated, man's capacity for gratification atrophied. The stenches of the cities reduced the urbanite's sense of smell; the cold relations of the marketplace diminished the merchant's abil-

ity to love. Thus the promise of a harmonious social order included not only the satisfaction of wasted potentials, but the
expansion of the potentials themselves. The introduction of rational social institutions would be followed by a wakening of
deadened potentials for joy, love, and delight, markedly trans-
forming human nature into a kind of super-humanity, a richer,
more enhanced species resembling Adam before the fall, with its
faculties—sensory, rational, and emotive—both sharper and
deeper.

WORK AND LOVE IN UTOPIA

Instead of the unplanned congregation of men into cities,
Fourier called for the creation of Phalansteries, ideal communities of less than two thousand people, organized according to
the prescriptions of the passions into integrated lives of work and
love. Fourier's plan for the Phalanstery, worked out down to the
most trivial detail, borrowed heavily from the round of life of
the French aristocracy, embodying the ideal of luxurious, play-
ful self-indulgence. The architectural plans were taken from
the Palace and the institutions of utopia from the Court; every
man a Prince and every woman a Princess. Stately and sensual
but without haughtiness and arrogance, the people of the Phalanstery embodied the best attributes of Europe's nobility. What
is significant in this reincarnation of the Old Regime is Fourier's
disdain for the bourgeois way of life with its cramped, ascetic,
and banal virtues of prudence, frugality, temperance, and
sobriety. No calculating, puritanical stinginess in utopia; rather
the tone of life would be gracious, sensual, generous, and joyful.
To the incredulous petit bourgeois who doubted the practicality
of all this luxury, Fourier responded that industrialization would
end scarcity, allowing a sumptuous level of well-being for all.
Alone among the prophetic socialists Fourier grappled imagina-
tively with the prospect of an affluent society.

The unique attribute that made the activities and relationships in the Phalanstery so harmonious was simply freedom—
man in touch with his own passions and his true needs worked

and loved voluntarily, without the necessity of social coercion in any form. Capitalism erred in compelling men, at the point of starvation, to work. In order that the activity of work be fulfilling, it must be chosen freely, for its own sake, as Marx would later agree. Here at last was a substantial conception of free labor to counter the hypocrisy of the capitalist notion of the "free" sale of oneself into the slavery of the factory. To the obvious objection that many jobs were inherently odious and demeaning, Fourier retorted that the interlocutor's vision was distorted by civilization. No job was essentially repugnant. The diversity of human tastes would account for them all, including the disposal of refuse. Careful observation of the behavior of children, Fourier noted, revealed their love of filth. They could be organized into "little hordes" which would happily dispose of the Phalan-

AN AVERAGE DAY IN UTOPIA FOR A RICH MAN

Time	Mondor's day in summer
	Sleep from 10½ in the evening until 3 in the morning
at 3½	rise, preparation for the day
at 4	"cour du lever public," news chronicle
at 4½	breakfast, the first meal, followed by a parade of workers
at 5½	a session in a hunting group
at 7	a session in a fishing group
at 8	*lunch,* newspapers
at 9	a session in a group for cultivation under tent
at 10	a session at the Mass
at 10½	a session in a group at the pheasant house
at 10½ [sic]	a session at the library
at 1	*dinner*
at 2½	a session in a group for plant cultivation in a glass house
at 4	a session in a group for exotic plants
at 5	a session in a group for the live-fish tanks

> at 6   *a snack* outdoors
> at 6½   a session in a group for merinos
> at 4 [*sic*]   a session at the bourse
> at 9   *supper,* the fifth meal
> at 9½   "cour des arts," concerts, balls, performances,
>   receptions
> at 10½   *going to bed.*[9]

stery's garbage. With considerable satisfaction at having proved the superiority of his ideas, Fourier concluded his argument by berating the obtuse blindness of the bourgeois who justified his repressive organization of work only by his obsession with cleanliness, an obsession which prevented him from grasping the humanity of all social tasks. This type of circle of stupidity and moralizing was, for Fourier, the major obstacle to the perfection of humanity.

Once labor became voluntary men would not work at any given task for more than two hours, usually only one. This schedule was imprinted on the passions which were distorted by the monomaniacal obsession with one type of work for a whole day, month, year, even lifetime that characterized bourgeois civilization. Recent psychological experiments[10] have partially confirmed Fourier's intuition by finding a cycle of brain activity, during the day as well as at night, of one-hour periods. In addition to short work intervals, Fourier proposed a vast range of tasks for each individual, an idea that Marx borrowed in his well-known description of the non-alienated worker as a hunter, a fisher, and a critical critic. Thus the Sisyphean drudgery of the vocation of man would become transformed in the future Phalanstery into delightful, spontaneous play.

Love relations in the Phalanstery also required a thorough-

[9] From O.C., VI, p. 68. Cited in *The Teachings of Charles Fourier* by Nicholas Riasanovsky (Berkeley, University of California Press, © 1969), p. 50. Reprinted by permission of The Regents of the University of California.

[10] This research has been done by Dr. Gordon Globus at University of California, Irvine, among others.

going reversal of civilized notions and institutions. Paralleling his rejection of the bourgeois style of consciousness which fixed on one God, one Law of Nature, and one vocation, Fourier scrapped the custom of monogamous marriage. The passions no more suited men and women to one mate than to one job. Fourier depicted the relations of love and friendship in the future for each individual as a complex network of liaisons. In fact, the major preoccupation of life would become relationships, the only concern Fourier considered truly human. Just as the passions required a diversity of tasks, so they demanded a full range of love relationships. For a man, one woman might be a Platonic friend, another a work companion, a third a lover, a fourth a spiritual inspiration; the same would hold for women. Furthermore, in sexual relations all forms were permitted—heterosexuality and homosexuality, partners of two and orgies of ten, everything from mere lust to a full integration of sensual and spiritual passions. The walls between people and the limits on their affective relationships were smashed and discarded by this lonely seer.

COMMERCE AND THE FAMILY

Fourier always etched out the design of utopian institutions in close juxtaposition to his criticism of bourgeois civilization. The commercial enterprise and the family were his primary targets. With every sentence, the cloth merchant's son attacked the positions that justified commercial, industrial, and patriarchal society. However, his picture of competitive capitalism remained on the moral level, never penetrating to the structure of the economy in the manner of Saint-Simon, Proudhon, and Marx. As a result, Fourier did not abandon private property at least for the early generation of utopians. Far more incisive than his understanding of free enterprise was his analysis of the bourgeois family.

Given Fourier's emphasis on the passions, his insight into the relationship of the family structure and the social structure should not be surprising. After all, did not the family imprint the patterns of psychological gratification that stayed with people throughout their lives? To Fourier the bourgeois family—two parents, a servant, and a small number of children, usually two—was the worst possible organization of the emotions, limiting love to the smallest number of people. Each family saw itself in hostile competition with all other families, contracting emotive ties to the narrow household. To my knowledge Fourier never placed the nuclear family in a line of historical development from the tribe to the extended family of the middle ages.[11] His comprehension of the bourgeois family was in this sense flat and one-dimensional. Still, he did not absolutize the nuclear family into a "natural" institution that was unchangeable, like many liberal apologists including Freud. Rather, his criticism focused on the perpetuation of atomistic individualism by the shrunken affective bonds of the family. In essence, the bourgeois household destroyed the wider community typical of the village organization. In its place Fourier suggested an expanded family, one that would emotively bind all members of the Phalanstery, a new community of brothers and sisters.

From this general structural criticism of the family, Fourier penetrated the heart of the emotive tone of the sanctified relations between parent and child. Anticipating Freud's notion of the Oedipus Complex, Fourier characterized the relations of father and son as a mutual death wish. Cramped together so closely with the parents having absolute authority over the children (Fourier called it "tyranny"), the members of the bourgeois household could not avoid an atmosphere of cold acrimony. A bourgeois home was no place to bring up children. Blindly self-confident in their authority, the parents failed to understand the passionate needs that were unique to childhood. Here Fourier echoed Rousseau's recognition, in *Emile*, that children have needs that adults do not perceive and that they are trampled on in the family.[12] The child's interests and tastes, so different from those of his parents, were in continual conflict with the

11 P. Aries, *Centuries of Childhood* (New York: Vintage, 1965), *passim.*
12 Trans. by B. Foxley (London: Dent, 1963), 123.

desires of his father and mother, the latter being justified by
the halo of morality. Deferred gratification, rigid rationalism,
and calculating self-interest dominated the home and loomed
over the child, oppressing his impulses and appearing to him
not as moral but as arbitrary.

The family, the only emotionally supportive institution of
civilization, had been infested by mercantile values. Marriage
contracts resembled business contracts and the arm's-distance relations of the marketplace were duplicated in the home. Incompatible personalities were brought together and, like caged
animals in a zoo, had no chance of escape. In the psychological
environment of the home, the passions were distorted and
choked, setting the stage for the larger misery of society.

EDUCATION IN HARMONY

The remedy Fourier prescribed for the emotional plague of
bourgeois child-rearing practices was a new form of education
that would allow the child to develop his passions. In utopia,
children would educate other children through the natural tendency of emulation. In a communal setting, very much like the
kibbutzim of twentieth-century Israel,[13] the children spontaneously looked to their immediate elders as models. Society would
make use of this phenomenon by structuring the environment
of the child in such a way that emulation would be uninhibited
by adults. Fourier presciently advocated the socialization of children by peer groups, clearly understanding what today is
called the neurosis stemming from the nuclear family. Marx
and Engels praised Fourier's pioneering insights into the family,
without taking seriously their implications. The Marxist tradition vaguely called for the abolition of the family along with
private property, largely neglecting the closely related issues of
women's liberation, sexual reforms, and psychological revolution. Socialism had to wait until Wilhelm Reich, in the

[13] M. Spiro, *Kibbutz* (New York: Schocken Books, 1963) *passim*.

1920s,[14] connected the authoritarian nature of the family with capitalism, reopening the debate over issues Fourier had raised a full century before.

FOURIER'S SOCIALISM

After this brief review of Fourier's main concepts one can try to fix his position more securely in the traditions of European thought. Given his faulty education, Fourier managed to apprise himself of contemporary intellectual issues only through newspapers, journals, and by word of mouth. Deliberately placing himself on the outskirts of the centers of philosophical ferment, he took a perverse pride in being aloof, an obscure outsider. Yet Fourier did fit into the central trend of early-nineteenth-century thought which reacted violently against the Enlightenment.

For the utopian socialist the Enlightenment did not mark a sharp new beginning or even a watershed in European thought; it was yet one more round of lamentable disparagement of the passions. The Enlightenment merely continued the line of wrong-headed moralism that went back to Greece and the Church Fathers. When Fourier bothered to mention the *lumières* of the eighteenth century—Voltaire, Condillac, Rousseau, and Diderot were the most popular names in his pages—it was only to denigrate them. Their abstract view of man, their rationalism, and their legalistic egalitarianism were the center of their thought to Fourier, and this is what he condemned. Although Fourier's conception of the Enlightenment was terribly oversimplified, he was accurate in describing the essential elements in the bourgeois world view. Nevertheless, his attack on the Enlightenment did not free him of its influence; he was deeply indebted to the *philosophes* for his most fundamental positions, especially his basic premise of human perfectibility and historical progress. Like the more optimistic moments of the Enlightenment, Fourier saw no inherent flaw, no principle of

[14] "Dialectical Materialism and Psychoanalysis," *Monthly Review*, 1968, 5–56.

evil in man's nature. What is more, he adopted their first principle that the goal of society was the fulfillment of all man's
powers.

The direction Fourier took away from liberalism was determined by the incapacity of bourgeois thought and bourgeois
society to realize its own program. The market economy and
le ménage bourgeois prevented the realization of human powers.
The laissez-faire state promoted only the greatest happiness of
the bourgeois-aristocratic ruling class. Like Rousseau, Fourier
saw the individualism of the merchant as incompatible with the
full development of man. As a means of overcoming the *amour-
propre* of the privatized bourgeois who played being "natural
man" when in fact he was a dependent creature, Rousseau suggested a new social contract that would fundamentally transform human nature from the false independence of the
bourgeois into a social self, a man who realized his social or collective nature.[15] But Rousseau was pessimistic about the
prospects of such a new society.[16]

Fourier's utopian thought may be viewed as a detailed program designed to realize Rousseau's wistful dreams. Concretely,
Fourier mapped out plans for social reorganization that would
transform the isolated bourgeois into a truly social creature who
could realize all his faculties. The entire thrust of Fourier's
thought was directed toward this end of erasing the contradiction of natural or egoistic man who lived in a state of interde-
pendence. Psychologically, the program consisted in transcending the structures of bourgeois consciousness that impeded his
relating to other people as ends not as means. Fourier's theory
of group formation embodied a dialectic that took the isolated,
frustrated ego of bourgeois society, passed it through a moment
of uninhibited lust, and finally, when the bourgeois could at
last recognize and accept his own desires, which were normally
unconscious, permitted the coming together of people in full

[15] *The Social Contract,* ed. by G. D. H. Cole (London: Dent,
n.d.), 14.
[16] J. Shklar, *Men and Citizens, A Study of Rousseau's Social
Theory* (New York: Cambridge University Press, 1969), 184.

spiritual and sensual love relations. A careful reading of "The Group in Action," on p. 125 below, confirms this statement. Utopia was thus a land where people realized themselves in full, human relations with others, a true community where the lives of men and women were fully integrated, not a mechanical society where people related to others for self-interested, utilitarian purposes in a perpetual and ubiquitous series of business contracts.

It is Fourier's concept of community as individual self-realization through the creation of social institutions permitting human encounters that defines him as a socialist. Although he did not completely abandon private property, Fourier was in the socialist tradition because he rejected liberal ideology and bourgeois society as vehicles of human perfectibility, while he projected a society, as Marx would later say, without alienation, that is, without the tendency of human powers to become separate forces dominating men.

MARK POSTER

PART ONE

THE FOUNDATIONS OF UTOPIAN KNOWLEDGE

I. THE METHOD: *L'ÉCART ABSOLU*

Agricultural association, which in all ages has been deemed impossible, would produce results of unbounded magnificence; the rigorous demonstrations, the mathematical calculations by which these results will be verified, will not, however, prevent the picture of the future harmony and happiness which they present from repelling minds habituated to the miseries and wretchedness of our present civilization.

Were I to assert, for example, that association would in a brief period—in the course of a few years—triple the annual product of Industry or the wealth of nations, so that that of France, estimated at the present time [1822] at five thousand millions of francs a year, would be augmented to fifteen thousand millions, I should incur the charge of extravagant exaggeration; and yet after a perusal of this work it will be seen that this estimate, instead of being too high, is in fact placed entirely too low.

If, on the other hand, I were to promise some great political result as a consequence of association, such for example as the fusion and absorption of all political parties, and a complete termination of their dissensions, I foresee that distrust would increase and that my views would excite complete derision.

This miracle of social concord would result not from direct conciliation, which would be impossible, but from the development of new interests, and especially from the amazement with which the minds of men would be filled on being convinced of the radical falseness of the civilized social order by comparison with the associative or combined, and of the errors in which the social world has been so long plunged—misled by *speculative philosophy*, which upholds and extols this order with all its defects to the entire neglect of the study of association.

Speculative philosophy, which has so long governed and misled the human mind, is composed of four branches: 1. metaphysics. 2. politics. 3. moralism. 4. political economy. These speculative and uncertain sciences will fall at once before the theory of association of which it is said, "it is too perfect for man, therefore it is impossible." Their errors and illusions are at length to be dispelled; the theory of association is discovered and in all its details. Its practical realization depends upon the application of the law of universal distribution and arrangement in nature, which I will call the *"series of groups, contrasted, rivalized and interlinked."* In the course of this treatise it will be shown that association is impossible, unless based on this fundamental law of nature's plan of organization.

The *series of groups* is the method adopted by God in the distribution of the kingdoms of nature, and throughout the whole realm of creation. The same method ought, according to the law of *unity of system,* be applicable to the passions and to human relations: the problem was to discover the mode of application.

I do not propose, then, an unknown method, one of my own invention. I employ that which God applies throughout the universe, and this, I think, is a guarantee which should entitle the theory to a provisional confidence—that is, until tested by experience.

There is no idea more novel, more surprising, than that of associating three hundred families of different degrees of fortune, knowledge and capacity. It is a proposition that will be immediately met with the objection that it is impossible to associate even three families, much less three hundred. It is true that three families cannot be associated; and I, who am conversant with the theory of association in all its degrees, can affirm that in the lowest degree, more than thirty families are requisite; it may be organized with forty, and from that number up to three hundred. To explain an operation so entirely new, so incomprehensible, when judged by our present methods, we must first refute the errors and prejudices on which these methods are based.

The possibility of associating two or three hundred families in agricultural and manufacturing industry depends upon a system so entirely different from what now exists, that it will open to the reader a new social world. He must consequently, in the study which opens before him, follow the guide with confidence, bearing constantly in mind the gigantic results which will flow from association. Such results are well worth the sacrifice of a few prejudices. Every sensible reader will be of this opinion, and will concur to follow the advice which I shall constantly give, namely, *to neglect the form and style of presentation, and occupy himself solely with the substance of the theory, seeking to determine whether the process of association is really discovered or not.*

There is a class of writers who are ever boasting of the progress of civilization and of the human mind in modern times. If we were to credit their pretensions, we should be led to believe that the science of society had reached its highest degree of perfection, because old metaphysical and economic theories have been somewhat refined upon.

In answer to their boasts of social progress, is it not sufficient to refer to the deeply-rooted social evils which exist, and which prey upon our boasted civilized social order. We will mention but a single one, the frightful increase of national debts and of taxation. Where is a remedy to be found for this scourge? Can our political and economic sciences suggest one? They tend only to increase the evil, if we may infer from the fact that the countries which have produced the greatest number of political economists with the most subtle theories are the most deeply involved in debt; witness, for example, France and England. These debts, gigantic as they are, could easily be extinguished by the immensely increased product which would result from a scientific organization of industry and from association. This is but one of the immeasurable advantages that would grow out of the inauguration of the combined order, against which the four philosophic sciences will direct their attacks, declaring it to be *impracticable, impossible.* How grossly have the moderns been deceived in giving credit to these sophistical sciences, which, to sustain the present system, and the pride and position of their authors, would persuade the world that needed discoveries are impossible, and, under this pretense, foreclose all inquiry in this direction.

Other sciences—mathematics, physics and chemistry—are making real progress, but so far from being vain of their success, students in these departments admit that there yet remains much to be discovered. Political and moral theorists pursue a contrary course; the greater the increase of social evils, and the greater the ignorance that exists as to the means of exterminating them, the louder are their praises of the progress of civilization. The political experiments of modern times, however, demonstrate that nothing is to be hoped from their doctrines, and that efficient remedies for existing social evils must be sought for in some new science.

All minds are more or less imbued with and misled by reigning philosophic theories and teachings; even those who think they are opposed to the doctrines of speculative philosophy are filled with the prejudices they inculcate, and disbelieve in the possibility of any great social changes. Religious minds, which are distrustful of philosophic dogmas, fall into the error—inculcated by philosophy—of supposing that Providence is limited in its action; that it does not extend to the social world or the social relations of mankind, and that God has not determined upon any plan of social organization for the regulation of those relations. If they had a PROFOUND FAITH IN THE UNIVERSALITY OF PROVIDENCE, they would be convinced that all human needs must have been foreseen and provided for, and especially that the most urgent of them all could not have been overlooked— namely, the need of a social order for the regulation of our industrial and social relations.

I do not speak of political relations; the error of science is that it has been for thirty centuries past almost exclusively engaged in administrative controversies, which serve only to excite commotions; it should have devoted its attention to the question of industrial and domestic organization, to the art of associating isolated households or families, and of realizing the colossal economies, the enormous profits, which such association would produce.

It is well known that agricultural and domestic association, were it possible, would give rise to a gigantic production, to vast economies, and, as a consequence, to universal wealth. The Creator could not have been ignorant of this. What, then, must have been his design in regard to it? When he determined upon a system for the regulation of the industrial and social relations of mankind, he could only choose between association and the isolated, individual method. Which of the two has he designed for us? If he has decided in favor of association, as may be reasonably supposed, we should have sought for the laws which he must have framed for it. Had human reason devoted its attention seriously to the solution of this problem, it would soon have solved it by the discovery of those laws.

But to have entered upon such an investigation would have been to run counter to existing philosophic prejudices, and to have cast suspicion on our political and economical doctrines. Those who uphold these doctrines must necessarily reject the idea of a social providence, extending to the industrial and political relations of man, and of a social order precalculated by God for the regulation of human societies.

Hence it is that no one has thought of making any serious study of association, which must necessarily be the system, designed by an economical providence. To enter upon this study and pursue it with impartiality, we must free ourselves from the prejudices which are accredited by the four speculative sciences, and which are everywhere dominant through their influence. These prejudices are truly a kind of *original sin* in the minds of men, beclouding their intellects, and can only be dispelled by constant and repeated criticism.

It is but too true, that for five and twenty centuries since the political and moral sciences have been cultivated, they have done nothing for the happiness of mankind. They have tended only to increase human perversity, to perpetuate indigence, and to reproduce the same evils under different forms. After all their fruitless attempts to ameliorate the social order, there remains to the authors of these sciences only the conviction of their utter incompetency. The problem of human happiness is one which they have been wholly unable to solve.

Meanwhile a universal restlessness attests that mankind has not attained to the destiny to which nature would lead it, and this restlessness would seem to presage some great event, which shall radically change its social condition. The nations of the earth, harassed by misfortunes, and so often deceived by political empirics, still hope for a better future, and resemble the invalid who looks for a miraculous cure. Nature whispers in the ear of the human race, that for it is reserved a happiness, the means of attaining which are now unknown, and that some marvelous discovery will be made, which will suddenly dispel the darkness that now enshrouds the social world.

The theory of association will fully justify this hope, by assuring to every one that amplitude of means which is the object of universal desire. The sciences will have done nothing for social happiness, until they have satisfied the primary want of man, that of wealth, and secured to the poorest individual a *decent minimum*—that is, a comfortable subsistence. If the theory of association were to give us science alone, nothing but science, instead of securing us that wealth which is our first want, our unanimous desire, it would be but a new dishonor to human reason.

As for civilization, from which at last we are about to escape, so far from being the social destiny of man, it is only a transient stage—a state of temporary evil with which globes are afflicted during the first ages of their career; it is for the human race a disease of infancy, like teething; but it is a disease which has been prolonged in our globe at least twenty centuries beyond its natural term, owing to the neglect on the part of the ancient philosophers to study association and passional attraction. In a word, the savage, patriarchal, barbaric and civilized societies are but so many stages, leading to a higher social order, to social harmony, which is the industrial destiny of man. Out of this order, the efforts of the wisest rulers cannot alleviate in the least the miseries of nations.

It is in vain, then, philosophers, that you fill volumes with discussions as to the means of attaining social happiness so long as you have not extirpated the root of all social evils, namely, INCOHERENT INDUSTRY, or non-associated labor, which is the very opposite of the economic designs of God.

You complain that nature withholds from you a knowledge of her laws; but if you have been unable, up to the present time, to discover them, why do you hesitate to admit the insufficiency of your methods, and to invoke a new science, a new guide? Either nature does not desire the happiness of man, or your methods are condemned by her, since they have been unable to wrest from her the secret of which you are in pursuit.

Do we find her frustrating the efforts of the natural philosophers as she does yours? No, because they study her laws instead of dictating laws to her; while you only study the art of stifling the voice of nature, stifling attraction which is her interpreter, and the synthesis of which leads in every sense to association. What a contrast between your blunders and the achievements of the positive sciences! Every day, philosophers, you add new errors to the errors of the past, whereas we see the physical sciences daily advancing in the path of truth, and shedding as much luster upon the present century as your baseless visions have cast opprobrium upon the eighteenth.

TSO, I, pp. 5–11

II. GOD, NATURE AND SOCIETY

In publishing a discovery which the world was so far from expecting—namely, the theory of general destinies—let me explain why it has been missed by the great men of the past—among others by Newton, who discovered one branch of the system of nature—and how it happens that the prize has fallen to the lot of a man not engaged in scientific pursuits. We often see fortune baffle the efforts of genius, and accord to chance the most important discoveries; should we be surprised, then, that she has acted thus in respect to the great question of the mathematical calculation of destinies? Besides the favors accorded to chance, there are also those granted to audacity. *Audaces fortuna juvat.* We often see the bold succeed where men of learning and professional skill fail, and even the latter often owe their success to mere accident. Kepler confessed that he was speculating at random when he discovered the famous law that the square of the periodic time is proportional to the cube of the distance. It must be admitted, then, that in respect to discoveries, boldness and chance divide the honors with genius and science. Newton, we are told, was indebted to a lucky incident, to the fall of an apple, for the discovery of the law of gravitation, which Pythagoras had a glimpse of, but missed, twenty-five centuries before. This is a sufficient reply to objections of this nature. Right or wrong, I hold the prize, which has escaped the favorites of science.

Modern philosophers, especially those of France, pretend generally to explain the principle of the *unity of system in nature;* never, however, was the world farther from any regular study of the subject; hence it has not acquired the least idea of the theory of UNIVERSAL UNITY, which consists of three branches, to wit:

Unity of man with himself;

Unity of man with God;

Unity of man with the universe.

It will be demonstrated in the course of the present work, that the philosophers have for three thousand years neglected to study the first of these three unities, that of man with himself, and especially with his passions, which, out of the combined order, are in a state of general discord, and lead to perdition the individual whom they direct.

This duplicity of action, this dissidence of man with himself, has given rise to a science, called moral philosophy or ethics, which considers duplicity of action the essential condition, the immutable destiny of man. It teaches that he should resist his passions; that he should be at war with them and with himself —a principle which places man in a state of war with God, for the passions and instincts come from God, who has given them as a guide to man and to all creatures.

In opposition to this view, certain learned sophisms are urged in regard to the intervention of reason, which God, as it is said, has given us as a guide and a moderator of the passions, whence it would follow:

1. That God has subjected us to two irreconcilable and conflicting guides—*passion* and *reason.* (*Theoretic duplicity.*)

2. That God is unjust toward the ninety-nine hundredths of the race, to whom he has not imparted that degree of reason necessary to cope with the passions; for the masses in all countries, civilized and barbaric, do not reason; as for the savages, they are guided only by their passions. (*Distributive duplicity.*)

3. That God, in giving us reason as a counterpoise and a regulating agent, has miscalculated its effects; for it is evident that reason is powerless even with the hundredth of men who are

endowed with it, and that the oracles of reason, the greatest intellects, are often the greatest slaves to their passions. (*Practical duplicity.*)

Thus our theories as to the unity of man with himself commence by supposing him subject to a threefold duplicity of action—a monstrous absurdity, and a threefold insult to the Creator of the passions.

Nothing in either of these three hypotheses is admissible; they will be examined and fully refuted in another part of the work, where it will be demonstrated that all these aberrations of civilized metaphysics arise from the neglect to study passional attraction and to determine analytically and synthetically its properties and tendencies; by this study we should have discovered what functions God assigns to passion and to reason, what equilibria he establishes between them, how in the combined order they would harmonize in all respects, and how in the civilized or incoherent order they must be in a state of continued discord and antagonism.

Ignorant as regards the unity of man with himself, the world is still more ignorant in respect to the two other unities—unity of man with God and the universe. Is this surprising, when we reflect that men have neglected to study the first, the theory of which would have furnished the key to the two others?

Thus there has been, up to the present time, no integral investigation, and science has succeeded only in discovering a few fragmentary branches of the system of nature, as, for example, the Newtonian theory, a branch of the third unity. The discovery of this theory should have led men of science to follow up the success achieved, and to extend the calculation of attraction from the material to the passional world, in order to determine the social and domestic organization which God has assigned to our passions and to our industrial relations.

It has been vaguely laid down as a principle, that man was made for society; but it has not been observed that society may be of two orders—the isolated or the associated, the incoherent or the combined. The difference between the two is as great as that between truth and falsehood, light and darkness, the comet and the planet, the butterfly and the caterpillar.

The age in its presentiments as respects association, has pursued a vacillating course; it has feared to trust to its inspirations which led it to hope for some great discovery. It has conceived the possibility of the associative order without daring to proceed to the investigation of the means of realizing it; it has never thought of speculating upon the following alternative:

There can exist but two methods for the exercise of industry: namely, the incoherent and fragmentary, or industry carried on by isolated families, as we now see it; or, on the other hand, the associative method, or industry carried on by large combinations of persons, with fixed rules for the equitable distribution of profits according to the CAPITAL, LABOR, AND TALENT of each individual. Which of these two methods is the order intended by God—the incoherent or the associated? To this question there can be but one reply. God, as the supreme economist, must have preferred association, which is the guarantee of all economy, and must have devised for its organization some method or process, the discovery of which was the task of genius.

If association is the divine method, it follows as a necessary consequence that the opposite one—namely, fragmentary and incoherent labor—is the DIABOLIC METHOD, *and must engender all the evils and scourges which are opposed to the spirit of God, such as indigence, fraud, oppression, carnage, etc.*

And since the societies—the barbaric and civilized—based on fragmentary and incoherent labor, perpetuate these evils in despite of all the efforts of science, it is evident from this fact that they are THE DIABOLIC METHOD, PORTÆ INFERI, the antipodes of the designs of God, to which designs man can conform only by discovering and organizing the system of associative industry.

Starting from this principle, the age should have proposed the investigation of the associative theory; but neither governments nor individuals have thought of doing this. The authors of the speculative sciences have not occupied themselves with this problem, as it would have cast discredit upon their theories of fragmentary or civilized industry—the system of cultivation by isolated families.

At last the discovery is made, and made in all its degrees, but it will have this fault in the eyes of the learned world, namely, that of casting ridicule upon all previous theories of social organization, and of exposing the fallacy of the four sciences, called metaphysics, politics, moralism, and political economy.

It is not very complimentary, I admit, to an age so advanced as ours in the physical sciences, to say of it, that in respect to other sciences, it possesses only erroneous opinions, and that of many opinions it has no conception whatever, as for example, the four following:

INDUSTRIAL ASSOCIATION;   PASSIONAL ATTRACTION;
AROMAL MECHANISM;   UNIVERSAL ANALOGY.

If the pride of the age is offended by this assertion, let it judge of what it has accomplished by a reference to the following table of the various branches of the system of nature, from which it will appear that the civilized mind has traversed hardly a tenth part of the career which was open to it.

TABLE OF THE FOUR CARDINAL AND
PIVOTAL MOVEMENTS.

4. THE MATERIAL. The theory which astronomers have given of this branch of universal movement explains *effects*, but not *causes*. It has made known the laws by which God regulates the movement of matter, but it remains silent upon everything which relates to *causes*.

3. THE AROMAL, or system of distribution of aromas,[1] known and unknown, operating actively and passively on the animal, vegetable, and mineral creations. We have no regular theory of these aromas, nor do we know the causes

[1] By the term aroma, Fourier designates the imponderable fluids—light, heat, electricity, magnetism, galvanism, and others which remain to be discovered. They constitute a kingdom by themselves, which he calls the AROMAL.—Note of A.B.

of the influences which they exercise, especially on the revolutions of the heavenly bodies, which are regulated by aromal affinities.

2. THE ORGANIC, or the laws according to which God distributes forms, properties, colors, savors, etc., to all substances created, or to be created on the different globes. We are ignorant of the *causes* of the distribution of the above attributes in existing creations, and of both the effects and causes of distributions which will be made in future creations.

1. THE INSTINCTUAL, or the laws which regulate the distribution of passions and instincts to all creatures of past, present and future creations on the various globes. We are ignorant alike of the distributive system of instincts, and of the causes which have regulated their distribution.

PIVOT. THE SOCIAL OR PASSIONAL, that is, the laws according to which God has regulated the order and succession of the various social systems on all globes. Of this pivotal movement, our sciences have explained neither the effects nor the causes; nor have they conceived of any means of establishing on our earth the reign of social unity, which implies the harmony of the passions without resort to repressive methods.

It results from this table, that of five branches, constituting universal movement, we are acquainted with but one—the MATERIAL—which is the least important of the five; and even this has been known only since the time of Newton, who has explained *effects* and not *causes*—that is to say, but half of the theory of one of the five branches.

A strange oversight on the part of science is, that the existence of the third branch of movement, the AROMAL, is hardly suspected, and has never been an object of research. It plays nevertheless an important part in the harmony of the material universe—a harmony which men of science, owing to their ignorance of the aromal system, have been unable to more than half explain.

Propose to them problems like the following on aromal equilibrium:

1. What is the law which regulates the distribution of satellites? How is it that Herschel, which is so much smaller than Jupiter, has, nevertheless, a more numerous train?

2. What is the law which regulates planetary revolutions? Why does Vesta, the smallest of the planets, revolve around no other, not even the enormous Jupiter, near which it is placed?

3. What is the law which regulates the position of planets? Why is Herschel, which is only a fourth the size of Jupiter, four times further from the Sun? In analogy with this distribution, the earth should have been located far beyond the orbit of Herschel.

On these problems, and others of the same kind, which I shall bring up in the course of this work, the scientific world is reduced to silence, as upon all other questions which relate to CAUSES.

Their knowledge is limited to the analysis of EFFECTS, and in but one of the five branches of movement; that is to say, in the study of Nature and of the system of the universe, *but a tenth part of the work to be accomplished has been done.* Newton, who led the way, began with the inferior branch, which the age would have readily perceived, had there been prepared a regular programme, an integral plan of studies, such as I have just given, the primordial branch or pivot of which should be the study of man, or the analysis and synthesis of passional attraction. This was the true starting point.

Newton commenced the study of universal movement with the last and least important of its five branches—the material. It was none the less a great step in advance—a brilliant initiative. As a geometer, nothing more could have been required of him. But his success in the material branch of movement gave him the right to summon other men of science to explore the *organic, aromal, instinctual* and PASSIONAL branches. (The latter I call the pivotal branch, because it is the type of the four others.)

Newton referred all questions of metaphysics to his friend Clark. Might he not have assigned to him the calculation of passional attraction,[2] which is the primary branch of metaphysics, and called upon him or others to proceed to its investigation? He could have taken the ground that the theory of material attraction having led to the discovery of the laws of one branch of the system of nature, they should have consulted the same interpreter—attraction—in respect to the four other branches, remaining to be discovered, and *deduced from the principle of* UNITY OF SYSTEM *the conclusion, that if the regular calculation of material attraction explains the mechanism of the material harmonies of the universe, it is just to infer that the regular study of passional attraction, by analysis and synthesis, would determine, in like manner, the mechanism of passional and social harmony.*

The age has not adopted this course, and despite its high pretensions in the matter of abstract calculations, it has not risen to the consideration of those transcendent abstractions which embrace the universality of the system of nature. Hence it has made no progress in the most urgent of all studies—the integral investigation of the five branches of movement. Partial success, like that of Newton, has not yet led to further exploration; the geometers and naturalists, reposing on their laurels, have neglected to summon the other classes of savants, and remind them of the precept so well expressed, but so little followed, "to explore the system of nature integrally, and to consider nothing done while anything remains to be done," especially, since of

[2] The term *passional*, as the reader will perceive, is derived from passion, as material is from matter. By passional attraction is to be understood the tendency of the passions, their gravitation to the ends or foci to which they are destined. The passions—variously called sentiments, affections, instincts, etc.—are the motor forces, the springs of action in man; they are the parts of a unity or a whole, which is the soul or the spirit. God, in implanting in man these impelling forces, must have calculated mathematically their mode of action, their tendencies, and their functions. Passional attraction implies all these; it is equivalent to the mode of action and tendencies of the passions. As the passions come from God, this attraction expresses or reveals to us the will of God; it is his voice speaking through the soul: it is the power which he employs to impel us to fulfill the destiny he has assigned us.—Note of A.B.

the five branches constituting universal movement, only the least important, the material, has been explored.

When we reflect that inventions the most urgent and the most easy to be made, like the stirrup and the carriage-spring, unknown to the Greeks and Romans, were overlooked for thousands of years, though within the competency of any one, we are forced to admit that there reigns on our globe some fatality, some radical defect of method, which thwarts all discoveries. Is it heedlessness, or negligence? poverty of genius, or imperfect methods of investigation? Certainly it is one of the four, or possibly they all concur in paralyzing genius. The human mind must have been very ill-directed not to have had its attention drawn to the most important subject, the discovery of domestic association, for upon this depended the systematic organization of industry, the securing of universal abundance, and what is still more important, the elevation of the world to SOCIAL UNITY.

That a discovery is delayed should never be a reason for despair. For three thousand years mariners suffered for want of the compass; at last this invaluable guide was found. A success so long deferred should have called attention to the defects in our methods of scientific exploration, and led to the inference, that as the branches of knowledge of which we are still deprived may be more numerous than those already discovered, measures should be devised for organizing a system of general and integral investigation. Without some such system we are certain to fail, not only in great discoveries, but even in those of minor importance. What a reproach that so trifling a thing as the wheelbarrow should not have been invented before the time of Pascal! It is almost always accident or chance that supplies the deficiency of our methods, which is a proof that the course adopted by our explorers is without order or concert.

Our imperfect methods of study and exploration have cost the moderns very dear. The world should have possessed the theory of association a hundred years ago, for it is a natural deduction from the Newtonian theory of material attraction, and applies to the passional or social world his theory of the equilibrium of the material universe.

Other sciences would have effected the same result, if their authors had followed a methodic and integral system of exploration. The political economists, for example, whose special function is the investigation of all problems relating to order and economy in the industrial world, should have proposed as their primordial object the *study of association*. It was the subject the most important to investigate, for association is the basis of all economy.

We find numerous germs of it even in the present social mechanism, from powerful corporations, like the East India Company, to small combinations organized in our villages for carrying on specific branches of industry. We find among the mountaineers of the Jura a combination of this kind, formed for the manufacture of the cheese called *gruyère*; twenty or thirty families take their milk every morning to a central depot, and at the end of the season each of them receives its part in cheese, obtaining a quantity proportional to the contributions of milk as credited on the daily accounts. Thus, on a large scale and on a small, we have under our eyes the germs of association, the rough diamond which it was the duty of science to cut and polish.

The problem was to develop and combine in a general system of unity these fragments of association, which are scattered among all branches of industry, where they have sprung up by accident and from instinct. Science has neglected this task, though none was more urgent.

An age guilty of such negligence in the details of scientific study could not have failed to misconceive the work of integral exploration; hence it has neither classified the different branches of the general system of movement, nor the three unities above mentioned—a classification which would have demonstrated that both the social and the material world are in a state of *duplicity*, that is, of conflict with the principle of unity.

As to the duplicity of the social world, we see each class interested in the misfortunes of other classes, and placing everywhere individual interests in conflict with the collective. The lawyer, for example, desires dissensions, particularly among the rich, to give rise to expensive litigations. The doctor wishes the prevalence of disease; he would be ruined if people died without sickness, as would be the lawyer, if all disputes were settled by arbitration. The soldier desires a good war that will kill off half his comrades, so as to procure him promotion. The sexton is interested in deaths, especially among those that will secure to him profitable burials. The monopolists want a good famine, which shall double and triple the price of grain. The architect, the mason, and the carpenter want good fires that will burn down a hundred houses and give activity to their business.

In fine, the civilized social order is an absurd mechanism, the parts of which are in conflict with the whole and with each other. The folly of such a system cannot be appreciated till after a study of the combined order, in which interests are associated, and in which every one desires the good of the whole as the only guarantee of the good of the individual.

The civilized order, on the contrary, while advocating unity of action, sanctions political and moral theories, the whole tendency of which is to uphold *universal duplicity of action*. It is admitted, however, that we should aim at unity, the means of realizing which are entirely unknown; they are to be found only in association, with which science has never occupied itself, and out of which the social world falls necessarily into that labyrinth of duplicity and misery, the aspect of which caused Rousseau to exclaim: "These beings whom we see around us are not men; there must be some perversion, the cause of which we cannot penetrate." Nothing is more true, and the human race is, in the language of Christ, "a generation of vipers," a demoniac breed, so long as the true and unitary order of society—ASSOCIATION, which is the destiny of man—remains undiscovered, and unorganized. To discover it, it was necessary that men of science, having first analyzed existing social evils, should have proceeded to the investigation of each of the unities, and especially of social unity, of which the societies now existing on the earth are evidently the antipodes: first, by their antagonism one with another, and second, by the conflict of action that exists in all the departments and interests of each.

The theory of association being inseparable from that of the unity of the universe, it will be necessary to treat briefly of the three branches of unity, which I shall do in future volumes, in order that my calculations may not be chargeable with incompleteness.

As for the unity of man with himself, that is with his passions, it is the special object of this work; I shall here treat it in its application to internal or domestic relations. Its complete theory, embracing commercial and other external relations, will be treated hereafter.

In studying the problem of social development and progress, we must rise to the conception that the human race, considered as a whole, must pass, like the individual, through a regular career, subject to the four phases of infancy, youth, manhood, and old age; I shall show that it is now in the first of these phases.

The social infancy of the race is much shorter in proportion to the other phases than that of the individual man; but the effects in both cases are the same; that is, a social world in the phase of infancy may be compared to a child that at the age of six or eight, wholly absorbed in childish sports, has not yet any knowledge of the career of manhood. In like manner the human race on an infant globe, or a globe in the first phase of its career, does not rise to the conception of a future state of harmony, in which the social world will pass from indigence to opulence; from falseness to truth and justice; from a state of social discord to social unity.

If association can be demonstrated to be practicable, it is certain that the existing societies—the civilized, barbaric, and savage—will disappear before it, and that the social world will pass from the phase of infancy to that of adolescence—to the essential and happy destiny which awaits mankind—the duration of which is seven times that of the ages of social chaos and misfortune.

I shall endeavor to prepare the mind to conceive the possibility of this great social change, which will absorb all party contentions and all conflicting interests in the grandeur of new hopes and interests. The prospect of such a vast social transformation should rouse the minds of men from their present lethargy, from their apathetic resignation to misfortune, and especially from the discouragement diffused by our moral and political sciences which proclaim the impossibility of the reign of social unity and happiness on earth, and assert the incompetency of human reason to determine our future social destiny. If the calculation of future events is beyond the reach of the human mind, whence comes that longing common to all mankind to fathom the secret of human destiny, at the very mention of which the most passive natures experience a thrill of impatience, so impossible is it to extirpate from the human heart the desire to penetrate the future. Why should God, who does nothing without a purpose, have given to us this intense longing, if he had not reserved the means of some day satisfying it? At last that day has arrived, and mortals are about to rise to the prescience of future events. I shall give, in the chapters on cosmogony, an outline of universal analogy, which will reveal to us these mysteries, and open to us the book of eternal decrees. Philosophy, unable to explain them, would deter us from their research by declaring that they are impenetrable. But if nature is really impenetrable, as the philosophers assert, why has she permitted Newton to explain the fourth branch of her general system? This was an indication that she would not refuse us a knowledge of the other branches. Why, then, have our men of science been so timid in pursuing the secrets of nature, who has encouraged them by allowing a corner of the veil that covers her mysteries to be raised? With their brilliant paradoxes, they communicate the scepticism and doubt with which they are filled, and persuade the human race that nothing can be discovered where their sciences have been unable to discover anything.

Meanwhile, they delude us with the idea that civilized society is progressing rapidly, when it is evident that it moves only in a vicious circle, and that there can be no great improvement but in the discovery and establishment of a new social order, higher in the scale than the present; and that human reason, under the influence of existing prejudices, is incapable of conceiving and executing any radical good. Twenty scientific centuries elapsed before any amelioration was proposed in the condition of the slaves; whence it would seem that thousands of years are necessary to suggest to the civilized mind an act of justice and social progress.

Thus our scientific guides are utterly ignorant of the means of promoting the real welfare of mankind. Their efforts at political reforms produce only commotions and disasters. The sluggish progress of our societies may be compared to that of the sloth, whose every step is attended with a groan; like it, civilization advances with an inconceivable slowness through political storms and revolutions. In each generation it gives birth to new schemes and experiments, which serve only to bring disasters upon those who try them.

At length the end of our social miseries, the term of the political infancy of the globe, is at hand. We are on the verge of a great social transformation, which a universal commotion seems to announce. Now, indeed, is the present big with the future, and the excess of human suffering must bring on the crisis of a new birth. Judging from the continual violence of political convulsions, it would seem as if nature were making an effort to throw off a burden that oppresses her. Wars and revolutions devastate every part of the globe. Political storms, for a moment lulled, burst forth anew, and party conflicts and hatreds are becoming more and more intense, with no hope or prospect of reconciliation; the policy of nations has become more tortuous and crafty than ever, and diplomacy is familiar with every variety of political turpitude and crime; the revenues of states fall a prey to the vampires of the stock exchange; industry, by its monopolies and excesses, has become a scourge to the laboring classes, who are reduced to the fate of Tantalus—starving in the midst of wealth and luxury; the ambition of colonial possession has opened a new volcano; the implacable fury of the negro race threatens to convert whole regions of the New World into a vast charnel-house, and avenge the exterminated aborigines, by the destruction of their conquerors; commerce, with a cannibal cruelty, has refined the atrocities of the slave trade, and treads under foot the decrees for its abolition; the mercantile spirit has extended the sphere of crime, and at every war carries devastation into both hemispheres; our ships circumnavigate the globe only to initiate barbarians and savages into our vices and excesses; the earth exhibits the spectacle of a frightful chaos of immorality, and civilization is becoming more and more odious as it approaches its end.

It is at this crisis, when the social world seems to have reached the bottom of the abyss, that a fortunate discovery brings to it a guide out of the labyrinth—association, based on the laws of universal harmony, which the age, but for its want of real faith in the universality of providence, might have discovered a hundred times over. Let it know, and it cannot be too often repeated, that providence must before all things have determined upon the plan of a social mechanism for man, since the social is the most noble branch of universal movement, the direction of which belongs to God alone.

Instead of comprehending this truth—instead of seeking what were the designs of God in respect to the organization of human society, and by what means he must have revealed them to us, the age has rejected every principle which admitted the UNIVERSALITY OF PROVIDENCE, and a plan of social organization devised by God for man. Passional attraction, the eternal interpreter of his decrees, has been defamed; the social world has confided itself to the guidance of human legislators and philosophers, who have arrogated to themselves the highest function of Deity—the direction of the social movement. To their disgrace, humanity has, under their auspices, bathed itself in blood for twenty-five sophistical centuries, and exhausted the career of misery, ignorance and crime.

But fortune has at length become propitious; fate is disarmed, and the discovery of the associative theory opens to us the means of escape from that social prison called civilization.

On what conditions is this discovery entitled to an impartial examination, and to a practical trial? Only so far as it is in unity with the universe, with its known harmonies—the planetary, the mathematical and the musical—and is substantiated by the fundamental principles on which those harmonies are based. If there is unity of system between the material and spiritual universe, the equilibrium of the passions must be based on the same laws that establish equilibrium in the material creation.

If this condition is fulfilled by the theory of association which I present, there is nothing more urgent than to make a practical trial of it, which can be done on a small scale with a hundred families. If the age is wise enough to lay aside its prejudices, and make such a trial, the whole face of things on this globe will be changed; humanity will elevate itself at once from the social abyss in which it is now struggling to a state of happiness and harmony; the change will resemble the shifting of the scenes on the stage, where Olympus is made to succeed to Pandemonium. We should behold a spectacle which can be witnessed but once on any globe, namely, the sudden passage from a state of social incoherence to unity and harmony. This is the most brilliant effect of movement which can take place in the universe. Every year, during this grand metamorphosis, would be worth an age of ordinary existence, and would present a succession of events so marvelous, that it would be premature to describe them until the reader was prepared to conceive of their possibility.

Disheartened by long-continued misfortunes, bowed down under the chains of habit, men have believed that God destined them to a life of privations, or at most to a moderate degree of happiness. They will be unable to conceive the idea of the blessings that await them, and should there be exhibited to them without precaution a picture of the combined order in all its grandeur, they would reject it as impossible and visionary.

The combined order will, from its commencement, be the more brilliant from having been so long delayed. Greece might have undertaken it in the age of Pericles, her industrial and other resources having already reached the necessary degree of development. Its organization requires the aid of an advanced state of industry, which necessarily does not exist on any globe during its early generations, whom God for this reason leaves in ignorance of the happy destiny which awaits them—a destiny to which no globe can rise during the phase of its social infancy.

At the present day the resources of art, industry, material elegance, and refinement are at least double what they were among the Athenians; we shall accordingly enter with so much the more splendor upon the combined order. It is now that we are to reap the fruits of the progress made by the physical sciences; hitherto, while multiplying the means of wealth and luxury for the few, they have increased the relative privations of the masses, who are destitute even of the necessaries of life. They seem only to have labored for the happiness of the idle-rich and great, while they have aggravated the moral sufferings of the toiling multitude; and this odious result leads to one of two conclusions: either the malevolence of Providence toward man, or the falseness of civilization. Rationally we must adopt the second. Philosophers, instead of taking this view of the subject, have wholly evaded the problem presented by human misery, the extent of which should have led them either to suspect civilization, or to suspect Providence. Confounded by the spectacle of so much evil, they adopted during the last century a side issue—that of Atheism—which, assuming the non-existence of a deity and the absence of a social providence, turned the attention of that age of innovation and revolution from all study of the divine plan of social organization, and authorized the philosophers to propose their own capricious and contradictory theories for the government of the social world. They hold up as perfect the civilized order, the aspect of the results of which bewilders them nevertheless to the extent of making them doubt the existence of God.

The philosophers are not the only ones at fault in this matter. If it is absurd not to believe in God, it is equally absurd to believe in him half-way—to believe that his Providence is incomplete; that he has neglected to provide for the most urgent of our social wants—that of a social order which would secure our happiness. When we behold the prodigies of our industry—as for example, a three-decked ship and other marvels which are premature, considering our social infancy—can we reasonably suppose that God, who has lavished upon us so many noble sciences, would refuse to us a knowledge of the most important of all— that of the social organization, without which all others are comparatively useless?

Would not God be inconsistent with himself, if, having initiated us into so many sublime branches of knowledge, they were only to produce societies, disgusting by their vices and their crimes—societies, such as barbarism and civilization, from which humanity is at last about to be delivered, and the approaching end of which should be a signal of universal joy.

TSO, I, pp. 12–28

III. COSMOGONY AND HISTORY

ON ASTRAL HARMONY

Some moderns have rightly suspected that there exist among the heavenly bodies bonds of harmony other than those of weight and gravity. Chateaubriand says in *Les Martyrs*, "that in the other life various elected ones occupied themselves in studying the mysteries of the harmony of celestial bodies." As the number of the elect will be very small however, according to the evangelical augury, *Multi enim vocati, pauci vero electi;* nine out of ten of us cannot look forward to participating after death with the elect in the knowledge of sidereal harmony, and can, on the contrary, expect to be plunged into Hell, where there will be only tears and the gnashing of teeth. Consequently, it will be prudent for the lovers of science to seek in their present life to initiate themselves into a field of knowledge that must be extremely interesting since it comprises the amusement of the most learned among the elect—the mysteries of the harmony of celestial bodies.

Those who have taken the planets to be inanimate bodies without function, limited to traveling geometric paths, resemble idiots who would believe that the brain is inanimate because it has no visible function, or that the stomach is idle because it does no visible work as do our limbs. *Civilizees*[1] have always been reproached for believing nature to be limited to known

[1] Fourier's neologism for bourgeois.—Ed.

effects. If the planets were not animate creatures endowed with functions, God would then appear to be an advocate of laziness. He would have created universes furnished with large inert bodies spending eternity in purposeless meandering as do the idlers in our society. This common opinion is based on our ignorance of the planets' workings—it is as if one thought that the leaves of a plant did not contribute to the work of bearing fruit because one sees no exterior sign of their production of sap.

The creatures of various degrees of the polyversal keyboard all have use of the twelve radical passions, but they differ in their exercise of them. Man's exercise of them is crude since he is last on the keyboard, a creature of transition. Thus man nourishes himself from solid matter and planets from ethereal matter called aromas. The unsophisticated, who believed that the sun swallowed comets, undoubtedly committed a gross error, but an error less ridiculous than that of the learned world which believes that the heavenly bodies fail to nourish themselves at all, and that they have not the use of five senses as we do: sight, hearing, smell, taste, and touch. Heavenly bodies possess them to a much more perfect degree than man. . . .

Each planet has not only the twelve radical passions as we do, but has in addition twelve radical aromas analogous to these passions and susceptible, as they are, to countless combinations. It is through aromal communication that the relationships between these large bodies exists. They execute work as active as it is varied, even though invisible to us. Nevertheless we can acquire some very interesting insights into these mysteries that were erroneously believed to be reserved for the elect.

The theory of aromal movement will dispel numerous misconceptions, especially those about comets which alarm the people. Comets are an aromal swarm destined to nourish the sun and the planets, and their approach is a joyful event for all the astral bodies. They are incapable of causing the least damage. Each heavenly body inhales various essences and nourishments essential to their well-being, which are given off by the comets.

Planets and comets throw out jets or rockets of aromas at the speed of light, which travel more than 4,000,000 leagues per minute. Light is the only visible aroma among the radical passions holding the same rank as the universalist passion, which is a composite of all the others. This aroma contains many colors other than the seven visible ones. It radiates thirty-two colors not including white, but our globe is not able to receive them, as it is the least receptive body to aromal communication. Hence only seven colors are perceived; our planet will not receive a larger number until after it has regenerated its atmosphere.

Each planet has, according to its degrees, one or several dominant aromas, plus the tonics. The distribution of aromas is similar to that of characters.[2]

A planet of low or first degree, like the moons of Jupiter, Saturn, and Uranus, have only one dominant aroma. The planets of second degree, like the three principal cardinals of our globe, have two dominant aromas of which one is pivotal. These classes of bodies correspond to the indicated characters called monogynes[3] and digynes.[4] Our sun, of a pentagyne[5] degree, has five dominant aromas. The stars Mars, Venus, Bellone, and Sapho are of mono-mixed degree and have a mixture of aromas. Let us remember that the dominance of an aroma does not hinder the heavenly body from having the eleven others or from utilizing them in certain ways.

The sidereal aromas have essences which are known to man—the jonquil furnishes us with the pivotal aroma of Jupiter; the violet contains the pivotal aroma of our globe; the rose gives the dominant aroma of Mercury. Each of these flowers was created by the planet whose aroma it transmits. Later on it will be seen how the heavenly bodies execute these creations; it is the most interesting part of their mechanism. . . .

I foresee many questions that will be asked, namely about the reproduction of these bodies. "How do the planets reproduce themselves? One does not see them engendering offspring.

---

[2] That is, personality types.—Ed.

[3] People with one dominant passion, a low order of personality in Utopia.—Ed.

[4] People with two dominant passions.—Ed.

[5] A person with five dominant passions.—Ed.

Why don't they grow up as we do? Are they fixed in size? If they are animate bodies they should be subject to the phenomena of growth, reproduction, death, etc; one sees not a hint of these processes."

My answer at this point is that these notions are not the most important ones; there are others more closely related to our interests, namely that of the work of planets, of which I will speak in the following chapter. Meanwhile I shall give the following bit of information which although outside our framework will make the delay easier to bear.

The seeds of heavenly bodies are deposited and cared for in the Milky Way, from which they emanate in swarms of comets that travel a long time and ordinarily gravitate toward various suns before becoming fixed in an orbit.

These seeds are engendered by aromal copulation between the planets and their sun. But it is not yet time to enter into the details.

We see reproduction take place before our eyes in many ways; a dog, a chicken, a carp, and a bee differ greatly in the details of fecundation and gestation. Planets follow still another process. Nature is infinitely diversified as to means, but her functions are similar in aim—reproduction in its various forms. It cannot be too often repeated that we must not believe nature to be limited to the effects that we see, nor think that the planets do not raise progeny because we are ignorant of the means they employ. . . . A planet is an androgynous body, provided with both sexes and functioning as a male through copulations at the north pole, and as a female by those at the south pole. . . . Each substance of the various animal and vegetable kingdoms is the product of an aroma radiated by one of the heavenly bodies combined with that of another. Cattle are born of an aroma sent out by Jupiter; horses of an aroma from Saturn; roses of an aroma from Mercury; carnations of an aroma from Hebe, the eighth moon of Uranus. The operation is roughly similar to that of our gardeners—they sow seeds containing a germ which combines in fermentation with the earth's sap. Thus, when Jupiter sent to earth the seeds of cattle they were received and nurtured in the heart of the planet, then thrown out upon different areas of the earth's surface, where they produced the first herd of cattle.

In truth, we see nothing whatsoever of the mechanisms of the heavenly bodies; likewise aromas are invisible to us. If we were able to perceive them, we would find the atmosphere obstructed by a crowd of aromal columns which cross it in all directions. We fail to see, for example, the magnetic fluid whose circulation around our globe is well established by the movement of the compass. Neither do we see the seven colors which exist in the solar rays before they are divided by a prism. Neither do we see certain aromas which we nevertheless feel acutely, thunder and electricity among others. Must we be astonished if we fail to perceive the agents of communication between the planets or the aromas and other substances that flow between them, from which our planet is excluded? Space is furrowed with these columns of aromas which radiate everywhere, and cross one another like bullets on a battlefield. The planets absorb and reabsorb these aromas in various places; an aroma of copulation is absorbed by the poles; an aroma of mastication by the Equator; one of planting or sowing by the various latitudes where the germs develop; and so on as the planet has points especially concerned with the exercise of each of the aromal functions. All these mechanisms, invisible to us, nevertheless exist. It is necessary to remind ourselves again that nature is very erroneously judged when one believes her to be limited to known means, to the effects and phenomena perceived by our senses.

AP, pp. 227–32

THE MOVEMENT OF SOCIETY

Every great discovery, when first announced and judged by what is already known, appears to be either impracticable or absurd. The inventor of gunpowder, when he first explained its results, was doubtless listened to with incredulity, and charged with being an arrant visionary. Nevertheless, what is better established at the present day than the astonishing effects of this discovery?

It will appear, I confess, an improbable statement when I announce that the means have been discovered of associating three hundred families of different degrees of fortune, and remunerating each individual—man, woman and child—according to his or her labor, capital and talent. More than one person will think it facetious to say to the author, "Let him try to associate even three families, to unite under the same roof three households, establish combination in their purchases and expenses, with harmony of feeling and perfect agreement as to the exercise of authority, and when he shall have thus succeeded in associating three households, it may then be believed that he will succeed with thirty, or with three hundred."

I have already replied to this objection, which, however, it is well to bring up again, as repetition in this matter will often be absolutely necessary. I have observed that, *as economies can result only from large associations, God must have adapted his plan of social organization to large numbers, and not to three or four families.*

An objection more sensible in appearance, and which it will often be necessary to refute, is that relating to social discords. "How," it will be asked, "will it be possible to conciliate the passions, the conflicts of interest, the incompatibilities of character, in a word, the numberless disparities which are the sources at present of so much discord?"

It has been shown that I make use of a lever hitherto entirely unknown, and the properties of which cannot be judged of till I have explained them. The contrasted passional series operates by these very disparities which so much embarrass our political sciences. By its action, the passions which now produce so many discords will be changed in their development, and become the sources of concord and harmony; the greater the passional dissonances and contrasts, the better the series will be graduated, contrasted and interlinked.

Care should be taken not to raise objections against a system until its processes have been explained. We must believe, according to the precepts of the philosophers, that nature is not limited to known means, and, according to the dictates of reason, that God, whose providence is universal, has not created the passions—the elements of the social mechanism—without providing some means for their useful employment—means, the discovery of which has been delayed up to the present day by our false methods of investigation. The stirrup and the carriage spring which any simpleton might have discovered, were unknown to Greece and Rome; should we be surprised then, that an intricate discovery like that of the passional series has escaped modern science, which has not even searched for it, or suspected its existence?

The greater the advantages which a discovery promises, the more exacting we should be in respect to proofs. If my theory were not in accord with the positive sciences, men would be justified in accusing me of constructing arbitrary systems, and might claim to modify my plan of association according to their fancy. It will be worthy of confidence only so far as it bases the theory of the harmony of the passions on other known harmonies of the universe. But to demonstrate the unity of the passions with the general system of the universe, this system must first be understood, which at present it is not, though so many writers have pretended to explain it. Hitherto men have speculated vaguely on the unity of the universe; it is now about to be demonstrated by reasoning from the passional world to material, guided by the analogy which exists between the two.

We shall thus have two new sciences to study concurrently—that of association, and that of the harmonies of the universe. This is enough to alarm many a reader who will fear that we are about to engage him in abstruse studies, which is not the case; for to explain the unity of the universe, the accord of the material with the passional world, I shall have recourse only to analogies drawn from the most interesting objects in the animal and vegetable kingdoms.

Let me first dissipate the prejudice which would assign limits to the power of God, and to the progressive development of nature. It would seem, if our sciences may be believed, that the present social order, called civilization, is the ultimate limit of human progress; that it would be impossible for Divine wisdom to invent a more perfect system than this labyrinth of misery and duplicity. There can be no greater error. Humanity is destined to organize many happier societies, and there exists a regular calculation for determining their properties, and the order of their succession. I will here point out the eight first societies that are to exist on the earth, including those which are now established.

TABLE OF THE FIRST PHASE OF SOCIAL MOVEMENT.

1. PRIMITIVE SOCIETY, called Eden or terrestrial paradise; confused series. Association by instinct and from circumstances.

   1½. The finer tribes of South-sea Islanders.

2. SAVAGISM, or the savage state, transition to, and commencement of the subversive societies.

   2½. Tartars and other wandering tribes.

3. *Patriarchalism.*

   3½. Circassians, Corsicans, Arabs, Jews.

   4. *Barbarism.*

     4¼. Chinese.   4¾. Russians.

   5. *Civilization.*

(Societies 2–5 are bracketed as "Subversive Societies.")

6. GUARANTISM, or semi-association; transition to the harmonic societies.

7. SIMPLE ASSOCIATION; commencement of the series.

8. COMPOUND DIVERGENT ASSOCIATION.

9. COMPOUND CONVERGENT ASSOCIATION.

(Societies 8 and 9 are bracketed:) Complete organization of the series, and passional harmony.

[The ninth society forms part of the second phase of social movement.]

In the four periods numbered 1, 7, 8, 9, which are organized in series, truth and justice predominate, and lead to fortune and consideration, whereas duplicity and injustice would lead to ruin and dishonor.

On the other hand, falseness and injustice must reign in the periods 2, 3, 4, 5, because in them they lead to wealth and distinction; this is an inevitable effect of the system of incoherent and fragmentary industry, or industry exercised by non-associated families. As to truth and justice, they lead to wealth and honor only in the combined order—that is, in the periods organized in unitary passional series.

Of the nine periods indicated in the table, four only are known to us; they are the four false or subversive periods.

2. The savage.   3. The patriarchal.
4. The barbarian.   5. The civilized.

I define them as *subversive societies*, because they are based on an inversion of the principles of unity and harmony, and are so many labyrinths in which the human race gropes its way by instinct towards its destiny. During the continuance of these periods, humanity is reduced to mere dreams as to the primary objects of its desires, which are

Proportional Wealth,
Individual Happiness,
The Reign of Justice,
PIVOT. Unity of Action.

Instead of attaining these ends, it has succeeded only in establishing

Relative Poverty,
Individual Anxiety,
The Reign of all Vices,
PIVOT. Duplicity of Action.

The duplicities of action will alone furnish us an immense catalogue of social evils, the most striking of which is the conflict of the individual with the collective interest, and the indifference of every one to operations of general good, such as the preservation of forests.

In the above table I have inserted four transitional or intermediate societies, placed at the intervals; they will be sufficient to exercise the reader in classifying mixed or transitional periods.

For example, Chinese society, as we know, unites in about equal proportions the characteristics of barbarism and of civilization: it has its seraglios like the barbarians, and its tribunals of justice like the *civilizees;* it is then a mixed period to be classed between periods 4 and 5, of the characteristics of which it partakes about equally.

The mixed or transitional order is found throughout the whole system of nature. It exists in the social as well as in the material movement. The transitional periods are to the others what the polypus is to the animal and vegetable kingdoms, what the bat is to the order of quadrupeds and birds, between which it forms the link. We shall return to the consideration of these transitional or mixed social periods, which it is not yet time to describe.

Let us confine our attention to the main subject—the distinction of the social periods into associated and non-associated, or the harmonic and the subversive, between which we remark the following principal contrast, namely:

1. That the associated periods, numbered in the table 1, 7, 8, 9, have the property of rendering virtue, justice and truth more honorable and advantageous than vice, injustice and fraud; and, as a consequence, of causing virtue to be preferred to vice, and inspiring men with a love of practicing truth and justice.

2. That the non-associated periods, numbered 2, 3, 4, 5, confer wealth and honor upon fraud and injustice, disguised under the colors of virtue, and, in consequence, lead the immense majority of men to the practice of them. They are as a consequence subversive social states, social purgatories, in which man, sunk in social darkness, is ignorant of the means by which wealth, happiness, truth and unity could be established on the earth.

The comparison between these eight societies, four of which are happy and four unhappy, leads us to lay down the principle of *duality of development* in the social movement, and to distinguish between the harmonic, or true and happy order, based on the series, and the subversive, or false and unhappy order, based on the system of isolated households and families.

In respect to this problem the ancients, guided by instinct, had more correct ideas than have the moderns, guided by reason. The latter have not recognized this law of duality of movement. The former admitted two principles in the universe—the one good, the other evil—as for example, in the Persian mythology, Oromasdes and Abriman. They extended this idea to the social movement, in which they introduced demons acting concurrently with gods. By giving a further extension to, and modifying this idea, the different social periods would have been divided into harmonic and subversive, or divine and demoniac. This would have led to the conclusion that our globe is in the subversive periods, under the reign of evil, for we see upon it all the effects that would be produced by the influence of evil spirits. The social world presents nothing but the spectacle of indigence, fraud, violence, carnage and other similar results, which are calculated to make us doubt the intervention of Providence in human affairs, and lead us to conclude that the social movement is in the phase ruled by the evil principle; this should prompt us to seek for other systems of society regulated by the good principle, and productive of the reign of universal liberty and peace.

We see in every sphere of nature these two classes of effects—the harmonic and the subversive. If there is unity in the system of the universe, this contrast of development, this duality of action, must exist in the social world.

It required no great effort of genius to suspect an analogy between the social and the material movement, and to conclude that as human society might be subject to this double development, means should be sought for escaping from the subversive and unhappy periods—the savage, barbarian, patriarchal and civilized—and for establishing the harmonic or happy periods—that is, the societies based on the divine law or the series.

The sixth period, indicated under the name of guarantism or semi-association—which is the transitional period between the subversive and the harmonic societies—has not been discovered, though active researches have been instinctively made for it. It would present a mixture in about equal proportions of truth and falseness. It is the object of the dreams of the philosophers, who in their utopias reason only of guarantees, counterpoises, balances and equalibria. To rise to this degree of social good, this partial reign of truth, it will be necessary to discover the sixth period, which is higher in the scale than civilization. The latter is incompatible with any regular guarantees; hence all which men have sought to establish has been vain and illusive.

The conclusion to be drawn from the study of the preceding table is that the subversive periods—the societies 2, 3, 4, 5, in which the principle of association is unknown, and industry is prosecuted on the incoherent system by isolated families—are four sinks of vice, four boxes of Pandora, spreading over the earth all social calamities, such as poverty, fraud, anxiety, duplicity, etc.

When we see all these evils springing up in place of the good results promised by science, and becoming aggravated by the antidotes applied to them, is it not evident that the human mind is completely in the dark on social questions, and that the true principles of human society remain to be discovered? Why does philosophy refuse to acknowledge errors which experience points out? Other sciences are more modest; it is admitted in medicine, for example, that there is a deficiency of knowledge when diseases like the gout, hydrophobia or epilepsy, resist all known modes of treatment. In this case it is frankly confessed that the science is behind hand in discoveries, and that the antidote remains to be found.

Let us here point out an inconsistency which has not been remarked. On the one hand, prejudice leads us to neglect all study of association under the pretext that it is *too perfect for man;* while on the other, the evils under which we labor, lead us to invoke one by one all the benefits which would flow from association. Our desires in this respect may be reduced to four, which have already been enumerated, and which include all the others. They are:

> Proportional Wealth,
> Individual Happiness,
> The Reign of Justice,
>   PIVOT.   Unity of Action.

I employ the expression, *individual happiness,* which is the source of general happiness, as the latter can only be based on the contentment of each individual; until this condition is fulfilled, general happiness cannot exist.

All the desires expressed by our moral, political and economic sciences are summed up in the four lines of the above table, which indicate the general results of association. Now, to wish for these results, is it not to wish for the cause that can alone produce them?—for the associative regime, which no one has thought of exploring.

Political science, which promises to secure to us the four blessings of wealth, happiness, justice, and unity, establishes only the four opposite evils.

1. It promises to enrich nations and individuals; but instead of this, we see that nations are becoming more and more involved in debt, and that individuals, whose wants are increased by the progress of luxury, find their fortunes too limited, even among the opulent classes; while the laboring multitude have not even the necessaries of life, and find themselves more liable to be thrown out of employment since the progress made in manufactures and the mechanic arts.

I have already showed that the civilized order cannot guarantee to the masses the means of a livelihood, because labor being repugnant out of association, the people would give themselves up to idleness the moment they were certain of a *minimum* or an ample sufficiency of all the necessaries of life; this cannot be secured to them except in the combined order in which industry is rendered attractive, so that each association can, without risk, make an advance to the members of two-thirds of what they would earn in devoting themselves to congenial labors—that is, labors rendered attractive, and transformed into pleasures. At the present day, the repugnance for labor seems on the increase, and for the reason that the poverty of the masses is relatively greater now than it was at periods when there was less luxury; there is no more frightful misery, for example, than that which is found among the English, who hold nevertheless the first rank in industry.

2. Political science aims, as it asserts, to elevate the social world to happiness; but it is difficult to understand how it can do this when it does not even know what constitutes happiness, and has given no positive theory of it.

To understand wherein happiness consists, we must consult the desires of the majority. Now we see the rich leading a life of idle ease, or if they engage in industry, exercising those functions which are agreeable, honorable and lucrative. We see, on the other hand, the middle class and the common people, who constitute the immense majority, seeking also to lead this easy life of the rich, and to take part with them in the affairs of government. Thus, it is evident that every one places happiness in the possession of fortune and leisure, or in the exercise of attractive and honorable functions.

It is necessary, then, if we would elevate the whole people to a state of happiness, to transform the repugnant labors to which the great majority are now condemned into pleasures, that is, into attractive pursuits.

Such will be the effect of association organized in series; it will secure the happiness of the people by offering them the means of wealth and pleasure in productive employment—in agricultural and manufacturing labors, which it will render as attractive as any known pleasures now are, and which in this order will be made so enticing as to allure to them even the rich and great.

3. Our moral science would establish the reign of virtue, of good morals, and the practice of truth and justice. Nothing can be more laudable than such aims but where are the means of accomplishing them? They do not exist in the civilized social order, in which virtue is but little practiced, since truth conduces less to fortune than falsehood and injustice. We can hope for the reign of virtue, truth and justice only in a society which will render them surer avenues to success than iniquity, wrong and falsehood. This effect can only take place in the associative order, which comprises the periods 7, 8, 9, of the table.

To obtain these important results, it has been supposed that genius should invent codes and systems of laws, and the means of enforcing them; in the place of these useless levers, a single method will suffice, namely,

Produce by unitary series.

Consume by unitary series.

Distribute by unitary series.

Here is the method, stated in its simplest form, by which association operates; it consists of a single process, attractive in all its details and workings, and applicable to the three industrial functions, *production, consumption, distribution*. Everything will be effected by this single means, and the only thing to be studied will be the art of organizing and developing the series, and applying them to industry.

As regards the guarantee of labor and a *minimum* to which we have often referred, the age seems to be retrograding; it will be seen in the chapter devoted to the analysis of commercial errors, that civilization is declining towards its fourth phase, which is more false and oppressive in its industrial and commercial arrangements, than is the third, which now exists.

The age, though actively occupied with industrial questions, has failed in discovering the means of real progress, that is, in discovering intermediary measures between isolated individual industry, exercised by families, and combined industry, exercised by associations; the latter once inaugurated in any country will be everywhere imitated, owing to the immense advantages which it will secure, both as regards the increase of wealth and the happiness of the people.

It is very difficult for a globe to rise at once to the discovery of the combined order and the passional series. If I have made it, it is because I was, from the outset, favored by fortune; but few globes accomplish this without feeling their way slowly and making many experiments, the successive trial of which consumes centuries.

I regret that, in publishing my discovery, it is necessary to accommodate myself to the commercial spirit of the age, and dwell constantly upon the pecuniary advantages of association as the best means of interesting the public mind. In other ages, nobler incentives might have been presented, such as the guarantee of the reign of universal harmony, of practical truth in all relations, of unity of language, weights and measures, of the equilibrium of climate, and many other advantages which would result from the combined order; but these grand results will seem of slight importance to an age absorbed in commercial and stock-jobbing operations.

To gratify its mercantile mania, I might show that association with its industrial organization will attract to labor a hundred million of Africans, who, though at the very gates of Europe, are of no commercial advantage to it; it will do this by its property of imparting a charm to agricultural and manufacturing industry—a property reserved to the combined order alone, organized in passional series.

The adoption by the African race of productive Industry will render abundant those tropical products which our habits have rendered indispensable; sugar will then be exchanged, pound for pound, for flour; a few years will be sufficient to effect this brilliant operation, which by elevating Africa in the social scale will abolish forever the infamous practice of the slave trade, now such a reproach to civilization. Shall I add the perspective of industrial unities, especially the guarantee of a free intercourse on all the seas and continents of the globe, facilitated by unity of language? These advantages, the idea of which is so dazzling, the combined order will diffuse by the thousand. In the divine plan of social organization, in the mechanism which God has devised for the industrial concert of the passions, everything is wonderful. And is it not in the nature of things that a social order given to the world by divine wisdom should cause the reign on earth of as many blessings as the laws of man—which violate that order—have produced scourges?

If our age were animated by a real faith and hope in God, far from doubting the possibility of attaining the immense advantages which association promises, they would look upon them as the probable design of providence; they would feel that the Supreme Being must have reserved for man some lot less humiliating than that of the miseries and the degradation of civilization. But the spirit of the age leads the nations to despair of divine aid, and to doubt of a social providence; it inclines them to believe that God has left to feeble human reason the task of directing the passions, and of organizing human relations. The world is about to be fully disabused on this point by the trial of the associative order; and though our age is one of scepticism, materialism and of irreligious opinions, I can bid defiance to its doubts, and guarantee that after a single experiment of association, the sceptic, the materialist and the indifferent in religious matters will be so fully convinced of the existence of a social providence, of the Divine generosity and of the *harmonizability* of the passions, that we shall see them transformed into fervent adorers of the Deity, honoring that religious spirit which now they disdain. Irreligion is the result of the permanent reign of evil on earth, and of the immensity of human sufferings, which, to a superficial observer, seem to accuse the Creator of incapacity, or of indifference.

Doubtless if we consider only the four subversive societies— the savage, patriarchal, barbarian and civilized—we shall feel justified in condemning the passions; but to appreciate the wisdom of God who created them, we must wait the explanation of the effects which they will produce in the harmonic societies, organized according to the Divine law.

After having read the description of the wealth and harmony which association will produce in these periods, and of the lustre which virtue, justice and truth will enjoy in them, we shall then be able to judge of the solicitude of God for the happiness of mankind, and of the incredible thoughtlessness of the scientific world in having neglected for so many centuries to make researches for some other societies than the four subversive ones in which the human race has hitherto vegetated. Simple association might have been organized as early as the time of Pericles, and even in ancient Egypt; how much bloodshed and misery this delay in social studies has cost the world, especially during the present century with its terrible revolutions and devastating wars!

It is natural that a generation which has suffered so much from political errors and failures should be very distrustful as to any new theories; hence I propose a practical trial of association on a small scale, limited to four hundred persons, and I insist on the difference between such an experiment and those which from the very outset commence by convulsing a whole empire. If modern nations have suffered so much from wars, revolutions and civil commotions, it is because our political sciences have not been restricted to local experiments. Since the time of Descartes, experience has been extolled as the only guide; how is it that men who recommend it in all cases where innovations are proposed do not apply it to their social and political theories? This policy of a local practical experiment is the course which would be followed in testing association, from which in consequence no danger need be apprehended. The trial might be limited to a small nucleus of sixty or eighty agricultural families. No confidence need be placed in the theory till it has been fully sanctioned by a practical trial—in other words, till after having proved by this limited experiment that association organized in *series* would *render labor attractive, triple the general product of industry, and establish unity of interests, by remunerating each individual in the ratio of his* CAPITAL, LABOR *and* TALENT, and, especially, of providing for the first want of man—namely, *the certainty of employment and a minimum of support.*

It has been believed for a century past, that the means of improving the condition of the people were to be found in the theories of political economy, and its treatises on national wealth; but, could it teach the method of increasing the wealth of nations, does it follow that it would be any guarantee of individual happiness? No, for individual happiness depends first of all upon *attractive industry,* without which it is impossible to guarantee to the masses either pleasure in their labors or a *minimum,* that is, the guaranteed certainty of a comfortable support; they would, if once guaranteed the means of subsistence, abandon industry. National wealth, then, if possible, would fail entirely of securing social and individual happiness; there would still remain two problems to be solved:

1. That of rendering industry attractive; without pleasure in

his occupations, the laborer is miserable; he envies the rich who can live comfortably without being forced to repugnant toil.

2. The establishment of distributive justice in industry, that is, a distribution of profits according to capital, labor and talent. This condition can be fulfilled only in the combined order, operating by Series.

Considering that the above problems are intimately connected, and that their solution depends exclusively upon the organization of the series which has not been discovered by political economy, it is evident that this science is far from having fulfilled its promises of elevating the social world to happiness; in fact, it has occupied itself only with the first of the three problems, that of national wealth; and even in this it has shamefully failed, as is shown by the legions of beggars who abound in the most opulent nations; as, for instance, England.

The achievements of our speculative sciences—politics, political economy, etc.—may be summed up in the following table.

TABLE OF THE NINE PERMANENT SCOURGES
INCIDENT TO THE SUBVERSIVE SOCIAL PERIODS.

1. INDIGENCE
2. FRAUD
3. OPPRESSION
4. CARNAGE
5. CLIMATIC DERANGEMENT
6. DISEASES ARTIFICIALLY ENGENDERED—LIKE THE
   PLAGUE, CHOLERA, ETC.
7. CIRCLE OF ERROR

PIVOTS. { UNIVERSAL SELFISHNESS
         { DUPLICITY OF SOCIAL ACTION.

Each of these scourges includes by implication many others; every social evil may be referred to some one of them. National debts, for example, are included under the head of indigence, for they are a result of general poverty; stock-gambling and speculation are included under the head of fraud; usury and monopoly under that of oppression; the congelation of the polar regions and the obstruction of the northern seas under that of climatic derangement; the destruction of forests, one of the causes of climatic derangement, comes under the head of circle of error, for it is an evil resulting from incoherent and disordered cultivation.

The philosophers, ashamed of these disgraceful results which are constantly reproduced in the civilized social order, propose as the only remedy political innovations; in place of really useful measures, they recommend continually the same old experiments, which have produced nothing but the three social furies, called civilization, barbarism and savageism.

They should have been restricted in their experiments to operations really new in social and domestic organization—operations which, when tested by experience, would produce the nine benefits opposed to the nine radical evils engendered by civilization. These benefits which the combined order will secure are summed up in the following table.

TABLE OF THE NINE PERMANENT BENEFITS
OF THE COMBINED ORDER.

1. GENERAL AND GRADUATED WEALTH
2. PRACTICAL TRUTH IN ALL RELATIONS
3. EFFECTIVE GUARANTEES, AND REAL LIBERTY
4. PERMANENT PEACE
5. EQUILIBRIUM OF CLIMATE AND TEMPERATURE
6. UNIVERSAL SANITARY SYSTEM
7. ENCOURAGEMENT FOR ALL DISCOVERIES, TESTED BY PRACTICAL EXPERIMENTS

PIVOTS. { COLLECTIVE AND INDIVIDUAL PHILANTHROPY
UNITY OF SOCIAL ACTION.

Such will be the results of association. As soon as a practical experiment of it is made, even on a small scale, we shall see unrolled before our eyes the plan of God as to the employment of the passions and their tendency to, and concurrence with, industry and practical truth. At this spectacle, human reason will be confounded at having doubted the universality of Providence, and at having believed that God has created the passions without assigning to them a mechanism of social and industrial harmony. On beholding this divine order, this concert of graduated inequalities, the champions of the speculative sciences will be silenced, and the atheist, even, seized with a pious enthusiasm, will exclaim in the spirit of Simeon, "Lord, now let thy servant depart in peace, for my eyes have seen the masterwork of thy wisdom—the social harmony of the passions—the way to truth and unity, and the happiness that thou hast prepared for all thy people."

The multitude, addressing the scientific leaders of the world, will ask, "You who are the guides and oracles of nations, who promise them prosperity and happiness, who claim to have penetrated the depths of science, how is it that you have not seen that there is a God whose providence is universal, that it extends to all things and especially to human relations, and that the task of human reason was to seek for and determine the order of social and industrial relations which he has prepared for man?"

The spectacle of the wonders which the trial of association will produce, such as

      1. The tripling of the products of industry
      2. Industrial attraction
      3. Concord of the passions
      PIVOT. Unity of action

will suffice to transform the rich and great into active cooperators, eager to take part in the labors necessary to the organization of their associations. Thus the initial experiment will be universally imitated with the greatest rapidity. The first realization of the combined order will produce upon the existing incoherent societies the effect of a powerful absorbent; they will be replaced with inconceivable rapidity, and in the course of a few years the entire globe could be organized in association.

Discoverer of the theory of association, I find myself in the situation of a man who, in the age of Augustus, should have in-

vented gunpowder and the mariner's compass, but who, instead
of hastening to communicate his inventions, should have spent
twenty years in calculating their effects. Suppose at the end of
these twenty years of study he should have presented himself
before the ministers of Augustus, holding in his hand a cartridge
and a compass, and have addressed them in the following language: "I can with this substance—powder—change the tactics of Alexander and of Cæsar; blow the Capitol in the air;
batter down cities at the distance of a league; reduce Rome at a
given signal to a heap of ruins; destroy your legions a thousand
yards off, and render the feeblest soldier equal to the strongest.
With this other instrument—the compass—I can brave storms
and breakers in the darkest night; direct a ship as safely as in
broad daylight; and find my way everywhere, though neither
land nor sky are visible."

On hearing such language the grave dignitaries of Rome
would have treated him as an arrant charlatan, and yet he would
have promised nothing but what was quite possible, and is
known at the present day even to children.

It is the same with the two theories I announce, namely, *industrial association* and *passional attraction;* these two discoveries, which are intimately connected, and neither of which could
have been made without the other, place me in a position to
promise a host of marvels, the mention of the least of which
would cause me to be called a visionary; and yet, ere long, they
will seem perfectly natural and will be intelligible to the merest
child. They will be effected, as I have said, by a single process,
namely, the passional series, substituted in place of the present
individual and incoherent system, from which the human race
has reaped only indigence, fraud, oppression and carnage—a
system which, after having been a disgrace to human reason for
thirty centuries, is about to fall before the social laws devised for
man by Divine reason.

To minds exempt from philosophic prejudices, these laws
might be explained at once and without preamble, but minds
imbued with these prejudices are averse to the reception of
truth; their preconceived notions must be destroyed before they

can be brought to a common sense view of nature and her operations. We may draw an illustration from the architect, who finds less trouble in building on an unoccupied field than on one covered with the ruins of an old castle, the rubbish of which must first be cleared away. The human mind is in an analogous condition; it is a ground encumbered with old and worn out doctrines and theories, to which philosophy has given birth. Blinded by the false views and prejudices which they have engendered, it has been accustomed to look upon nature in a sense contrary to her true aim, which is harmony and unity based on duality of development.

Our political, moral and economical theories have inculcated opinions wholly opposed to the principle of unity; they have accustomed men to believe:

1. That the divine nature, the universe, and the system of movement are simple, not compound—that there is *monality*, and not duality in their action and development.

2. That providence is limited and partial, instead of universal; and that it does not embrace the direction of the social movement.

3. That man is a *simple* being, excluded from unity with the universe, and from divine guidance in his social relations.

4. That the social compact must be based on selfishness and duplicity, and that reciprocal guarantees of truth and justice are impossible.

5. That our passions are our enemies; which implies that God who created them is also our enemy.

6. That reason suffices of itself alone to repress and direct the passions, while it is evident, as experience demonstrates, that it cannot repress or direct even those of the men who claim to be its oracles.

7. That the reign of truth and justice is to be secured by smothering our desires and attractions, by disregarding riches and worldly interests, and by other similar means, and not by new discoveries in social organization which would secure the harmonious development of man's nature, and the reign of universal abundance.

PIVOT. That nature is limited, as respects social organization, to the societies already established, namely, the civilized, barbarian and savage, which implies that the passions are susceptible of but one mode of development—the subversive—and that the nine scourges, already enumerated, are permanent and irremediable.

We might fill pages with absurd opinions similar to these, to which might be added the modern doctrines of materialism and atheism, which did not exist in antiquity. It is evident, then, that human reason, notwithstanding its boasts of progress, is on all great social questions still sunk in darkness and ignorance. "When things have come to this point," says Condillac, "when errors have thus accumulated, there is but one means of restoring order in the domain of thought, and that is to forget all that we have learned, go back to the origin of our ideas, to first principles, and, as Bacon says, conduct the whole work of the understanding anew. This means is difficult of application in proportion as men believe themselves learned."

Conformably to the views of Condillac and Bacon, I shall return frequently to the attack of dominant errors. I cannot too often repeat, however, that in criticising the controversial sciences, I do not criticise their authors; to speculate in opinions and theories is no more reprehensible than to speculate in any tolerated branch of trade. The blame falls on civilization, which does not employ genius properly by encouraging useful discoveries, and then on the prejudice which would teach us that this disastrous order is the ultimate destiny of man, and that God was incapable of inventing anything better for organizing human relations. How can an age which lays claim to an enlightened religious faith, adopt ideas so derogatory to the wisdom and goodness of the Creator?

TSO, I, pp. 43–60

PART TWO

THE NEW THEORY OF SOCIETY

I. THE PASSIONS

REPRESSION IN BOURGEOIS CIVILIZATION

Let us consider briefly the suffocation of passion and its disastrous results. I will compare passion with mania, which is a diminutive form of passion.

All repressed passion produces its counter-passion which is as malevolent as the natural passion would be beneficial. The mechanism is the same for manias. Let us take some examples of this repression chosen from particulars of love, which is the subject of this . . . section.

Dame Strogonoff, a Muscovite princess, seeing herself grow old, was jealous of the youth and beauty of one of her slaves. She frequently had her tortured and she herself often stuck her with pins. What was the real motive of her cruelty? Was it truly jealousy? No. It was lesbianism. Without knowing it, this lady was a lesbian, in love with the beautiful slave whom she tortured. If someone had acquainted Mme. Strogonoff with the idea of lesbianism and had arranged a reconciliation between herself and her victim, these two would have become very passionate lovers. But the princess, failing to consider the idea, fell into a counter-passion, subverting her true feeling and persecuting its object, with whom she should have found pleasure. Her rage was proportionately greater as the repression came from a prejudice which, hiding from this lady the true nature of her passion, did not allow its ideal development. A repression of violence, which is the result of all forced deprivation, does not always result in such fury.

Others act out in a collective sense the atrocities that Mme. Strogonoff exercised individually. Nero enjoyed collective cruelty. Odin made a religious system of cruelty and de Sade a moral system. This predilection for atrocity is again but the counter-effect of the suffocation of certain passions. In the case of Nero and de Sade it was the composite and the alternating passions which were repressed, while for Mme. Strogonoff it was a branch of love that was subverted.

The suffocation of rare manias or extra-manias has the same disadvantages. If a man born to be a hair or a foot fetishist is unable to satisfy himself in love, if he finds only women and confidents who expose him to ridicule, he will be fettered by his special proclivity and will fall into malevolent manias. The humorous mania of Julius Cæsar is well known—"to be the wife of all husbands." Such a desire could not be satisfied today without exposing Cæsar to public derision. He would be thwarted and would perhaps fall into atrocious counter-manias to which all his empire would fall victim.

NMA, pp. 390–92

PASSIONATE ATTRACTION

If the immensity of our desires is compared with the limited means that we have of satisfying them, it would seem that God behaved inconsiderately in giving us passions so avid of pleasure, passions created to harass us by exciting a thousand longings of which only one-tenth can be satisfied in the present social order.

It is in view of these considerations that moralists claim to correct God's work, to regulate and repress these passions they do not know how to satisfy, and for the most part do not even recognize. Of the twelve passions which compose the principal springs of the soul, they recognize only nine; and they have only a very imperfect notion of even the four main passions.

These nine recognized passions are *the five appetites of the senses* which exercise varying control upon each individual, and *the four simple appetites of the soul,* namely:

6. Group of friendship
7. Group of love
8. Group of paternity or family
9. Group of corporation or ambition.

Moralists want to give to these nine passions a course contrary to the intent of nature. How they have harangued for the last two thousand years to subdue and change the five sensual appetites in order to persuade us that diamonds are ugly stones, that gold is a vile metal, that sugar and spices are worthless products meriting disdain, and that thatched cottages and simple, crude nature are preferable to kings' palaces. Thus have moralists sought to deaden the sensual passions. And they spare to no greater degree the passions of the soul. How they have vociferated against ambition! According to them, one must desire only mediocre and barely profitable occupations; if occupation brings an income of 100,000 pounds one must only accept 10,000 in order to gratify morality. Their opinions on love are even more absurd—they want to make constancy and fidelity reign. What is more incompatible with the intention of nature and more tiresome to the two sexes? No being will submit himself to tyranny when he can enjoy total freedom.

All these philosophical whims, called *duties,* have nothing to do with nature. Duty is man's creation; attraction comes from God. In order to understand the design of God, one must study attraction, nature itself, without taking duty into account, since it varies in each century and in each region, whereas the nature of passion has been and will remain invariable for all people.

Let us give an example of the study of attraction, using the relationship between paternal and filial love.

Moralists want to establish equality of affection between fathers and children. On this subject they allege sacred duties with which nature is not at all in accord. In order to discover nature's will we must forget duty, *what should be,* and analyze *what is.* We will then see that a father's affection for his children is approximately three times as great as that of children for their father. The disproportion seems enormous and unfair on the part of children; however this is to be considered in a study of *what is* and not of *what ought to be*.

If, instead of trying to correct the passions, we would search for nature's motives in giving the passions a direction so different from duty, we will soon see that these sacred duties have no connection with justice, as the disproportion between filial and paternal love will show us. And this inequality is founded on plausible grounds. If children return only a third of the love shown them by their parents, three reasons can be given.

First, until they reach puberty children are ignorant of what it means to be a father and to engender offspring; they can neither appreciate nor understand this title. In early childhood, when filial affection is formed, the nature of the act constituting paternity is carefully hidden from the child; he is therefore at that time only susceptible to *sympathetic* and not to *filial* love. We should not require that his attachment be one of gratitude for the care given to his education; this reasoned recognition is above the moral faculties of a child. It would be more childish than he is to expect such love from a being incapable of reflection. In any case that gratitude is *friendship,* and not *filial love,* which a child can neither understand nor feel.

Second, a child from the age of seven to fourteen years is importuned by the remonstrances of his parents, seasoned with harsh treatment among the lower class. Since the child has not enough reason to appreciate the necessity of the constraint imposed upon him, his attachment can only develop in connection with the kindness that he receives; thus one frequently sees that a grandparent, a neighbor, or a servant is dearer to him than his parents. And fathers have no right to complain; if they have some sagacity they must know that the child, due to the causes cited above, is responsive only to *sympathetic love,* and that such a love establishes itself in proportion to the gentleness and discernment with which fathers exercise their paternal role.

Third, as soon as the child learns what the status of father- and motherhood consist of, he perceives the self-seeking motives of his parents' love for him—for example, the hope that his birth furnished to their ambition or to their weakness, and the distraction that he provided when he was the charm of their leisure hours. After discovering the selfish nature of his parents' affection, a child cannot believe himself very indebted to them since they have procured so much pleasure in which he has not shared. These notions serve to cool rather than to increase his affection. He finds that he was engendered through love of pleasure and not through love of himself; that his parents perhaps created him against their wishes, maybe that they increased their already too numerous progeny through carelessness, or that they desired a child of the opposite sex. In short, during adolescence, when filial love can begin to exist in a child, a thousand considerations come to dissipate the prestige and even to make ridiculous in the child's eyes the importance attached to paternity. Thus, if parents have not known how to gain a child's esteem and friendship, they will see no filial love whatsoever spring up in him, not even the one-third return at which nature has fixed the debt of children to their parents, a return which will be sufficient in the new social order, where education will cause not the least hardship to fathers. It is in this direction that our globe is advancing, and to which our passions are predisposed.

As for the present, if the burden of education seems to give the father unlimited rights to a child's love, it is because the three attenuating reasons that I have brought to light have never been taken into consideration:

1. Young children's ignorance of the qualities constituting paternity;
2. Distaste experienced in childhood through the abuse or misunderstood exercise of paternal authority;
3. The contrast observed in adolescence between fathers' pretensions and the lack of real merits on which they stand.

Other accessory considerations, such as paternal preferences which justly offend the child, will help us perceive why the child commonly feels only a third of the affection given him by his parents. If he feels more, it is the effect of sympathy and not of family ties. A child will often have two or three times more affection for one parent than for the other, whose role is the same in his eyes, but whose character does not suit him.

Here are truths that civilizees neither want to admit nor want to base their social judgments upon. Poor in pleasure, they want to be rich in illusion. They claim for themselves rights of property upon the affection of the weakest. A sixty-year-old husband demands the absolute love and fidelity of his twenty-year-old wife—we know with what success. Fathers want to be gods, models in the eyes of their children; they cry ingratitude if they obtain the measure of love they deserve. Lacking the true affection of their offspring, they gorge themselves on delusions; they seek out books and plays displaying scenes of filial love and conjugal fidelity whose shadow is not to be found in real family situations. Civilizees, nourishing themselves on moral fantasies, become incapable of studying the general laws of nature; they see them only in relation to their whims and despotic pretensions. They accuse nature of injustice without wanting to consider her aims.

To discover the design of nature it is necessary, without stopping at ideas of *duty*, to proceed to the analysis and synthesis of that *passionate attraction* which seems evil to us, because we are ignorant of its objectives, but which, evil or not, has never been the subject of methodical analysis. . . .

THE TREE OF PASSION AND ITS BRANCHES

Let us begin with the first degree, bearing three branches; we shall speak later of the trunk, or *unityism*, considered to be the source of all the passions, which are in the first level three, in the second level twelve, etc.

There are in the first degree or first division of the trunk three passionate sub-foci or centers of attraction, toward which persons of all ranks and all ages incline; these three passions are:

1. *luxuryism,* or the desire for luxury;
2. *groupism,* or the desire for groups;
3. *seriesism,* or the desire for series.

Let us examine them in subdivisions according to the number of passions they furnish in the following level or second power, which bears twelve branches forming the passional scale analogous to the musical scale.

First sub-focus, luxury. It furnishes and governs the five secondary passions, called the sensory passions or desires of the senses.

Luxury is *internal* and *external;* it is internal with regard to the health that the free and direct exercise of each sense guarantees us; one has a healthy stomach and excellent appetite in vain if he lacks the money to dine. He who has not a penny is condemned to starvation, to the indirect suppression of the senses. The senses therefore cannot have full indirect development without the mediation of money, to which all is subordinated in civilization.

The case is similar for the other senses; each of them, without the aid of wealth, is reduced to minimum development. To what end does one have a perfect ear, if for lack of money he is refused entrance to operas and concerts, while seeing others enter who have a tin ear and a well-lined pocketbook? The possession of health or inner luxury, therefore, is not sufficient for happiness. We still desire the external luxury, or wealth, that guarantees free development of the senses, of which internal luxury secures only conditional development.

The exception itself confirms the principle. A young lady finds an old fogy who assures her a happy life and full exercise of certain sensual pleasures, opulent repast, adornments, etc., which she has lacked. In this case one of the five senses, the fifth, touch, intervenes in order to assure through wealth the external exercise of the four others which would have had only internal use or health. Without the aid of this old goat's wealth, they would have a capacity deprived of positive development, and would have been subjected to all sorts of privations; perhaps even including the sense of touch, since the poor have very little means of obtaining in love the one they desire.

We conclude that luxury is complex rather than simple, that it is both internal and external. This is an important principle to establish in order to demonstrate the vagueness of the physical sciences in all questions of unity or movement. Witness the debate on the simplicity or complexity of light; if light were a simple phenomenon it must be, by virtue of the unity of nature, that luxury is also simple. It is the first aim of passional attraction, as the pivot of light or the sun is the first aim of material attraction. But luxury, being complex as we have just seen, indicates that light must be complex as well, unless there is duplicity in the system of nature and in the parallelism of material and passionate movement.

Second sub-focus, groups. This branch furnishes four secondary passions, called *affectives:*

Major $\begin{cases} 1. & \text{Group of honor, or corporation} \\ 2. & \text{Group of friendship} \end{cases}$

Minor $\begin{cases} 3. & \text{Group of love} \\ 4. & \text{Group of family or kinship} \end{cases}$

Our legislators want to subordinate the social system to the last of these four groups, that of family, the group that God has almost entirely excluded from influence in social harmony, because it is a group of compulsory or physical bonds, and not one of free passionate association, dissoluble at will.

It has been typical for people who contradict nature in all their calculations, to take as the pivot of social mechanism the one of the four groups that exerts the least influence, since it excludes freedom. In harmony, then, this group has active use only when it is absorbed by the other three and operates in accordance with them.

All constraint engenders falsity, necessarily established by reason of the influence of the family group, which is neither free nor dissoluble; thus there is nothing more false than the two civilized and patriarchal societies where this group dominates. Barbarian society, more cruel, more oppressive than ours, is, however, less false, being less influenced by the family group, one of the greatest germs of falsity that there is in movement. An indissoluble bond is contradictory to God's spirit, which wants only to guide by attraction or by bonds of liberty and impulse.

Third sub-focus, the series, or group affiliations aligned in series and enjoying the same properties as the geometrical series. This third branch furnishes three of the twelve secondary passions—these are called *distributives* and tend toward a social and domestic arrangement unknown to civilization, although known to primitive society. This is the secret of lost happiness that must be recovered. Thus, the calculations of passional harmony must depend principally upon the art of forming and mechanizing the series of groups.

If savants believed in the unity of the universe that they have dinned into our ears, they would be of the opinion that, if all the universe and all created products are distributed by series, it will be necessary to establish a similar order in the play of social and domestic passions in order to align ourselves with unity.

It did not please them to admit to that analogy, nor to infer the necessity for research on the formation of the passional series, of which I bear the secret. . . .

Unityism is the penchant of the individual to relate his happiness to that of all who surround him, and to all mankind, today so hateful. It is an unlimited philanthropy, a universal good will, which can be developed only when the whole of mankind is rich, free, and just, conforming to the three passionate sub-foci—luxury, groups, and series—which demand:

First development, progressive riches of the five senses;

Second development, absolute liberty for the four groups;

Third development, distributive justice, for the passions of this name.

If unityism includes the three primary passions, from here on it will be proper to compare unityism to white light which contains the seven solar colors. It must be known that light contains five other invisible colors that are not perceived by us—pink, fawn, maroon, dragon green, and lilac (I am certain only of pink and fawn). Therefore white light truly contains twelve colors, of which only seven are visible, just as the musical octave contains twelve tones, seven of which are primary. There is therefore no exactitude in representing unityism as the union

of the seven passions of the soul, called affectives and distributives, since that union supposes the development of the five
sensory passions and consequently, development of all twelve
secondary passions.

This prospectus lacks a definition of unityism, the root of the
passions, but since this is not at all developed in the civilized
order, it is sufficient to fix our attention on the counter-passion,
egoism, that so universally dominates. The system or ideology
of perfectible perfectibility has made egoism, or the self, the
basis of all its calculations. It has been commonplace to observe
in civilizees only subversive passions, which have but an apparent likeness to those in harmony.

Our scholars are unaware of unityism or unlimited philanthropy; instead of this passion they have only envisioned its subversive development or counter-development, the mania of
subordinating everything to our individual convenience. This
odious penchant has various names in the learned world—the
moralists call it egoism, the ideologues call it the self, a new
word which says nothing new. It is but a useless euphemism for
egoism, of which civilizees have always been rightly accused
since in making hypocrisy and oppression reign, their social
condition tends to subordinate the twelve passions to egoism.
Thus egoism becomes a subversive focus and replaces unityism
or the focus of harmonious passion.

Since happiness—or the development of unityism, which includes development of all the passions—is our common goal, we
must, in order to simplify our studies, settle our thesis upon
the three primary passions, luxuryism, groupism, and seriesism,
or at the most upon the twelve secondary passions which are subdivisions of the three primary ones.

It is useless to prematurely expand the details of the 32 terti-
ary passions, still less of the 134 quartiary passions, since the
complete development of the three primary passions assures that
of all the following ones.

In this prospectus, therefore, it is amply sufficient to theorize
on the development of the three primary passions, called sub-

foci, and on those of the twelve secondary passions, called radicals of the octave and the passional scale.

We are very familiar with the five *sensory* passions tending toward luxury, and the four *affectives* tending toward groups; we have only, then, to become acquainted with the three *distributives,* whose combined development produces the series. This is a social method whose secret has been lost since the time of the first men, who were only able to maintain the series for about 300 years. This mechanism has at last been recovered with the disposition necessary to apply it to large industry.

Our task, reduced to its simplest terms, is thus to determine the game of seriesism, or the third primary passion; it is that which holds in balance the other two, luxuryism and groupism, whose discord is permanent without the intervention of seriesism.

When the three are in agreement, happiness is produced by assuring the development of unityism of the passions, which engenders all the branches of the various degrees.

I have given the classification or the degree of powers; let us repeat that the tree growing out of unityism, a passion unknown to us which is the opposite of egoism, gives in the first power three, in the second power twelve, in the third thirty-two, in the fourth 134, in the fifth 404, plus the pivot, which is never counted in movement.

Temperaments are classified in approximately the same order. They are four in the second degree, plus the focus; the fourth degree may vary from thirty to thirty-two, and so on.

It is possible to extend the analysis of passions, characters, and temperaments to the sixth, seventh, and eighth powers. The fifth will satisfy our curiosity to begin with, since it yields the totality of the Phalanstery of harmony or domestic destiny. I will go further in the treatise.

Conforming to the unity of the physical and passional universe, the system of attraction is very faithfully depicted and followed in sidereal mechanics; here thirty-two planets are seen to gravitate in the collective mode toward unityism, through the equilibrium and harmony of the solar system with the starry heavens, whose center it occupies. Passing to the subdivisions and beginning with the first degree, the system gravitates toward the three sub-foci:

First, toward luxury or the solar pivot;

Second, toward the four groups formed by the four lunary planets;

Third, toward the series formed by the accolade of the four groups and ambiguities toward the solar pivot.

We shall now proceed to the twelve radical passions of the octave in the second degree.

THE TWELVE RADICAL PASSIONS OF THE OCTAVE

I have given the following classification—five sensories, four affectives, and three distributives. The three latter are barely known in our civilization; one sees only glimmers of them exciting the anger of moralists, who are the relentless enemy of voluptuousness. The influence of these three passions is so negligible and their appearance so rare, that they have not even been distinctly classified. I had to give them the denomination *associative, diversifying* and *graduating,* but I prefer to designate them by the numbers ten, eleven, and twelve. I put off defining them because it will not be believed that God, despite all His power, could ever create a social order capable of gratifying three passions so insatiable. The seven affectives and distributives depend more upon spirit than upon matter; they are of BASIC rank. Their combined action engenders a collective passion formed of their union, as white is formed through the union of the seven spectral colors. I will name this thirteenth passion *harmonyism* or *unityism;* it is even more unknown than the tenth, eleventh, and twelfth passions of which I have not spoken. Even without being familiar with them one can reason about their possible influence, which is what I intend to do.

Even though these four passions—tenth, eleventh, twelfth and thirteenth—are completely smothered by society's customs, their seeds still exist in our souls; they fatigue and harass us according to their degree of activity in each individual. Hence many civilizees pass their lives in boredom, even though they possess every object they desire. Cæsar, for example, was astonished to find that sitting upon the throne of the world he experienced only emptiness and boredom. His anxiety had no other cause than the influence of these four stifled passions, and especially the thirteenth, which exercised an acute pressure upon his soul. His succession to the highest rank in the world left him no longing capable of distracting or diverting him from the strain of the thirteenth passion, dominant for him.

The same disfavor is generally extended to the great men of civilization, whose souls are rudely agitated by the undeveloped passions. One must not be surprised if common men are seen to be more satisfied by their banal happiness than are the great by their grandiose pleasures. These often-vaunted splendors— throne, dominion, etc.—are doubtless real advantages, no matter what the philosophers say. But they have the property of irritating rather than of satisfying the four stifled passions. Hence the middle class can enjoy more with fewer resources, because its bourgeois habits irritate only the first nine passions, to which the present order of civilization permits some development; while it permits almost none whatever to the three distributives, or toward harmonyism.

In general the influence of the three distributive passions produces characters accused of corruption, libertinism and debauchery. The thirteenth, harmonyism, produces people known as eccentrics who seem ill at ease in society, and who cannot accommodate themselves to society's mores.

Barbarians are almost ignorant of these four passions that are not awakened in any way by their social state. They are thus more satisfied than we are with their crude customs which derive from the nine physical and spiritual passions, the only ones by which they are troubled.

In short, if there is perfect happiness for mankind only in the order of group series or the combined order it is because full development is assured to the twelve radical passions, and consequently to the thirteenth, which is a composite of the seven principal passions. In this new social order, then, the least fortunate men and women will be much happier than the greatest king today; because true happiness consists in the complete gratification of the passions.

The twelve radical passions are subdivided into a multitude of nuances which are more or less dominant in every individual. The result is an infinite variety of characters, all of which can be related to the 810 principal characters. Nature distributes them at random among children of both sexes. Hence among 810 randomly chosen children will be found the germ of all perfection attainable by the human spirit; that is to say, each one of them will be naturally gifted with the aptitude necessary to equal one of the most astonishing people who has ever lived, like Homer, Cæsar, Newton, etc. Consequently, if the population of France (36,000,000) is divided by 810, one will find that there exists in this nation 45,000 individuals capable of equaling Demosthenes, etc., if they were prepared from the age of three, and if they were to receive a NATURAL education which would develop all the seeds distributed by nature. But this education can only take place in the progressive series or combined order. Since the population of France alone would furnish 45,000 people who possess every talent, we can imagine the abundance of famous people of all types in this new social order. When the globe is organized and the population reaches a total of three billion, there will be thirty-seven million poets equal to Homer, thirty-seven million geometrists equal to Newton, thirty-seven million dramatists equal to Molière, and so on for all the talents imaginable on the globe. (These are approximate estimates that the newspapers of Paris have taken literally.)

It is thus erroneous to believe that nature is sparing of talent; she is prodigal beyond all our desires and needs. But the means of developing these seeds remains to be discovered. We are as ignorant of this as a savage is of the discovery and exploitation of mines. We have no art, no touchstone to discern what nature has destined for individuals, or what seeds she has implanted in their souls. These seeds are trampled and smothered by civilizee education; barely one out of a million escapes. The art of discovering this will be one of a thousand wonders that the theory of the progressive series will teach us, in which each will develop and perfect to the highest degree the different seeds of talent sown by nature.

If the 810 characters are distributed at random among all children, one must not be astonished at the usual contrast seen to exist between fathers and sons. Thus the proverb, *a père avare, fils prodigue.*[1] From this arises the continual upheaval of family interests; a father is seen to build at great effort and expense an establishment that is neglected, degraded, and sold by the son whose tastes are in opposition to those of his father. For fathers this is the cause of interminable harangues against nature. The new social order is going to vindicate all of nature's apparent injustices, even the most revolting, like the abandonment of the poor who are the less protected for having a greater need of help and work; while the wealthy, who have no need, find themselves progressively overwhelmed with favors of fortune and situation. This influence of a malevolent demon emerges in all branches of civilization, showing nature in every sense set against the poor, the just and the weak. We find everywhere the absence of a divine Providence, and the permanent reign of a demoniacal spirit who allows a few glimmers of justice to shine only often enough to teach us that justice is banished from barbaric and civilized society:

> I do not know what unjust power
> leaves crime in peace, harasses innocence.
> Wherever in life I turn my eyes,
> I see misfortunes that condemn the gods.
>
> (*Andromaque*, Racine)

These temporary disorders will seem to be dispositions of the highest wisdom when it is recognized through the theory of attraction that the civilizee order has the faculty of developing the twelve radical passions in a *general counter-march,* and of

[1] "To an avaricious father, a prodigal son."—Translator.

constantly producing as many inequities and horrors as these passions would produce justice and benefits if they were allowed their natural course and combined development in a new social order. We shall admire the regular sequence of these calamities with which God crushes us, and will continue to crush us, as long as we persist in living in industrial incoherence. You will see that these so-called peculiarities of the play of passions stem from profound calculations by which God prepares us for immense happiness in the combined order. We will learn at last that passionate attraction, accused by our philosophers of vice and corruption, is the wisest and the most admirable of God's works. Passionate attraction alone, without constraint and without aid other than the charm of voluptuousness, is going to establish universal unity upon the globe, and will cause war, revolution, indigence, and injustice to disappear during the seventy thousand year period of social harmony which we will enter.

OC, Vol. I, pp. 72–86

THE FIVE SENSES

I shall abridge this chapter, because it proceeds upon minute details, but which require also much attention.

It is scarcely credible that after 3000 years of studies, men have not yet thought of classifying the senses. At present even our five senses are cited pell-mell; no distinction of rank is admitted between them. Nevertheless no equality exists between the senses—taste and touch play a superior part. Taste is evidently the first in rank among the sensual passions; you can exist though deprived of the active use of each of the four other senses, but you cannot live without eating, without the active exercise of the sense of taste. It is consequently the first as to the uses of necessity. Perhaps it is so too in regard to pleasures, for it is the first and the last enjoyment of man, it is almost the only resource of children and old men in matters of pleasure. Taste is therefore the chief of the five material passions, although others may procure pleasures superior to those of taste.

Long details are not required to prove that the sense of *touch-rut*, holds the second rank among the five. It has, like taste, the faculty of procuring active pleasures, whereas two other very valuable senses, sight and hearing, only yield passive pleasures, and are of a subaltern rank. Sight itself, although of inestimable value, is excluded from voluptuous sensations; it has very direct and positive sufferings; it has only pleasures indirect and subordinate to thought. It is an effect that must be explained to habituate the reader to recognize a gradation amongst the senses, as among the other passions, which are not equal to one another. Our eye finds a passive well-being in certain sights, like that of verdure, which has affinities with man's vision. Yet it does not procure him pleasure that is active, or backed by nervous sensation, as happens sometimes when you eat excellent viands. Our eye, as relates to pleasure, enjoys therefore negatively, like the foot which is incommoded on a rugged ground, and free from constraint on an even ground.

In the second case, there is only absence of uneasiness for the foot, but no real pleasure; in short, in every impression which affects vision, it is the thought alone which enjoys—the eye is only passive in the agreeable sensations that sight procures us.

The same thing happens with the ear, which gives pleasure without experiencing any itself. The most harmonious music cannot excite any tickling in the ear; harsh sounds draw the tympanum, true sounds delight us, but without any physical enjoyment for the tympanum. It is still thought which is the arbiter of this pleasure; and in proof of it, we see that in concerts and operas any distraction makes us lose the enjoyment of the sounds; an idea may absorb us suddenly, and cause us to forget the piece which the performers are singing; the ear becomes insensible to it the moment that it is not supported by thought and attention. Frequently at the opera a man whose head is full of something is angry with himself for having lost, by distraction, a certain passage that he wished, and even expectantly longed to hear. He only perceives this inadvertency in the middle or at the end of the passage. It is a proof that the ear, by itself and without the aid of thought, is unfit to enjoy the sounds that are most flattering to it.

It is not thus with smell. A tuberose that was placed under our nose, would make itself felt, and would stimulate, in spite of distractions, because smell is a sense of active irritability, though very inferior in importance to touch and taste.

We may deduce from these considerations the classification of the senses into

Two active senses—taste and touch.

One mixed sense—smell.

Two passive senses—sight and hearing.

I classify smell as a mixed or neutral sense because it participates in both the others; it enjoys actively, but without notable influence. It is like a subordinate guide destined to serve taste; it serves also vision and the other senses in certain researches. Finally, in all respects it occupies a middle rank between the active and the passive senses, of which it participates equally.

Here we have a distinction in the senses, indifferent at first glance, and yet very essential. How comes it, that an age all infatuated with analytical methods, thus despises elementary analyses in the study of the passions. It is by similar blunders that the calculus of passional attraction has been entirely missed. Science ever fails, by trying on the first start to rise to the clouds, before keeping its eyes fixed upon the humble region of common sense, in which are found the primordial notions of every science.

The two active senses, taste and touch, exert a colossal influence in material concerns, as much by necessity as by refinement. The two passive senses, hearing and vision, and the neuter sense, smell, have only a feeble empire in comparison with the two actives, which are really kings of the social world—for the furies of ambition, the inclination of the populace for insurrection and atrocities, only spring from the want of satisfying these two senses. The people would by no means perpetrate crime to slake the three other senses—to procure pictures, perfumes, or concerts. These three sorts of pleasures would not be able to move the mob, which on the contrary is entirely devoted to the impulsions of the two active senses—taste and touch. The mob requires to be fed and clothed. Everything is sacrificed, with the people, to these two senses, which are very powerful again in the opulent class, not in the light of necessity, but as a goad to gluttony, effeminacy, and lubricity.

These influences may appear vicious to us in the existing order of things; we must wait till we know what have been God's motives in giving so much influence to two sensual passions. We can only be initiated into this mystery by studying the mechanism of the passional series, in which the pleasures of the senses are accordant with propriety and virtue, and become the springs of general equilibrium.

The enormous and tyrannical influence of these two senses ought to make us suspect an affinity of functions between them. For instance, we see that *touch-rut*[1] is very intimately married to the affective passion called sentimental love, which is the cardinal hyperminor.[2] We ought to conjecture that taste may have a similar connection with the cardinal hypermajor, called honorism (ambition in the subversive vocabulary). There was an interesting enigma to be explained, touching this connection of good cheer and honor; the secret of it will be seen in the treatise on Gastrosophic Cabal. It is so extraordinary a subject that I cannot give an abridged notion of it. I shall only venture a word of prelude upon this great problem.

The human species being subject to the abuse of the five senses in the social limbo, or civilized, barbarian, patriarchal, and savage states of society, the philosophers have, for this reason, devoted the sensual pleasures to contempt. Yet it ought to appear very ridiculous to us that two senses, which so imperiously direct human and animate beings, should be reputed contemptible. How great would be the inconsistency of God were He to vilify the two principal springs which He employs to direct beings!

The moralists, to support their attacks against gourmandism, pretend that it assimilates us to the beasts, which are the slaves

---

[1] The word *rut* signifies the *sexual* element in touch.—Note of J.R.M.

[2] See Fourier's definition on p. 96.—Ed.

of their belly according to Sallust—*prona et ventri obedientia*. This subjection of animals and of men to the sense of taste is a sign of the eminent rank which that sense ought to hold in the balanced or harmonic movement. It is already balanced in beasts, since they do not abuse it. When men shall have reached the first degree of wisdom, good cheer will have nothing ignoble in their eyes, and will be able to rise to the rank of the first sensual spring, the most honorable spring of the five, and the one which ought to occupy the highest rank, since hunger is the most stimulating of the five sensual appetites. It is the one respecting which the human body cannot deliberate. The more its present excesses may have dishonored the sense of taste, the more lustre will this sense acquire when it shall have attained to equilibrium, and shall become the germ of all the agricultural and chemical studies, etc. Gourmandism once raised to this character (*rôle*), will be the magnetic needle of health and of wisdom; it will be a title to honor as a path of science; it will only lead man to work to satisfy the senses of others, at the same time that he is satisfying his own, and securing health to all. It will constitute the science named gastrosophy, which will place good cheer in strict alliance with honor and the love of glory.

Gourmandism being the most frequent of all our enjoyments, the first and the last pleasure of man, it ought to be the chief agent of wisdom in future harmony, where all concurs to satisfy the collective passions by the development of the individual passions. A clever gastrosopher, expert in the three functions of gastroculture and gastrohygiene, will be revered as an oracle of supreme wisdom; and the most clever gastrosophers will be in their life-time promoted to saintship, of which they will have the rank and the title. A major saintship and a minor saintship are admitted in harmony. The first is founded on the combined development of the two passions abused amongst us, ambition and good cheer. We only value in the present day the *gastronomer*, who understands good living; in harmony he will be required to be gastroculturist or experienced in the laws of agriculture, and the culinary preparations that a dish may require.

He will require, moreover, to be gastrohygienist, knowing the suitableness of a dish with the different temperaments, which will be classed into 810. The gastrosopher will therefore be a very eminent *savant,* in whom gourmandism must be allied to all the springs of scientific honor. Thus will be formed the alliance of the two passions, taste and ambition; thus the sense of taste, one of the two rectors, will be united to the hypermajor cardinal affective, called honorism, honor; just as the other rector sense, touch-rut, is united to the hyperminor cardinal, called sentimental love; and the two rector senses will be in marriage with the two rector affectives, honor and love, which, in this order of things, will only be able to develop themselves in perfect balance, free from all excess, balance being an inalienable property of the passional series.

Without this alliance, God would therefore have condemned to disgrace the principal spring of the movement, which is the sense of taste. It is surprising that men have not rather presumed the brilliant use which is in store for this sense.

For the rest, the civilizee mechanism is so remote from all kind of passional equilibrium that it would have foundered on all the problems of this description. It has made men able to believe foolishly in the infamy of the chief one amongst the springs that make us move. Hence it comes that gourmandism is dishonored in opinion; it deserves this affront in an order of things in which it has produced a Vitellius; but when the passional balance shall exist, gourmandism will hold a rank so eminent that it will be encouraged even amongst those children who are sufficiently inclined to it. It will no longer be a vice in them, when it will become a stimulant to labor and study, without ever leading to any excess. Consequently all children will be excited in harmony to systematic gourmandism (I do not mean gluttony), and a harmonian child will be as early as the age of nine years a cleverer gastronome than the Apicius's of our capitals, who, with all their pretended delicacy, could not on eating a dish of poultry, point out the errors committed in its education, nor rise to the rank of gastroculturists, still less to that of gastrohygienists.

We shall often be obliged to establish a distinction between the passions, which is that of major mode and minor mode. The major comprises the strong and free (shades), the minor comprises the slight shades that are compatible with suppleness of character. Hence it comes that the passions of women are commonly of minor shade, with some exceptions, and those of men of major shade, with some exceptions; but in either mode they are in all cases the same passions, always the twelve radicals.

Confining ourselves to the five sensual passions, which are the object of this chapter, the reader perceives that many inequalities and differences exist between them; amongst others that of simple, comprising vision and hearing; that of mixed or neuter, which is smell; and that of compound, which applies to taste and touch-rut.

A new omission of our analysts. They have committed the same inadvertence in the difference of the simple and compound as in that of the active and passive.

The two senses of taste and touch are compound. You find two very distinct pleasures in taste, which can be enjoyed separately. These are eating and drinking. You find in the same manner in material love, or love considered as a sensual effect, two distinct pleasures which can be separated; they are copulation and kissing. Besides this material ambiguity, they are moreover subject to a spiritual ambiguity, invisible in the sense of taste but very evident in the sense of touch, which unites two actions, two affections, the material or rutting, and the animic[3] or celadony[4]; an affective *penchant*, which is very distinct from the sensual *penchant*. This bi-composition is not found in the three other senses, which are of the simple order; it is one of the advantages which constitute the eminent superiority of taste and touch-rut. On these two senses reposes a great mystery of social equilibrium—I mean the balance of the directing passions.

I designate by the name of rector passions a quadrille of two sensitives and two affectives, married in the following order:

Minor—gourmandism and honor.

Major—lubricity and celadony.

[3] Fourier's word for spiritual derived from animus.—Ed.
[4] See note on p. 137.—Ed.

Bless me! they will say, what connection is there between gourmandism and honor? I have given farther back the outline of an answer on this subject. It is necessary, before solving the problem, to wait till I have depicted *social honor* in the mechanism of the series, and have dissipated the prejudices of the civilizees, of whom some place honor in precedence of ceremony, the contempt of labor, the exercise of tilting; others no less ridiculous, notwithstanding their title of sages, make honor to consist in stifling the passions, and robbing oneself of the most valuable possessions.

We shall have to dissipate these prejudices in order to make known true honor, in its harmonic or social acceptation, according to which no conduct is honorable but that which serves at once the collective and the individual interest. Amongst us the man is thought praiseworthy who sacrifices his personal interest to the good of the mass; he acts honorably, no doubt; he develops honor in a diverging or negative sense; the positive or converging development must favor both the collective and the individual passions. It is only under this condition that honor becomes harmonic. For the rest, the above specified condition of honor adapted to the collective and individual necessities will thin out of the ranks of men of honor that crowd of civilizees who plume themselves upon their idleness, and style themselves very proper people, *gens comme il faut,* because they do nothing, and produce nothing; so that if all the world were as it should be, *comme il faut,* conformably to civilizee honor, the human race would die of hunger the following year. Harmony will not suffer these absurdities of *comme-il-faut* idleness; it will only reckon that honorable which will concur in producing, in enriching the mass; true it is that its industrial functions will be sufficiently attractive to catch even the class called proper people, *comme il faut,* and to make it acknowledge that in civilization it was very improper, *comme il ne faut pas.*

We are at present engaged only about corporeal or sensual studies. Before inquiring about the perfection to which the senses may attain, and about the immensity of the means of nature on this head, we must previously become convinced of their material and artificial imperfection. This is what I am about to treat.

If luxury is internal by means of the physical faculties, and external by means of riches, the same is the case with poverty. It is internal and external with each of the five senses.

1. Internal poverties, or deficiency of faculties.

Internal poverty is composed of the faculties in which our senses are wanting, and which they will acquire in the future. Thus the want of co-nocturnal vision, like that of the lion or cat, is an internal poverty of the fourth degree to us. The absence of the telescope was, for the Romans, an internal poverty of a mixed degree, between the sixth and seventh.

This said possession of the telescope is an internal luxury for us, since it gives a great extension of faculties to one of our senses. But this luxury is still only simple internal, inasmuch as the glasses of our telescopes are of a subversive material, which has not the compound properties that will accrue to glasses manufactured of substances that will be yielded by the harmonic creations.

Our senses, besides the want of faculties which constitute internal negative poverty, are subject to a host of maladies which cause internal positive poverty. To confine our remarks to sight, how many infirmities may attack it from the natural ones, such as myopia, down to those that are accidental, like cataract. These maladies, considering their present frequency, become poverty relative to the future order of things, which will prevent all these disasters, or will reduce them to the minimum. Then Egypt and Lapland, at present so dangerous from ophthalmia and blindness, will be regions as favorable to the health of the eye as can be now the healthiest provinces; and immediately on passing into harmony, the internal positive or internal negative poverties will cease at once.

The greater number of the positive internal poverties are accidental, such as the hydrophobic, psoric, syphilitic, pestilential poisons; and so many besides, which a good administration might extirpate or prevent in every part of the globe, even before the foundation of harmony. All these poisons no longer exist even in the sixth society, called guaranteeism. When we consider that civilization, far from having extirpated them, has recently hatched three new plagues, the yellow fever, the typhus, and the new choleramorbus of Bengal, which is a contagious disease, we may judge of the excess of internal poverty that afflicts the limbic societies, and of the impudence of the jugglers who trumpet perfectibility.

Harmony is a social system, so admirably suited to the sanitary wants, that scarce a hundredth part of our civilizee infirmities will be seen in it. The harmonians, one out of twelve of whom will reach the age of 144 years, will be, in the course of this long career, so little subject to diseases, that many phalanxes of about 1500 persons of all ages will be heard to boast at times of not having a single invalid, except in the two ages of transition, babes and patriarchs, who cannot escape some infirmities. I also except the accidental cripples, a fall and the fracture of a limb not being a vice of diet or of insalubrity. But, putting these three sorts of inevitable accidents out of sight, you will often see, in the whole body of the fourteen amphichoirs, number two to fifteen, the entire phalanx in full health; and it is then that the doctors will gain most, for each Phalansterian pays them in proportion to the general health.

It proceeds in the same way as those who, in civilization, subscribe to a doctor, say £25 per annum. It is for the interest of a doctor that such a subscriber should enjoy a long life and sound health. The physician has thus so much more profit and so much less trouble. Each Phalanstery enters into treaty in the same way with the groups of physicians and surgeons. But civilization, which styles itself perfectibilized, acts in the contrary fashion, since it makes all the doctors and lawyers interested in there being many law-suits and sick: hence we ought not to be surprised that they wish for an abundance of patients and plaintiffs; or that, on the other hand, those of harmony should everywhere agree in preventing maladies and disputes.

The state of general health will not, however, amount to internal luxury; it will be nothing more than the absence of internal poverty, which comprises diseases avoidable by a wise regimen. As to internal luxury, it will be requisite in order to possess it that each sense should enjoy all its potential faculties in a scale analogous to those of vision.

These advantages can only be accorded to the generations of several (quarters) of harmony. The co-nocturnal vision will not be acquired with the first generation. It will take a number of (successive) quarters to give by degrees to the human race the forces necessary to develop in it these useful properties, and it will only be at the ninth (quarter) that men will begin to possess them in complete gamut. Some of them will be deferred to the sixteenth.

As to the state of general healthiness, of which I spoke above, it will only begin to be complete for the first generation of harmony. The present one, which is the product of civilizee and barbarian education, has not been able to acquire, in the existing social order, half the strength that the children born and bred in harmony will enjoy. This is a parallel which can be made as early as the fourth year, when the effects of harmonian education will already be apparent; it will make itself slightly felt in the civilizee children of a tender age, who will already participate in the benefit of the natural institution, the system of which will be shown farther on. As to the adults, who will pass from the existing order to harmony, they will gain by it, in matters relating to health, the absence of accidental diseases, such as the plague, etc., which will be extirpated by a general quarantine; next the rapid diminution of the essential diseases, fever, gout, rheumatism, etc., which will be almost entirely prevented by the property of passional and sensual equilibrium inherent in harmony.

2. External poverties or want of riches.

Independently of the numerous chances of internal poverty that I have just passed in review, we have a vast series of *external poverties* in our present privations. It is seasonable to observe some of their details in each sense, in order to confound the pretensions of our chanters of perfectibility.

External poverty comprises all the avoidable privations and inconveniences, such as want of carriages, or clumsy carriages.

These privations are very immense, even in the case of kings. Let us judge of them by an examination of some sensual injuries.

First, HEARING. A king, like any other man, is exposed to hear rude brogues (*patois*) that he doth not understand, disagreeable sounds around his palace, cries in the streets of his capital, voices out of tune, which he will find at every step in France; this nation, that has neither ear nor measure, being the most savagely determined to hum tunes.

If this king wants to pass through the country, to enjoy the charm of simple nature, he will hear the croaking of some thousands of frogs and toads, which neither spare the ears of kings nor of shepherds. The king will suffer even more than the shepherd by all these shocking noises of the country and of the town. And what will it be, in case he takes a journey in countries whose language he does not understand? He will be like every one else, in a state of blockade *relative to hearing*, since he will not be able to make use of the most precious faculty of hearing. It is in vain that he will pay interpreters; to be obliged to have recourse to interpreters is to lose all the pleasures of conversation.

The difference of tongues—the shame of civilized societies—is the most distressing of the disasters experienced by the sense of hearing. Habit makes us almost indifferent to this hindrance, very real though little observed.

A host of *lesions* of hearing are met with. I have observed that often a workman hammering, or a learner of the clarinet, suffices to desolate a whole district, particularly people who like to sleep in the morning. I refer the reader for details of these nuisances to an English author, who has filled three volumes with a collection of these civilizee bores and sensual kill-joys, from the cackling of geese down to that of discordant singers, far more detestable.

Our philosophers have inoculated us with a sort of fatalism respecting these sensual *lesions,* from which we suffer every instant. They have fashioned us to consider these miseries as necessary, and to habituate ourselves to them as apathetically as Turks do to the plague. It is necessary to be convinced of their extent to appreciate the benefit of harmony, which is about to deliver us from them. Every man could, like the English author, fill volumes with these material misfortunes, a few of which only I shall point out in each sense, by way of definition of the five external poverties.

Second, SIGHT. It will be maintained again that the poverties on this head are relative, imaginary. Yet it is quite certain that a man transported from the verdant banks of the Saône to the arid regions of Provence, where you see nothing but naked rocks, print-steps of the ravages of the elements—that such a man, I say, has his sight continually offended, unless he is a vandal, incapable of distinguishing between a graceful and a hideous landscape. It is a real pain for every man of good sense; he suffers positively by the sight of a frightful landscape, and relatively by the memory of the beautiful scenes, and the cultivated and woody mountains that he enjoyed in other places. The same thing happens to him who, coming from the clean and well-built villages of Flanders and Brisgau, perceives the disgusting structures of the French peasants, the villages of Picardy, of Bresse, of Champagne, their miserable mud huts, their dirty wooden barracks, heaped together as if space were wanting in the fields. When he visits the inside of these hovels, he will find them as dirty and miserable within as they are ugly without; he will quickly change the name of *belle France* into that of *sale,* dirty France, a name truly deserved by the far greater number of its provinces; for you scarcely ever find there cleanliness and elegance in the buildings, except in those like Flanders, which have formerly belonged to another power.

Amongst all these nuisances that affect vision, none is more frequent than the sight of the people and of the peasantry, especially in the lands of dirt, such as Spain and France. The sight of rags saddens us as effectually as that of the fogs of Holland, on arriving from the fine climate of Tuscany. Now in what country can you avoid seeing a populace in rags?

Again, the sight of ill-cultivated lands, of puny animals and plants, becomes a *lesion* relative to sight for a man who reflects on the improvements of which agriculture is susceptible. This visual disgrace will become more sensible when men shall have pictures of harmony; when they shall know that instead of mud huts, in which two or three hundred Picard families are piled up, we ought to see a vast and regular edifice, which even without ornament would be beautiful by the general effect and unity of the component parts, by the choice of situation, the judicious distribution of the stables, workshops, water-conduits, reservoirs, etc. Thus, although the ugliness and poverty of the civilizee towns and countries even now wound our eyes in all directions, the evil will become much more intolerable when men shall know the beautiful order that would reign in harmony, and even in the sixth period (guaranteeism), still little removed from civilization.

Third, SMELL. Fetid odors and stinks are so general a nuisance in civilization, especially in the tenements of the poor, that some nations, like the Germans, have invented a plan of remedying it by one absorbent stink, which is tobacco smoke, grown rancid by the heat of stoves, and concealing the bad smells which are fused into a single one. This is replacing numerous infections by another, which at all events is not unhealthy.

France is more intrepid on this head, and the workmen of its great factories, Lyons, Rouen, pass their lives with great apathy in stinking garrets, where they are huddled together by scores, and where prevail perpetually putrid smells, which spread abroad, infect the stairs, the court and the narrow alleys. Many of these streets preserve a mouldy and close smell, while the philosophers cry out about the perfectibility of the sensations of perceptions. They have never passed through these sickening streets in which the French populace dwell; and where the din of the trades, of the hammers, quarrels and beggars, the sight of the hanging rags, of the dirty dwellings and unpalatable labors of the poor, the stifling smell of the drains in which they swarm, so painfully affect the sight, hearing and smell, and so well belie the boasts of the perfection of the sensations of perception that our ideologists find in their *belle France!*

Would they not deserve—these babblers of perfectibility—that they should be condemned to dwell in the little country towns, in their dirty streets answering the purpose of privies, where reigns, ever since the creation of the world, an antique crust of fœcal matter, kept up every day by the "vases of ordure," which these provincial bumpkins insolently throw upon the heads of passengers with the cry, *"Passarés na'a degun."*[5] What would the ideologists and perfectibilizers of Paris think, if they saw, like dom Japhet, their face and clothes suddenly covered with this commodity? Thus bathed and perfumed, they would understand, by the sensations of perception, that if they have raised their *belle France* to perfectibility, it is not at least in what relates to smell, as ill-used as sight and hearing in *la belle France!*

Instead of this system of perpetual infection, we shall have to describe an order of general perfume. Independently of the salubrity of the air and of that of the buildings, the luxury of smell will be pushed so far as to give to the high roads the accidental perfume of plants, and to give to the street-gallery (warmed and ventilated communication on the first story) the perfume of the unitary aromas, which have, like the orange blossom, the double property of salubrity and olfactory charm.

Well! but what will the districts do, bordering on the Pontine marshes, the marshes of Egypt, Polesia, Guyana, Louisiana, and others? Let us wait till we hear how the harmonians work, and what is the power of the work carried on by passional series and attractive armies. When the reader shall have studied this theory, it will be seen that the impossibilities which arrest feeble civilization, such as the drying up of the Pontine marshes, will be only child's play for the industrial armies of harmony.

[5] A stranger knows not what the word *passarés* means. He thinks that they are calling an individual bearing that name. Moreover, the people of Provence are not so nice about it, and throw without caring on whom the article may alight. All is justified by that one word *passarés*. They have many other perfidies on this score, such as furnishing their window-sills with their unclean vases; so that an ideologist, lodging on the second floor, and placing himself, in the morning at the window to enjoy the charms of sweet nature, and reflect on the perfectibility of the sensations, would perceive the steam mounting to his nose; then, looking about him to the window below and crying out, "Where the deuce does this stink come from?" he will have the perfections of sensations of perfectibility of beautiful Provence.—Fourier.

Fourth, TASTE. We are so new in all relating to the sense of taste and to the perfection of good living, that my criticism would not be understood if I confined myself to the surface of the debate. I defer it to the section that treats of gastrosophy, a science of which some sybarites have given a caricature in their gastronomical pretensions. Let us remark only that civilization deteriorates incessantly in good living, owing to the progress of the spirit of trade, which alters the nature of all eatables, applies all the discoveries of modern chemistry to falsify and poison aliments, to multiply cheats, such as beet-root sugar, and poisons like chicory coffee, wine of Kinarodon, and mercantile tricks of all kinds.

The perfectibilizers will proceed to reply that the class of respectable people lives very well, and does not eat beet-root-sugar. That is false; the rich people, even while paying well, are gulled at every step. I have not frequented the great, yet I have happened to be sometimes at their board, and I have perceived that they are still more deceived than the middle class (*bourgeois*). For a shop-keeper who wishes to give a dinner, looks twice at all that he buys, and sees with his own eyes; a prince is obliged to delegate his business to a house steward, who wishes to gain and divide with the tradesmen; hence it comes that the great have commonly very indifferent things at their table, especially in the article of wines, which they give out as good on the word of the tradesman, or the steward, and no guest will go and tell the Amphitryo that his wine is not good. However, even were it true that respectable people live very well, have on their table nothing but dishes of excellent quality, that would at most only prove that civilizee philosophy only labors for respectable people, who are infinitely few in number, and that it simply ends in multiplying the relative privations of the multitude. Men ought to value so much the more a new science that teaches how to augment the pleasures of the rich man, at the same time that it increases those of the poor; this is what the reader will learn in the treatise on the passional series, and on their kitchen, distributed like all their labors by graduated and contrasted shades even for the poor.

Fifth, Y[6] SIMPLE TOUCH. To give a measurement of our imperfection in this sense, I refer to the section where I shall treat of the street-gallery, by means of which you can, in harmony, attend to all your occupations, pass through all the workshops, the stables, the public saloons, the assemblies of pleasure, without being affected either by heat or cold, or any inclemency. The reader will judge, by this single arrangement of harmony, how far the great are from procuring the pleasures of touch, even those of which the enjoyment is possible to the civilizees, and does not depend on an organic regeneration of which I shall speak in the following chapters, potential luxury.

If we consider that, in the regions which style themselves perfectibilized, like France, the people have not the means of warming and clothing themselves, we may say that they are in the sense of touch in an equal degree as in the sense of taste, reduced to live on nettles and other filth in years of distress.

Let us not lose sight of the fact that the position applies to the rich as well as to the poor. I shall prove that the opulent class doth not reach, in any of the senses, a fourth part of the pleasures that harmony must procure for it. The single annoyance of travelling would suffice to prove this assertion. A king, notwithstanding the most costly preparations, cannot, on a journey into the *interior of his kingdom,* find a fourth part of the pleasure that a private individual will find over the whole earth in harmony. What shall we say, then, when the king leaves his states to travel in a barbarous country; and what must happen with a man of the middle classes who travels in a semi-barbarous country like Spain, which has not even inns, and in those perfectibilized countries like France, where vermin swarm by myriads in the inn-beds of Provence and Languedoc?

Fifth, Λ TOUCH-RUT, or *ambiguous touch.* I shall speak elsewhere of this subdivision of the fifth sense. Let us conclude about the imperfection of *external* luxury in civilization.

You must call to mind here the distinction that I have made

6 These are apparently arbitrary symbols throughout Fourier's writings. They are best explained as pseudo-mathematical symbolization of the emotions.—Ed.

in the development of the senses, the difference of harmonic and of subversive development.

I have named *harmonic development* the gradation of pleasures that our senses will obtain when a material regeneration of the race shall have raised the senses to the accords of all internal degrees, of which I shall give an idea in the following chapters.

I call *brute* or *mean development,* the dose of pleasure which the present state of the senses can admit.

I call *subversive development* the scale of privations, which, in the present system, extend more or less to the various classes, and reduce the lot of the multitude so far beneath that of kings and sybarites, who yet only attain to the brute or mean development.

You may judge by this analysis or rather this view of external luxury, of the sad condition of the civilizees, of whom the immense majority is reduced to run through the scale of privations, and of whom a very small number, which is named the class of sybarites, only arrives at the mean degree in external luxury, and at the brute degree, in internal luxury, which can only be enjoyed after the sensual regeneration of which I shall treat in the following chapters.

I have proved that civilization only develops the five luxuries for the purpose of creating five scales of poverty, each terminated by a shadow of happiness that is only reserved for the rich, and which serves to drive to despair the immense mass of the unhappy, whose relative privations increase in proportion to the progress of luxury. It would be impossible for the council of devils to organize the sensual persecution of the human race more scientifically than it is in this perfectibilized civilization, in which the unhappy have not even the double stay of fatalism and brutality that supports the barbarians, and in which refined executioners communicate enlightenment and the reasoning power to the people without giving it the means of enrichment. So that the people only becomes enlightened to be more apt to judge of the extent of its miseries—only that it may see positive suffering increased by relative suffering.

PHS, I, pp. 29–36, 41–52

GOURMANDISM

It is now that the powerful affinity established by nature between gastronomy and honor can be recognized. When I [   ] the immense cabal through which self-esteem and gourmandism will become [   ] in harmony, I recognize that it is difficult for anyone in civilization to understand the springs by which harmony will establish this affinity. Two springs, however, can be seen; one is the gradual effect or triumph by the globe, the other is the gradual hygiene or application to 405/810 temperaments in the fourth power and to 33/66 in the second power.[1]

Other objects will furnish scales in the third power. Pears, for example, of which nature provides about 150 varieties, will well be able to compose the classification analogous to 133/266 temperaments in the third power. Other comestibles will be varied enough to be classed by analogy in the fourth power for 405/810 temperaments.

For natural species, like the pear, the honor of the triumph will fall more to nature than to the cultivator, whereas for a product of art like pastry, the triumph will be all to the worker and to the corporate body that will know how to determine the foods most suitable for each temperament. By imagining the intensity of cabal to be established between the gastronomers and those learned in the culinary arts of the various regions and communities, one can thus envision that in a social order devoted to pleasure and especially to gourmandism, this gastronomic and gastrohygienic cabal, becoming a voluptuous and learned cabal of the highest utility, will hold first rank among the cabals of the globe. It will particularly merit the title of palladium of wisdom since it associates the most useful of sciences, the guaranteed hygiene of health, with gourmandism, even today the most frequent and constant pleasure of all ages, and which will become even more so in a social order of general opulence. In harmony

[1] These figures represent intensity of passion.—Ed.

each person will be assured five good meals a day, not including the interludes (or feasts of transition), which will consist of four light snacks of about five minutes each, or the harmonious re-unions, where less than two hours' time is generally spent in dining, appropriate to the season and to each individual's taste.

The gastronomical cabal, found only in harmony, is thus a truly new bond between honor and gourmandism, a bond that could not even be imagined in civilization. I have advanced that this bond will be of the same strength as the bond in the minor mode between the two elements of love, the physical or cynical, and the spiritual or celadonic. That is to say that in the major bond the power of gastronomical cabal will acquire as much influence as that of amorous voluptuousness in the minor bond. One must be acquainted with this concept, which is foreign to our customs, in order to understand the balance that nature would establish between the major and the minor passionals.

In the contemporary social order we see this equilibrium entirely destroyed. The two passions which constitute the material and the spiritual are in natural and indestructible league with one another—they know no balance, no counterpoint. Love produces in society each day monstrous violations of the social conventions, such as the union of Mohammed and Roxalana, where a turned-up nose overthrew the laws of an empire. Love's scandalous despotism is found everywhere, in all families and in all social relationships. No counterpoint exists. Ambition, for example, is not at all in balance with love. These two tyrants of the social order, these two passional giants ravage the social world and ceaselessly commit monstrous and scandalous injustices, each in its own way. What do our philosophers place in opposition to these two evils? *Morality!* A grotesque obstacle to love and ambition. Are not children who build a dike of pebbles to stop the Rhine or the Danube less foolish than the moralists who construct a dike of 100,000 volumes to stop love and ambition?

Nature would have us proceed systematically in regard to this grave problem; she would wish to oppose in counterpoint the two minor passions, cynicism and celadony, which compose love, and the two corresponding major passions, honor and gourmandism. From their union, impossible today, will emerge love's natural counterpoint. When the gastronomic and hygienic cabal, called wisdom in harmony, is in balance with love in the order of the passional series, ambition will find itself completely absorbed by new interests and by the new course established in all relationships by the mechanism of the series. Such is the problem of mixed harmony to which we will return, and which must be kept in mind so as to distinguish spiritual harmony—which rests on the balance of the four cardinal passions—from mixed harmony—a balance of material and spiritual springs. This balance is no less important than the other one, since the mixed and the ambiguous in harmony has the same force as the combined and the spiritual.

We have noted that the two pleasures work together in harmony in all their degrees. In the armies of which we just spoke, for example, both love and wisdom (gastronomy) express themselves in the omnimode[2] or infinitesimal sense, and are consequently in counterpoint, supporting one another in other circumstances. In the lower degrees, such as the amphimode and the polymode,[3] we will see them in counterpoint. They always work together in whatever degree. The polymode that exerts itself in the army is a very strong attraction for self-esteem, and in [   ] for gastronomy and for the desire of amorous variations or erotic manias. Both act in such a way as to form a bond with the whole world.

Is this also true for trifles such as pastry? The whole world will judge the debate. We have just seen how such an affair in Babylon was handed over to a combined council, attended by the 240 empires, with all of humanity as arbiter. This is not a negligible spring in a mechanism that violently irritates the self-esteem of the industrialists, as we saw in the treatise on the passional series.

In love the same vehicle is established through the omni-

[2] The expression of all passions at once.—Ed.
[3] Amphimode and polymode are words for multiple passions at various degrees of intensity.—Ed.

mode or infinitesimal regime developed in the armies. It is
here that one of the rarest fantasies, like foot fetishism, has
the whole world for support. The 300,000 souls reunited at the
battle of Babylon furnished perhaps thirty foot fetishists of both
sexes, equally impassioned for the active and the passive role.
The clever Pontiff Urgèle knew how to have them meet immediately through his methods of [   ]4. None of the thirty, scattered among the tourbillons of the various empires, had discovered a means of sharing his mania, and each one found himself
reduced to speculating as to the willingness of others.

Accordingly, this mania was merely absurd to the thirty sectarians. But they are cleansed now of that attitude and are united
by a bond proportionately stronger as it is more difficult to satisfy. Each of them will sustain the most lively affection for their
fellow foot fetishists from the various empires. All will keep a
list of their groups and will thus prove to the world that their
passion is far from being ridiculous since it assembled out of
Euphrates' army, independently of those absent, 130 (sic)5
passive and active sectarians. They have created from this
mania a truly universal bond, since it unites men and women
from all parts of the world. Such is the goal of passional harmony—to form bonds that embrace the globe.

From this alliance the mania of foot fetishism, disdained until
now, will take its place on the scale of amorous variations and
will occasionally intervene to augment other variations; each variation is one more potential means to charm and unite large assemblies. Had Pontiff Urgèle not known how to put this spring
into play, there would have been thirty unhappy men and
women who would have each said to himself: all these varieties
of love don't attract me, I would rather encounter foot fetishists;
that is my supreme pleasure. Instead of thirty unhappy people,
there were thirty enthusiasts who satisfied their active and passive fantasies, because they were able to divide themselves into
three groups forming adjacent or adjoining circles of men and
women where, each person being able to develop his mania both

4 Illegible word in the manuscript.—Ed.
5 Fourier probably meant to say 30 rather than 130.—Ed.

actively and passively, found himself doubly satisfied in the end. This gave an infinite charm to the other pleasures which it pleased them to add to their supreme pleasure.

Fantasies divide themselves into physical, spiritual, and mixed, as do manias.

What would become of this [   ] of universal bond if all the amorous and gastronomical manias were smothered, as morality would have it? What if we all had only uniform habits in love, and uniform tastes in food? There would exist no great unity between strangers, and the social world would be an incoherent abyss as it is today, under the regime of this philosophy (the Enlightenment) that only wishes to put into play springs of discord such as moderation and uniformity; both are incompatible with the play of the series which is the mainspring of harmony. This philosophy is more ridiculous than the philosophy I set forth, which brings about unity.

Amorous love fantasies, whether infinitely rare as is foot fetishism, or common as are the sects of flagellation, cannot be subject to debate regarding honor or proper comportment, nor can they require the intervention of a council. Everyone is right in matters of amorous manias, since love is essentially the passion of unreason. It is thus only industry, especially gastronomical hygiene or the hygiene of wisdom, which is the object of the assemblage of council. In light of the great glory attached to the council's vote it is gastronomy which is the principal field of honor, because it is within the competence of all. A victory concerning the manufacture of cloth and fabric, even though obtained by vote of the council united from the 240 empires, does not interest everyone as does a victory concerning food. Threefourths of the inhabitants of a tourbillon will attach little importance to the debates, rivalries, and prizes devoted to a fabric, while the whole tourbillon will be interested in a debate about whipped cream, which everyone consumes. In addition, everyone is interested in knowing whether this whipped cream is hygienically suited to his temperament. Practical gastronomy or the culinary art is thus the branch of industry which most lends itself to glory and to rivalries in harmony. The gastronomic cabal holds the highest rank in all eyes not only as a path of science, but as a path to health and pleasure. Other objects of debate are unable to constantly interest the immense majority of all ages and at all times. Hence, one sees that gourmandism in harmony is as intimately allied with honor as cynicism is with celadony. These two alliances of passion are two giants in comparison with other physical and spiritual marriages of passion; they are therefore essentially the two pivots upon which the mixed system of harmony is based.

The other passions in their physical and spiritual alliances attract only a small number of individuals; for example, when honor and hearing are united, the result is musical ambition or the desire to distinguish oneself in music. This will electrify the Glucks, the Puccinis, and their impassioned followers who form only a portion of the population. But in order to arouse the mass of humanity, there is no mixed passional marriage other than the two already cited—that is, honor and gourmandism (gastronomical cabal) in the major mode, and love composed of celadony and cynicism in the minor mode. It will be agreed that all other passional marriages are but pygmies when compared to these two giants; or if they have a great intensity, it will extend only to a small number of people. Thus, spiritual friendship and sensual vision may very well ally to stimulate those who live in an unpleasant environment, to make them find attractions in their joyless region. But at two leagues' distance that enthusiasm no longer exists, and the sad and uncultivated countryside loses to foreign eyes all the enchantment that it holds for the natives. This is not so for love and opulent repast. Narcissus and Phryne and the wines of Bordeaux and Champagne, transported a thousand leagues, find as many, if not more, partisans than in the very place where they are found. They will charm the great majority of people, while a painting by Raphael or a composition by Pergolesi will enrapture only a small number. This is enough justification for the title of mixed pivot of harmony that I have given to the two passional marriages composed of wisdom or gastronomical cabal in the major mode, and love in the minor mode. These two pivots of voluptuousness are regulated very differently in the politics of harmony, where a gradation exists on the major side, and an equalization on the minor side.

In fact, the customs that I mentioned relating to gastronomy tend to classify very [   ] the pretensions and titles of superiority of each dish and of each contestant. Such is the function of the councils responsible for judging contests. In love, however, the job of the Pontiffs is to give everything equal value, to protect the fantasy of the foot fetishists as well as the love habits extolled by today's morality, such as the simple and mechanical copulation of peasants. The courts of love are based on the principle that every fantasy is good; they look for the most unknown, the most disdained, in order to give it prominence and to unite its partisans the world over. As we have seen this is a means of increasing bonds and of multiplying the amorous series.

NMA, pp. 379–86

II. THE GROUP

THE INDIVIDUAL, AN INCOMPLETE BEING

Man, in the material sense, is composed of two individuals—one male, the other female. Analyze a hundred couples of both sexes, and on dissection they will be found (except in cases of malformation) to possess a uniform number of muscles, nerves, viscera, etc. No one among this hundred couples will be found with eleven or thirteen pairs of ribs, twenty-three or twenty-five vertebræ, fifteen or seventeen pairs of teeth; variations are infinitely rare, like the absence of a pair of teeth; the addition of a sixth finger or sesamoidal bone are deformities and not differences of species. The human species, then, in the material sense, is composed of two bodies, a male and a female; and one such couple, taken at random, furnishes the complete type of the material man. It is not so with the passional man; he is a compound whole, composed of 810 individual souls or distinct characters, distributed in series in about the proportion of twenty-one males to twenty females.

A hundred couples, compared in a material sense, will be found anatomically homogeneous; but the same couples compared in a passional sense, or according to their characters, will be found radically different from each other—among some, avarice would predominate, among others prodigality; one would incline to frankness, another to deceit, and so on. Whence it is evident that the passional man is nowise complete in a single couple, as is the case with the material man; he is as far from complete in 100 couples, and would also be in 405 taken at random, since the assortment of characters might be defective and very discordant. To compose an integral or combined soul, the characters of various degrees must be brought together in graduated proportion, and arranged in classes, orders, genera, species and varieties, as we arrange progressively the pipes of an organ. Let us add that among the 810 individuals forming the 810 characters, there must be 415 men and 395 women, so that there are not 405 of each sex.

When the 810 characters are brought together and fully developed, forming the complete passional man, we shall see them attracted naturally, without the least constraint, to all the functions of agriculture, manufactures, science, and art—the children spontaneously with their parents, and all with enthusiastic ardor. It will be seen that in this new order the poorest individual may develop and satisfy many more of the passions of the soul than the richest potentate can do in the present day, and the greater the inequalities in fortune, intelligence, etc., the easier will association rise to a general accord, which will be as perfect as that of the muscles of the body, or the various instruments of a good orchestra—the latter being an image of the human passions, which constitute an orchestra of 810 instruments.

In speaking of the integrality of the soul, we have to rectify a fundamental error as respects the passional man. Every individual believes that he possesses a complete integral soul; this is an error more gross than would be that of a soldier who should pretend that he formed by himself an entire regiment; the reply would be (supposing the regiment to contain a thousand men) that he formed but a thousandth part of it. The error of such a soldier would be far less absurd than that which has been committed in respect to the integrality of the soul, for the soldier is of the same nature as the captain and the colonel; he may replace them, whereas in the great scale of characters, a soul with one dominant passion, or passion fully developed, is of a very different nature from a soul with two, three or four dominant passions, and can not take its place. Let us make use of a familiar illustration. If we wished to form a pack of cards, and a thousand aces of hearts were offered us, but one of the thousand would be of use; a second would be superfluous. It is the same in the passional mechanism, the 810 characters composing which may be compared to 810 different cards. Now as a card of one particular kind, or a thousand such, would represent but a fifty-second part of a pack, so any one particular character, or a thousand such would represent, not an integral soul, but only the 810th part of it; hence in association but one of the thousand would be of use, and the 999 others would have to be rejected as superfluous.

This truth, which will be distasteful to many, is but an extension of the principle of corporal divisibility; if a thousand men were presented to form a human body, we should have to reject 999, and to the one which remained add a woman. Now if, as is evident, the integrality of the human body requires two different bodies, should we be surprised that the integrality of the soul may require two or even two thousand souls? This is a truth of the most simple and palpable kind, the oversight of which has led the philosophers into a labyrinth of errors in respect to human nature. Had they reflected upon the subject, they would long since have proposed the following problem. Since a human body, taken isolatedly, is not an integral body, we must believe from analogy that a human soul, taken isolatedly, is not an integral soul; and if two different bodies are necessary to form an integral body, how many different souls are necessary to form an integral soul? Are we to conclude from analogy that the number is 2, 3, or 4, or perhaps 200, 300, 400? and what rules should be observed in order to arrive at the solution?

The human body is not androgynous like most plants—that is, it does not possess the faculty of reproducing itself without a distinct male and female body.

A cabbage, if it could speak, might boast of constituting fully the cabbage species, for it reproduces itself, being provided with the male and female principles. It is not so with the human species, which, sexually considered, is divided into a male and female body, and is unable to reproduce itself isolatedly. Other creations are composed of three sexes—the bee for instance. Now if nature, which distributes everything by progression, has established the sexual progression of 1–2–3 respectively, for the bodies of the cabbage, the man, and the bee, it may well have established the progression of 1000–2000–3000, etc., for the integralities of souls—witness the bee, of which it takes as many as 20,000 to form a hive or the integral soul of the bee; this soul, then, is composed of about 20,000 souls, distributed among three sexes.

Can it be said that the three sexual bees—the queen, the working-bee, and the drone—form one integral bee? No, since the three can not form a hive; they are only parts which, associated with a large number of similar parts, form the integral soul, capable of developing in full the faculties of the bee.

A man would show that he knew nothing of bees, if, after passing his life in a country like Lapland, where there are no hives, he should judge this insect to be pernicious from the sight of a few isolated bees which had stung him. We should say to such a man, "You are in error; this little insect in its associated state is the most admirable of creatures." Every one must admit that a being is spiritually incomplete so long as he is not associated with a sufficient number to enable him to fulfill his social functions. We should say of two beavers, for example, Here is the entire specie, in the material sense, but it would take a hundred couples at least to form the species integrally in the spiritual sense—that is, to develop and exercise the natural social faculties of which the beaver is susceptible.

It is thus with man. There has never been seen on our globe an integral human soul in a natural and attractive social mechanism; we see only parts of the integral soul, existing without harmonic association—as would be the state of bees working isolatedly in a country where there were no flowers, which are the elements of their association; they would be wild bees, social abortions, and not integral or associated bees. Such is man in the savage horde; he is not an integral man; he is not in his natural state, since he lacks two elements—a knowledge of industry, the arts, and sciences, and the theory of passional attraction—both of which are necessary to enable him to elevate himself to his destiny, to social harmony. And in the barbaric and civilized orders, he possesses but the first of these two means; as a consequence he can not rise to his destiny nor develop the integral soul. We shall not understand the nature of the integral soul till we have seen man exercising without constraint the social and industrial faculties of which he is susceptible; in the civilized order he acts only from constraint; the proof of this is that if the prison and the scaffold should be abolished, this order would be overthrown at once by the uprising of the masses.

TSO, II, pp. 285–88

THE THEORY OF THE GROUP

The series of groups is the method adopted by God in the distribution of the kingdoms of nature and of all created things. Naturalists, in their theories and classifications, have followed this system of distribution unanimously; they could not have departed from it without conflicting with nature and falling into confusion.

If the passions and characters of man were not subject, like the material kingdoms, to distribution in series of groups, man would be out of unity with the universe; there would be duplicity of system in creation, and incoherence between the material and the passional worlds. If man would attain to social unity, he should seek for the means in the serial order, to which God has subjected all nature.

A passional series is an affiliation, a union of several groups, each animated by some *taste, inclination or shade of passion*. The series represents the SPECIES, of which the groups are the VARIETIES. Twenty groups, for example, cultivating twenty kinds of roses, constitute a series of rose-growers—the series embraces the species; the groups cultivating the white rose, the yellow rose, the moss-rose, etc., are the varieties.

Again, twelve groups are engaged in the cultivation of twelve different flowers; the tulip, for example, is cultivated by one group, the daffodil by another, the dahlia by a third, etc. These twelve groups united constitute a series of florists, whose collective or generic function is the cultivation of flowers, which are distributed according to a scale of tastes, each group cultivating the species of flower for which it has a special taste or attraction. The groups would be divided into sub-groups which would cultivate different varieties of the flower with which each principal group was occupied.

Tastes limited to a single individual are not admissible in the serial organization. Three persons, A, B, C, admiring three varieties of a species of pear, would form only a graduated dissonance, not adapted to serial accords, which require a number of groups distributed in an ascending and descending order.

A regular group, in order to be susceptible of equilibrated or balanced rivalries, should have from seven to nine members at least. In the series, then, we cannot base our calculations upon isolated individuals. Twelve men cultivating twelve different fruits could not furnish the conditions necessary for the rivalries of a series. Meanwhile it should be borne in mind, that the term *series* signifies always a collection or affiliation of groups, and never of individuals; thus the individuals above mentioned, A, B, C, could not form a series.

If, instead of three, we suppose thirty, namely, eight of the taste of A, ten of the taste of B, twelve of the taste of C, they would form a series, that is, an affiliation of groups, graduated and contrasted in their tastes. Their concerts and dissonances would create the incentives necessary to carry the cultivation of the pear to perfection.

The series have always in view a useful end, such as the increase of wealth or the perfection of industry, even when they are engaged in agreeable functions like that of music.

A series cannot be organized with less than three groups, for it requires a middle term to hold the balance between the two contrasted extreme terms. Equilibrium may also be well established with four groups, the properties and relations of which correspond to those of a geometrical proportion.

When the groups of a series are more numerous, they should be divided into three bodies, forming a center and two wings;

or into four bodies, forming a *quadrille*. In each body or corps of groups, the varieties which are closely allied and homogeneous are united.

The combined order must thus employ and develop in a regular and graduated scale all varieties of taste and character; it forms groups of each variety without deciding on the preference to which any particular taste is entitled. All are good, and all have their use, provided a series can be formed of them, regularly distributed in an ascending and descending order, supported at the two extremes by groups of transition or of a mixed character. When a series is arranged in this manner, according to the methods which will be explained in the body of the treatise, each of its groups, were they a hundred in number, would cooperate harmoniously with all the others, like the cogs of a wheel which are all useful, provided they interlock in their turn.

The calculation of the series will establish a principle very flattering to all characters, for it will demonstrate that all tastes which are not injurious or annoying to others have a valuable function in the combined order, and will become useful there as soon as they are developed in series—that is, according to a scale of graduated shades of taste, giving rise to as many groups.

The whole theory of association is based, then, on the art of forming and organizing passional series. As soon as this art has been discovered on a globe it can at once establish social unity, and attain to individual and collective happiness; it is, therefore, the most important of all studies.

The series must be *contrasted, rivalized and interlocked*. A series, failing to fulfill these conditions could not perform its functions in the mechanism of social harmony.

A series must be contrasted—that is, its groups must be distributed or arranged in an ascending and descending order; thus, if we would form a series of a hundred individuals classed according to age, we should distribute them as follows:

ASCENDING WING—groups of children and youths.

CENTER OF THE SERIES—groups of adults.

DESCENDING WING—groups of aged persons.

The same method of distribution should be followed in classifying series of passions and of characters.

This method, by bringing out contrasts, produces enthusiasm in the various groups; each becomes impassioned for the occupation in which it is engaged, and for the special taste which predominates in it, as also for the contrast corresponding to it in the scale; each group criticizes the branch of industry or the taste of the contiguous groups in the series, with which it is in rivalry.

From this system of progressive or graduated classification spring sympathies and alliances between groups properly contrasted in tastes and pursuits, and antipathies or dissidences between contiguous groups, or groups with tastes nearly alike.

The series has as much need of discords as of accords; it should be stimulated by numerous rival pretensions which will give rise to party alliances and become a spur to emulation. Without contrasts, it would be impossible to form leagues between the groups and excite enthusiasm; the series would be without ardor in its labors, and its products would be inferior in quality and in quantity.

The second necessary condition is to create emulation in the series and establish active rivalry between its groups; as this effect arises from the regularity of contrasts, and a graduated distribution of shades or varieties, it may be said that this second condition is fulfilled conjointly with the first, except in what relates to the means of creating emulation, of which it is not yet time to speak.

The third condition to be fulfilled is to connect or interlink the series. This can be effected only by the groups frequently changing their functions, say every hour and a half or at the most every two hours—for example, a man may be employed

At 5 in the morning in a group of shepherds.

At 7 in a group of ploughmen.

At 9 in a group of gardeners.

The term of two hours is the longest admissible in passional harmony, it being impossible to sustain enthusiasm for a longer period; if the labor is unattractive in itself, the term should be reduced to one hour.

In the example of alternation just given, the three series of shepherds, ploughmen and gardeners become interlocked by the process of reciprocal interchange of members. It is not necessary that this interchange should be general, that twenty men engaged in tending flocks from five to seven should, the whole twenty, join the ploughmen from seven to half-past eight; all that is necessary is that each series furnish the others with several members taken from its different groups, in order that the groups may be interlinked, and ties be established between them by the members alternating from one to the other.

A series formed and operating isolatedly would be of no use, and could perform no functions of a harmonic character. Nothing would be easier than to organize in a large city one or more industrial series engaged in the culture of flowers, fruits, etc., or in some branch of art or science; but such a series would be completely useless. At least fifty series are necessary to fulfill the third condition, that of connecting or interlinking; it is for this reason that the experiment of association cannot be made with a small number, as for example with twenty families or a hundred individuals, of whom it would be impossible to form fifty series composed of regularly graduated groups, distributed in an ascending and descending order. At least four hundred persons—men, women and children—would be necessary to organize regularly fifty series, which is the number required for *simple* association or association on a reduced scale; to organize *compound* association or association on a full scale, at least four hundred series, requiring fifteen or sixteen hundred persons, are necessary.

An apparent contradiction will be observed in this calculation of

> 1500 or 1600 persons to form 400 series, and
> 400 persons to form 50 series.

It will be thought that the four hundred persons should furnish a hundred series. This estimate would be *simple* and false. The calculation should be *compound,* that is to say, in the ratio of the number of individuals, and in the ratio of the combinations they admit of. Now as the smaller number is less favorable to combinations, it should not be thought strange that I estimate at fifty instead of a hundred the number of series which could be formed with the four hundred persons.

In the combined order, the profits increase in the ratio of the number of series which can be organized with a given number of persons; hence, *simple* association yields hardly half the profits which would result from *compound* association.

It will be thought that the experimental association should be of the *compound* order; this would certainly be desirable, but various considerations oblige me to base my calculations on the *simple* order, though, as I have said, it is much less brilliant and productive.

It has appeared to me necessary to give, at the outset, this slight sketch of the passional series. In order to simplify the study, I have adopted the progressive method, and commenced with a lesson limited to a few pages.

As all the operations of association are conducted by series of groups, our only study will be the organization of the series, their distribution, their rivalries, their equilibria, etc. The argument of the present work is, therefore, contained in the above outline, in which I have defined very briefly the main lever of association. It is the only system adapted to the requirements of the passions; the only one by which industry can be rendered attractive.

The necessity of connecting or interlinking the series, as above explained, shows why association is impracticable with the small number of ten or twenty families; if economy and profits can result only from large numbers and extensive combinations, God must have based his calculations on large associations; and our political theories which would base the accord of the passions on the smallest union possible, that of a single family, are utterly absurd. The isolated or family system is a complicated and ruinous one, which connects a thousand disgusts with the exercise of industry. Such an order is the antipode of the designs of God,

whose plans require unity of action, practical truth in all relations, and, especially, an economical organization of labor. The
latter can exist only in the series of groups, adapted to the different tastes and attractions, and alternating industrial pursuits
so as to prevent apathy and indifference.

It was in truth an intricate problem, that of associating individuals of different characters and degrees of fortune, and
remunerating them according to their capital, labor and talent;
but intricate or not, it was the primary problem for genius to
solve.

TSO, I, pp. 37–42

THE GROUP IN ACTION

While choruses and musical instruments ring out hymns of
gladness, the multitude advances amid a cloud of perfume and a
rain of flowers. As the crowd reaches the columned peristyle the
punches are lighted and a hundred different kinds of nectar
gush from the fountains. All the knights and ladies are dressed
in the most complimentary clothes, each best suited to display
the wearer's form and beauty. Two hundred elegantly dressed
priests and priestesses perform the honors of the introduction.
After refreshments they ascend to the hall where Isis sits en-
throned. Here the reception ceremony ends and the crowd
proceeds to the confession room after passing through the cham-
bers of ablution.

The leaders of the priesthood quickly begin the confessions
and receive written declarations. Some of the group, having confessed at a previous station, submit a written account of their
confession and sympathies drawn up by a prior confessor.

As soon as the light meal is announced, and as the group
seats itself, the priests proceed to the consistory to sort and classify the confessions. In light of the examinations of conscience
collated by the priests and priestesses who want to enter into
sympathy with the adventure, a list of five to six sympathies is
assigned to each knight and lady. During the meal the fairies

and genies finish the work of match-making and the lists of sympathies are given to the High Priestess and appended to each of the confessions. The disposition of sympathies is weighed for all possible combinations and is settled upon for those judged to be the most appropriate either to arrange partners based on previous impressions or to animate by contrast or identity the germs of fantasy that may exist in the soul of each adventurer.

I speak here only of the young class of female adventurers; the older ones treat their love affairs at the fakir's seances using other methods.

Even though they are especially consecrated to the travelling priesthood, the male and female dancers are not the only intervening class in these festivities since one wishes to reunite from the tourbillon, as well as from the surrounding area, all those of both sexes who can participate to advantage and who are not engaged by any prior bond of fidelity.

The first moments are given over to the ceremonial, which must always be accompanied by an informal meal. These preliminaries serve to satisfy the curiosity of the multitude, each one freely circulating and becoming generally familiar with the new arrivals who also need to familiarize themselves with the field. One could not imagine negotiating love affairs before the participants see and are seen by all. This delay is useful to classify the sympathies; each one finds his prepared list as he is ready to enter the court of love. Until this time the vestals and children are allowed to mingle with the crowds and to satisfy their curiosity. It would be very awkward not to take this precaution and to allow them to desire access to a place which they should not frequent. Only when the children drop from fatigue and have seen enough of the crowd, do the participants go to the High Priestess to obtain their confession and list of manifest sympathies. Here they also see the portraits of all those assigned to them according to their sympathies.

When the preludes are over the two groups gather in the salon. At the beginning of the seance the volley is set up—on one side of the room stands the crowd, and on the other side are placed the priesthood and all others drawn to the courtly affair by sympathy or desire. The priests are placed opposite the adventuresses, and the priestesses opposite the adventurers.

At the signal given by the fairy's wand the multitude surrenders itself to a bacchanal. The melee is general, the two groups throwing themselves into each others' arms. Everyone confusedly gives and receives caresses, quickly and spontaneously abandoning himself to the sensual delights of nature that come his way. The company flies from one to another eagerly and joyously kissing whatever charms appeal to him among the male and female champions. During the melee each tries to spend a moment with all who have captured his eye in the past. This short bacchanal serves to test pure nature and may dispose already of many sympathies for those who tend essentially or accidentally to the sensual.

Yet this confused skirmish alone does not indicate the tenor of the love matches to follow. It would even be in poor taste to fix one's choice from this initial encounter before tentative sympathy occurs. Those who found a suitable partner during the melee will meet again and will love one another better only if their calculated sympathy, of which they are as yet unaware, confirms the half-felt affinity revealed by the volley.

Some of the purely materialistic civilizees would like to stop the search at this point, imagining this melee to be sufficient to find the object of their desire. Such would be the judgment of the monogynes of touch. Nothing will prevent them, when they happen to meet some of their ilk in the melee, from relating in this manner to their cynical accomplices. But not one in twenty among the champions will follow this method, as it would form a bond of simple love based on a purely material affinity. Harmony works in a very different way, tending to engender unions of full sympathy for each couple—to which the melee is a necessary prelude—rather than unions of a simple sensual bond. Harmony conforms to the law of progression whereby movement is from the simple to the composite. It would be extremely contrary to the natural progression of love to first occupy the respective champions with spiritual and transcendent emotions. The first impulse of nature is toward the sensual, which must be

reinforced by a preliminary bacchanal and thereafter move toward the magic of sentiment. This magic, excited by the fairy's
tactics, will soon become associated with existing sensual impressions and will establish composite pleasure.

To conclude this scene, the rapid exchange of caresses and
the reconnaissance of the field should last barely seven or eight
minutes. There must be a dissolving factor to disunite the melee;
since in harmony all transpires by attraction, two groups are
cast into the multitude, lesbians and spartans, who will first
approach champions having the same proclivity as themselves.
They are easily recognizable during the melee since each wears
a pendant or an epaulet as a sign of his or her passion. As soon
as these two new groups have distracted the attention of a good
number of couples, and disunited them, they will lead off several individuals. The signal and entreaties of the confessional
mentor will then hasten and finally end the melee. From here
the multitude will enter the hall of sympathies.

The hall of reconnaissance is formed by two platforms, placed
across from one another and distributed in three tiers so that
those placed on one side of the hall may plainly see those across
from them. All the adventurers are placed on one side while
the novices of sympathy are placed on the other.

The priests and priestesses responsible for getting things under way lead in five or six athletes. Each of the villagers takes
a priestess of the adventure who knows all the members of the
group, and each of the group members takes a village priestess
who is acquainted with all the inhabitants of the area. Thus
each person, through the intermediary of the priesthood, is
shown the various individuals named on his sympathetic scale,
where he sees listed the details of their spiritual and spontaneous affinities. Now he can judge the physical suitability of the
men and women strolling about on the tiers, since they were
already surveyed more closely during the introductory bacchanal. Every member of the group is already more able to class
the range of his indicated sympathies and to have a feeling
for those between whom he will choose either by inspection or
by the indications of the priesthood.

To facilitate the inspection, alternate sides of the assembly are seated. The other side then strolls about and takes reconnaissance of the candidates in the group seated opposite them. In short, all possible measures are taken to insure alacrity. To that effect each one is careful to differentiate himself from the others by means of a nameplate or other visible sign to hasten and facilitate the indicating.

After having recognized his candidates in the ranks, each one can from the first round pronounce judgment on the sensual harmony of the individuals assigned to him since the priestess' notebook indicates their secret qualities. After this interview only that which touches the spiritual remains to be settled.

The inspections and reconnaissance terminated, the multitude enters the hall of festivities where the encounters take place. These meetings are arranged by the fairies and genies whose duties are much more subtle.

Let us now consider the complications. Many desires may center on the same individuals. A certain priest, for example, may be desired by ten female adventurers and another priestess by as many males. Such competition of sensual choice would be a great quandary in a bourgeois assembly where many preferences fall to the same person. But whosoever has loved knows that one often becomes passionately attached to beings for whom there is little attraction at first, but for whom there later develops a sympathy of souls. It is the goal of the court of love to determine such sympathies at the outset so as to avert a concentration of desires upon the same subjects resulting in a horde around a few, and a void around many others.

Physical charm will not have as colossal an influence in harmony as it does in civilization, where a beautiful woman catches all eyes. Harmonians will doubtless appreciate material beauty, and with more discernment than is found in our era. But the people of both sexes who are presented to a sympathetic gathering will not dwell upon material charm, as they will be distracted by three motives of [   ] and one of transition.

First, the adventurers never fail to ask for an exposition of simple nature, a procession in which the amorous notables of the region, in conjunction with those of the adventure, will display in the nude their most remarkable attributes. A certain woman who has beautiful breasts will be clothed in such a way as to show off only her most remarkable feature. A woman whose waist is beautiful will be dressed to show off only her waist. Those who wish to exhibit everything will appear entirely nude. It will be the same for men. After the assurance of this exposition of simple nature no one will doubt that he can admire all the physical charms to be found in the region.

Second, in addition to this exposition it will be possible to negotiate orgies for the following day that will be well assorted, and where full enjoyment will be had with the beauties seen at the exposition.

Third, the group has already been materially satisfied and has enjoyed this sort of pleasure at the preceding station. After any pleasure the first need is for variation by contrast. From this is born the desire for a sympathy of souls, which is the most immediate need of a troop upon arriving.

Moreover if, when the station is over, an adventuress has a whim for some fine priest that she did not have, she can ask for him at a session of general farewell. This is a courtesy of transition which should not be refused to a multitude upon its departure.

Since no one lacks physical satisfaction, solicitude is thus directed to the spiritual. Choices that are made in succession are often the most difficult to satisfy, as they have the fault of being simple. First there are the monogynes of touch or sight, people amorous of form and appearance, as well as those who need to give themselves over to the sensual to alternate with spiritual passion. These two classes fix their choice according to the inspection made in the hall of observation and at the preceding volley where they have already approached the most notable beauties. These simple unions are the most difficult to conclude because the two parties harmonize only slightly with one another. To prefer a certain person at first glance is not sufficient reason for the chosen to distinguish the chooser. It is much easier to associate those who have a sympathy of souls, which is the objective in the hall of festivities.

The various champions have noted their sensed sympathies before entering the hall. Clitie has noticed three of the six sympathies on her list, in addition to one that was not listed on her card. There is already a gradation established in her desires; she knows those whom she is most desirous of approaching and she numbers them accordingly on her list so that the fairy leading her will first present her to the athletes between whom she hesitates.

In these encounters the manoeuvers will alternate, that is to say that during a certain time the male and female adventurers, led by their male and female fairies, will approach the priests and priestesses and will make an ideal reconnaissance of their sympathetic choices. Then the priests and priestesses will approach the adventurers in a similar reconnaissance. Nothing will be concluded before everyone has encountered all his candidates. Each party in turn must be able to preview his longings, and must verify all the details of his character and habits, his temporary caprices, and his last passion and needs of alternation and contrast, which appear on his escutcheon.

Little by little the company will be reduced by sudden accords. Certain matches which include romanesque inspiration or pure sensuality will diminish the mass. Moreover these unions of first sight may very well be composed sympathies since everyone has augured his several sympathies by means of lists, inspections, and information. It suffices after this to verify firsthand the details that appear on the symbolic escutcheon, after which a brief interview will verify the accord. All those who are finally matched retire to another place which facilitates the operations of the other less well-suited unions. Reciprocal soundings are made without haste and by repeating the endeavor several times. Some unions are late and doubtful; it is possible to fail in the preliminary interviews and to decide only in the ballroom or at supper. These delays are frequent among those who wish to refine their choice.

Those who are the last to conclude do not risk being left out or badly matched because the fakir will intervene in order to satisfy everyone. But in general the last ones to decide are couples of [   ] who are better suited for having coquetted together during this time. In any case, if the sympathies that are decided last are much less intense than those decided midway or at the beginning, no one risks being limited to simple pleasure.

In all these encounters care is taken to save self-esteem, and to this end the male and female fairies intervene. As long as two people are under the guardianship of a fairy the offense of a delay or of a refusal is avoided. If after an interview someone wishes to refuse, the secret of his delay is communicated only to the intermediary who transmits the explanation in such a way that everyone's self-esteem is preserved. The fairies abandon their clients when they are sufficiently acquainted with their supposed sympathetics, and when their intimacy is well enough established to allow them to carry on alone.

Thus the court of love, of which I describe here only a simple operation, can operate a host of these fortunate unions of composed sympathy in two or three hours of work and gallant sessions. Civilization is often unable to operate even one union in a month of effort because one or two months are insufficient to know the character of civilizees, and especially of women.

The sympathetic intrigues are much more animated the second day because those which have just begun, or have miscarried, become reunited, and infidelities occur to vary the scene. The sympathies that endure are more brilliant as the occasions to slip away are numerous and tempting. There are hardly any adventurers who, during a station of three days, do not alternate their sympathies and return to those that they came in contact with at the first session. These interludes are entirely independent of physical distractions or orgies, or expositions of simple nature, bacchanals, etc. . . . , which are intermissions agreed upon by mutual accord between sympathetics. These moments of respite do not alter the union, as consciences in harmony are very accommodating about this sort of truce, which is not regarded as infidelity when it is reciprocally agreed upon. It happens very frequently that lovers, and even the most constant, agree in this way to an interlude after which they take up again with one another. These pacts are very common during brilliant happenings like the passage of adventurers and other delicate circumstances for the [   ] who could hardly avoid succumbing to temptation, and would thus lose the privileges of constancy. This is avoided by a truce registered according to the court of love and subject to certain rights of welcome. In any case these intermissions, despite registration, are seen as inconstancy when they are repeated more than three times, or in other cases provided for in the amorous code.

I have described a single operation of the court of love; let us observe some results. It is evident that young people would not be able to be responsible for the work of sympathies, as they lack the theoretical and practical knowledge required to quickly furnish the participant with all his soul's needs. The first of which is, in theory, to determine if one should be allied in love of contrast, alternation, or cabal, and to observe a suitable progression in these alliances by taking his former unions into consideration, and to discover the degrees of that progression by examination of conscience.

Second, in practice, to determine the persons with whom he may find some chance of the necessary sympathy, and to assign to him at least six, three of whom are matched chances, and three of whom are discordant chances.

These decisions require of the regional priesthood not only spiritual knowledge, but knowledge of momentary practices as well. Thus the sympathies must be managed by committees of fairies whereby affinities are classified by kind and species, and for each person a list is made of those people matching in sympathy. A single individual could never arrive at knowing enough people.

Let us add that a good match depends a great deal upon the orderliness of the examinations of conscience. Judicious confessors are needed here to help youth, who will often fail to bring analytical order to these examinations, and would thereby cause the [   ] of sympathy.

This operation, and others of equal importance, can be entrusted only to persons of age and experience. Without their help a troop upon arriving would not know how to match themselves in love and would be reduced to brutal unions, like the nasty and dangerous civilizee orgies, which are choices of simple love uniquely determined by physical suitability.

These same orgies in harmony will acquire a lively interest if they are posterior to sympathy. In fact when the adventurers of a station have carried on a fine passion with a certain priestess, she acquires value in the eyes of the multitude; she is desired by a crowd of people whose attention she had not attracted until then. Thus all couples, having once entered into sympathy, become interesting to one another. Consequently, when the group is on the point of departure, when they must take leave of one another, it becomes very piquant to reunite in orgy all those who were noticed either on the stage or in loves whose union may have excited longing. Every adventuress during these two days will have distinguished at least a dozen priests, and each adventurer as many priestesses. The orgy that will yield to them all these people will have the charm of multiple sympathy. If the same orgy had taken place at the outset it would be merely a very crude pleasure with no stimulant for the soul. From this will be judged the importance of pairing sympathies wisely at the outset, and the utility of the aged, with whom this task rests exclusively.

I have not spoken of the influence of the court of love upon intrigues of long duration, or of the benefits to be gained by its intervention. A whole section rather than a short account will have to be given this vast subject.

Let us go on to examine the benefits to the elderly in this amorous mediation, which will not be at all tiresome to them. An experienced pontiff who is well acquainted with the neighboring regions will make it a *point d'honneur* to easily manage all the unions, and to untangle in an hour's office work all the springs to put into play in each intrigue, and to completely satisfy the travellers by the skill of his council, his ministers and his officers. The pontiff of each tourbillon and his Aulic council will contend with neighboring tourbillons for renown on this point. The result will be that no horde, band, caravan or legion will want to be found lacking in gratitude. Upon departing each group will leave numerous couples of the odaliscate for the ministry of the pontiff. If he is a renowned pontiff he will not fail to receive these couples before a group arrives at the station.

It will frequently happen that travellers become enamored of their female confessor, since many have a penchant for mature people who are amiable. There will be instances in which this penchant will be provoked by the methodical progression of sympathy. A skillful confessor will know how to discern this need in her client's soul, and will even seek to encourage it. Moreover there can be no surprise in such an affair because the confessor must, according to the court of love's custom, be ornamented with an escutcheon which is worn as a medallion or an epaulet, to faithfully indicate her spiritual situation, her character and her most recent impressions. Confessors of both sexes will have a great advantage in forming these sympathetic unions between two extremes of age, should the occasion arise.

It is said that nothing in this world is free, and if it is fair that the old oblige the young in love affairs, it is equally fair that they be amply rewarded for their service. It was necessary to give a summary in support of the thesis of the rallying of love. I cannot repeat too often that customs so different from ours cannot be established in the first years of harmony, because it will be a necessary preliminary to purge the globe of syphilitic and dermatological maladies, etc. . . . Until then more circumspection must prevail in harmonian love than presently prevails in the civilizee era.

Furthermore, these unions similar to civilizee marriage, unions in which there exists no material and spiritual accord rather than the double accord of harmonian unions, will from the beginning be highly scorned in harmony. A union which depends only upon a physical accord will already be regarded as vicious and ignoble. It will be seen as debauchery and will be admissible only in transition, as in the bacchanals of the army, where not enough confessors and fairies can be assembled to carry on the work of sympathy. Here, then, it will be necessary for the majority to limit themselves to material unions, since there will be in the armies many other very brilliant sympathies, notably those of the vestals and of those people who have distinguished themselves on the stage. The others will have recourse to bacchanals and to orgies which in this case are ennobled as acts of unity and as a sacred function. But in all other cases unions which are pecuniary negotiations, as marriage and prostitution are for us, will be reputed to be ignoble and will be treated as commerce. Commerce is dishonored in harmony and even punished when one sells something arbitrarily, other than his person. Thus that negotiation so revered among us under the name of a proposal of marriage, in which men and women are esteemed by their weight in gold like animals at market, will be doomed to scorn. Those who participate will bear the defamatory title of friends of commerce, a title which in harmony is a superlative of depravity.

We have come to the quintessence of the passional domain, to the perfume of love, to the pure and unselfish flame that vulgar lovers are unable to experience. It is here that I must exclaim with Horace: Be gone, laymen, be gone! *Odi profanum vulgus et arceo.*

Pleasantries aside, harmonians would be very clumsy if they did not know how to cause the seeds of so many illusions to flower. Far from disdaining them, they will know how to cause true joy to spring from this source. We in civilization draw from this source perspectives of pleasure which are confined to novels, incompatible with our depraved spirits.

Sentimental society in harmony considers itself to be the high nobility of love. This is not a vexatious privilege since access to this honor is open to everyone and restricted only by the trials to be undergone. It is known in advance that the number of tested sectarians will barely exceed an eighth of the gallant class, and those of the semi-virtuoso class will not exceed a fourth. Thus it would be futile for the plebeian and material multitude to aspire to admission in this elite body. A man incapable of undergoing the trials would expose himself to affront and ridicule, which he will carefully avoid if he feels himself to be a slave of common penchants. Each candidate must be tested according to the degree of his character. The strength of sentiment that would be expected of an omnigyne, or character of the eighth degree, would not be required of a tetragyne, or character of the fourth degree. This sentiment would not be found at all in the case of a monogyne who, as soon as he is violently in love, is no longer impassioned of other women. But in order to have eight loves in one's title it does not suffice to elect and to designate them. It is necessary to evince sentimental love for them while having composed love for others. This is the touchstone of this kind of love.

We are not yet to a methodical picture of these tests which are all aimed at sentimental love, since material love in young people is not worthy. A pretender must first prove fidelity to his celadon[1] of the opposite sex. A man should have as many female celadons as he has passional dominants; thus the omnigyne has eight celadons to whom he must prove his boundless devotion. He must be assiduous in serving all their loves, even of orgy, without being permitted to possess them before the length of time necessary to prove celadony. (Either a vestalate or three female celadons serve as proof and are required of a monogyne.)

This is not at all an infringement upon liberty—it is a corporative statute. Everyone is free not to enter into the sentimental corporate body, or to resign from it. Moreover these interdictions are not perpetual. There is a fixed duration for the test of celadony, after which one can proceed to a material resolution, except to justify the complement, which is to say to justify a replacement in celadony. Consequently this liaison is the more honorable as its duration is more prolonged.

NMA, pp. 209–22

[1] A person who experiences purely spiritual love.—Ed.

SOCIAL CLASSES

Here we approach the most important subject in domestic harmony, the passionate accord between servants and masters, or the art of stimulating respective devotion between the two classes. Is there any art more foreign to civilization? Or rather, is civilization not antipathetic to all harmony between un-equals, namely between masters and servants? We will see how this branch of domestic unity, so impracticable in the present state, is established in association without any po-litical wisdom whatsoever through the development of the pas-sions alone. Nothing is more opposed to concord than the present condition of the domestic and salaried classes. By re-ducing this poor multitude to a condition very like slavery, civilization, on the rebound, imposes chains upon those who seem to dominate. Thus notables do not dare to amuse them-selves openly at times when the people suffer from poverty. The rich are subject to individual as well as collective servitude. A wealthy man is often the slave of his valets. However in har-mony the valet himself enjoys complete independence, while the rich are served with an assiduity and a devotion of which one sees not a trace in civilization. Let us explain this harmony.

In composed harmony not a single associate exercises house-hold duties; and yet the poorest of men have constantly fifty pages in their service. The announcement of such a state of af-fairs brings forth cries of incredulity, as is true for any of the mechanisms of the series, which nevertheless can be under-stood.

In a Phalanstery domestic duties are managed, as are all other functions, by the series which assigns a group to each variety of work. In time of service the members of the series bear the title of male and female pages. This title is given to those who serve kings; it belongs more rightly to those who serve a Phalanstery; for a Phalanstery is God in action. It is the spirit of God, since it is composed of the twelve passions harmonized,

by passional attraction,
practical truth,   and unity of action.
mathematical justice,

Hence collectively serving the Phalanstery is serving God; and it is thus that domestic duties are envisioned in harmony. If this primordial branch of industry were disparaged as it is today, passional equilibrium would become impossible.

Domestic service is not only idealized; it is also truly ennobled through the suppression of individual dependence which debases a man by subordinating him to the caprices of another. Let us analyze the mechanism of free collective service in an ordinary function such as that of chambermaid.

The female page Délie serves in the group of chambermaids assigned to the right wing of the building. She is on bad terms with Léandre and neglects his apartment when she visits the part of the building for which she is responsible. But others take her place, and Léandre is no less well served because Eglé and Phillis, two female pages of the same group who are fond of Léandre, assume responsibility for his apartment.

It is the same at the stables. If Léandre's horse is neglected today by one of the pages, he is taken later and groomed by a friend of Léandre's or by another page of the group. Thus in all branches of service everyone is eagerly served by those who are fond of him, or failing this he will be taken care of by the whole group. At another hour and in another function one may encounter those who have served him at a previous time, and who will perhaps be his superiors upon changing work. Eglé served Léandre at 7:00; but at 9:00 there is a session at the beehives where Léandre, who has taken part in this work for only six months, is one of the new associates. This duty is still new to Léandre while Eglé, who has done it since childhood, is very skillful. In his duties at the beehives Léandre finds himself under Eglé's orders.

Under such a regime no one need worry about obtaining domestic care; only the candidate has to be chosen. Among twenty pages who serve at the stables there will be at least ten who are closely related to Léandre through cabalistic affinity in several series (garden, orchard, opera); thus he will never lack a friend to care for his horse, who will be well cared for by the pages of the group in any case. But it is one of the charms of harmony, even in all the trifling branches of service, to see a friend busy himself for you, a friend more intelligent as harmonian service has many subdivisions and admits only experienced associates into each function.

Phillis and Eglé made Léandre's bed; someone else will air his suit. They take it to the airing room and give it to Clitie, who is also a friend of Léandre's. There is a spot on his suit and, after airing it, Clitie takes it to the cleaning room where it is attended to by Cloris, another of Léandre's friends. Thus each servant of both sexes is always motivated by friendship, love, or another affection in harmony, no matter what branch of service he devotes himself to.

The industrial cabals of gardens, orchards, workshops, opera, etc., create for everyone a group of friends of both sexes, and he is assured of finding several pages in every group who will affectionately serve him. The poor enjoy this advantage as do the rich, and a man without wealth finds a crowd of affectionate servants offering him their ministerings, just as a prince does, because *it is never the individual who is served who pays those who serve him.* A page would be ignominiously fired from the series if he were known to secretly accept reward from those whom he served. It is the Phalanstery that remunerates the groups of pages by a dividend based upon the share of work and talent, which is divided by the series between its members in proportion to their manifest aptitude and industry.

Thus individual independence is fully assured in that each page is concerned with service to the Phalanstery and not to an individual. Each member is therefore served with affection. This is a pleasure which even the rich cannot procure for any amount of money in civilization; because if one amply pays a servant in order to obtain his affection, ambition will render him careless, unpleasant, and often perfidious. This danger is inconceivable in harmony, where everyone is assured the friendship of many pages who adopt to serve him with the liberty to withdraw in case the affection cools, and with no pecuniary agreement.

Thus in harmony there is nothing mercenary nor servile in domestic chores; a group of chambermaids, like all other groups, is a free and honorable society that shares in the gross product of the Phalanstery by reason of the importance of its work.

Harmonian servants are as sensitive to *points d'honneur* as those whom they serve; every page avoids groups whose cabals he does not support. Thus companies, like individuals, simultaneously find in their pages affectionate and cabalistic preference. This double bond between he who serves and he who is served exists everywhere. Here, then, are already two motives for friendship between them, aside from amorous liaisons, which are possible when service is given by the other sex. But it is agreed that in our calculations on harmony we will never take love into account since, this passion being proscribed in civilizee morals, it is important to prove that enough resources exist to establish composite bonds in the experimental Phalanstery without having recourse to love.

Some domestic duties seem ignoble or debasing, like clearing away mud, refuse, etc. In harmony this service becomes a good work carried out by a series of children of both sexes. These children are destined by religion to the most repugnant duties, and are proud of that charity, just as doctors in civilization today pride themselves in caring for the indigent sick from whom they expect no payment. Guilds of penitents have been known to fetch and shroud the bodies of executed prisoners. Often it was a wealthy man who detached the criminal's body from the gallows. Religion ennobles these repugnant acts. It is similar in harmony for those duties which may seem vulgar to us. They belong to the noblest and proudest of corporate bodies, that of the little hordes of children of whom I will speak in the book on composed integral education.

A champion of the commercial mentality will object that if

harmony is immensely rich, . . . a large sum can be allotted
in wages for repugnant work. This will take place in the Hun-
garian association[2] which is unable to develop great springs
of attraction or to organize bodies of male and female pages.
But in harmony itself (eighth period, composed association) not
one farthing will be allocated for foul work; that would invert
the entire mechanism of high attraction which must, through
esprit de corps, triumph over the strongest aversion. Where attraction can do the most it can also do the least—when it is
known how to attract people to the work of clearing away refuse
and to hunting reptiles it will be easy to attract them to the cultivation of fruit and flowers.

I postpone this subject as it is treated in the article "Petites
Hordes," where we will see that the most subordinate service,
like sweeping a poor man's bedroom, will perhaps be performed
by a young ten-year-old princess enlisted in that corporate body
through honor and religious spirit, and this duty in harmony
will be of the highest order.

The extreme subdivision of duties in domestic service is a
guarantee of attraction to this kind of work. There will be many
series of pages because it will be possible to exercise a small
branch of service without accumulating, as today, either various duties or many details of a same service. Since one who has
a taste for cleaning wool will not like to clean silk or linen,
these two fabrics will be left to other groups. The large number
of sectarians will shorten and enliven the sessions. As a natural
consequence of their large number, and of the subdivision of
work, the poor are able to have fifty domestics in active service.
There will even be night lookouts to wake one at the hour decided upon the night before, by placing a sign on the door or
at an intersection where one's hall joins the main hall. Thus
the poor in harmony enjoy a multitude of services that in civilization the rich cannot procure, or only by mercenary means.
In harmony the poor obtain them through a composed bond of
cabal and affection.

[2] This is a fictional Phalanstery.—Ed.

It has been seen in this chapter that the mechanism of the passional series always substitutes a double attraction for the double disadvantages of the civilizee mechanism. I will explain.

On the part of a harmonian servant there is the double bond of affection and cabal, independent of all the other bonds, such as love, that might enter in. Let us limit ourselves to the particular charms of this service, to those created between people of the same sex. It will be shown that in harmony no matter how inferior a duty may be, like the caring for shoes, everyone has attending to his needs a male or female page that he cherishes in a double relationship through the bonds of cabal and friendship. It is thus a composed affinity; it will become super-composed if there is joined a third bond, like love; and bi-composed if a fourth is added, like kinship.

Service in civilization presents opposite results. There is among all servants, or at least seven-eighths of them, composed or bi-composed disaccord which is established by unsuitability of character, by mistrust and fear of theft, by impatience causing clumsiness or impertinence on the servant's part, by indignation at the master's exactingness, by jealousy of fortune, by rancor stemming from bad treatment, injustice or stinginess, or by ingratitude in the case of generosity. These many subjects of discord cause the rich to say that domestics are a source of tribulation, a complaint even more justly repeated by servants.

Hence a rich civilizee finds two, three, and four clashes in his relations with domestics. His bonds with servants are only composed, super-composed, or bi-composed discord, rather than an affinity of similar degree with which every detail of service will present him in harmony.

This contrast will be encountered in all civilizee relationships and their parallels in harmony—movement in the periods of limbo, second savagery, third patriarchy, fourth barbarism, and fifth civilization, is always carried to a degree of evil corresponding to its degree of good in harmony, where all relationships will assure super-composed and bi-composed pleasures, even for the poor class.

As relations with domestics, salaried workers, and the lower

classes are a permanent problem for leaders, and much more
so for subordinates, and as notables are heard to complain bitterly, I had to hasten to show them that in association this disadvantage will be transformed into a source of continual charm,
into an affectionate bond between leaders and valets. It completely delivers the rich of the expensive and onerous burden of
domesticity, while at the same time procuring for them a body
of servants as admirable for their devotion, probity and dexterity,
as those in civilization are distressing for the opposite vices.

OC, Vol. IV, pp. 526–35

THE ART OF FORMING GROUPS

In treating the measured series which are always distributed
in octaves of dozens as in music, and in demonstrating that these
kinds of series are very superior to the free series, whose groups
are of an indefinite number, I do not claim to establish any
prejudice for or against any number, nor to espouse the
opinion of authors predisposed to such discord. On the contrary, I am going to establish that harmony knows how to make
use of all numbers, except as the resources of each person
limit their use.

The mania for establishing exclusive systems in favor of a
certain number is as old as science. The Egyptian and Pythagor-
ian priests fell into this error; one would think the moderns
cured of this mania, but it has been revived, more vigorously
than ever. Even today I received an abstract from the work of
Saint-Martin, a modern philosopher, who sees the measure of
evil in the number 9 and the measure of good in the number 4.
It was not long ago that Bernardin de Saint-Pierre saw in the
number 5 the measure of all good; another will prove to us that
it is the number 6 that is the bearer of light.

These exclusive biases are signs of confusion.

It is foolish to think the author of nature so narrow-minded
that He is exclusively impassioned of a certain number, and that
He rejects all other distributions.

There are, in truth, numbers more or less suited to the good fortune of high harmony. These numbers are:

$$3--4--7--12$$

The last two numbers are products of the addition and multiplication of the first two; these are the four numbers whose combinations contain the principal subdivisions of the measured series. . . .

But, since certain numbers are favorable to the disposition of harmony, does it follow that the others are to be denounced and discarded? And that 2, 5, 6, 8, 9, 10, 16, 18—numbers more or less adapted to harmony—must be scorned and proscribed?

Let us here accuse all the sophists; let us first ask them about the inferior numbers 3 and 4. From there we will pass on to the higher numbers.

All of human kind has pronounced itself in favor of the number 3. Everywhere the trinity is a sacred number. But there are two philosophers, Saint-Martin and Bernardin de Saint-Pierre, who want to enlist us in favor of the numbers 4 and 5. Which of the two must we heed? Neither of them, since neither one nor the other understands the virtues of the number he extols.

The number 4 is as sacred as the number 3, since a simple series of 4 groups is as useful as those having 3 groups. Passional equilibrium is established as well upon one as upon the other, although by different methods. It follows that the trinitarian numbers and the cardinal or quaternary numbers are the two sacred lower numbers, being the most suited to combinations or harmony. The number 5 does not have the same advantage; it is usefully employed only when distributed in 4 touches co-ordinated to a pivot, like the 5 fingers of a hand, where one of them, the thumb, is a pivot and counterpoint to the other four.

Here is a harmony for the number 5, and consequently for the number 10. I will later indicate other harmonies for the numbers 6, 8, 16, 9, 18. It will be concluded that certain philosophers' biases in favor of particular numbers are unreasonable manias.

It is possible to give the lead to some numbers as principal agents of harmony; but it is necessary that the others conserve their prerogatives and that their useful employment be mentioned. It must be recognized that since all is progressive in nature's system, she can very well favor certain numbers and certain beings without proscribing the others.

I will be antagonistic throughout this work to the number 10 when speaking of numeration; I will scoff at civilizees because they count by 10s, like savages, but I will only express well-motivated railleries, of which it is not yet time to speak. I do not claim that the number 10 is a number to be banned, but merely that it is of less importance than the integral numbers of harmony, which are 3, 4, 7, 12; $3+4 = 7$ (addition); $3 \times 4 = 12$ (multiplication).

The number 12 has in its favor the evidence of spoken or musical harmony. God would not have assigned this number to music had he not judged it the most appropriate to the multiplicity of accords.

The same number 12 has mathematical harmony in its favor —12 is the number giving the most common factors in the least sum of units. In this double relationship it becomes a number of composed harmony, a title against which no other number can contend.

In the prolegomenon I announced the essential property of the number 7, which is that of forming the balanced series. With it are formed simple series of three groups, but the composed series can not be formed of fewer than seven groups, of which three are in the center, and two on each side.

The number 3 has the advantage of giving harmony of geometric proportion to four groups: 32 sectarians divided as 3, 5, 9, 15, can have properties of geometric proportion in industrial rivalries and in the payment of dividends. The combined influence of the two extreme groups will be equal to the combined influence of the two middle groups, either in relationships of interest and distribution, or in contests of emulation.

The series of three groups enjoys about the same properties, except for a slight difference. Thus, the numbers 7 and 12, being powers of 3 and 4, namely

      7, power of addition

      12, power of multiplication

are the most adapted to harmony.

These properties of the septaine and the dozen will not be judged fairly until the treatise on their use in the passional series has been read. It will then be concluded that these two numbers are the favorites of harmony, as well as the numbers 3 and 4, whose combinations engender the other two.

But because four numbers have a pre-eminence, must the others be discredited, and must systems be built that exclude from harmony numbers that the sophists dislike? Must division into five groups or into nine groups be excluded because Saint-Martin esteems only the number 4 and proscribes the number 9? Must division in four groups be excluded because Bernardin de Saint-Pierre only admires the number 5?

All these prejudices are foreign to harmony, which takes all the advantages possible from each number, and even though the octave, or dozen, is most favorable to accords, the other numbers are also used with success. A bi-octave, for example, like the ribs, is formed of twenty-four parts plus two foci or clavicles, which total twenty-six, doubtless a harmonic number. But if cultivation furnishes twenty-seven distinct groups, harmony will try other accords of twenty-seven. Maybe a particular culture does not admit division in octaves; in this case a free series of twenty-seven groups will be tried which may succeed by divisions of 7, 9, 11, forming a center and two wings, or perhaps 8, 9, 10, or 6, 9, 12 or 6, 12, 9, etc.

It is possible, then, either by free or by measured series, to find paths of accord for all numbers. Such will be the harmonian method. Harmonians will never espouse the civilizees' systematic spirit which, when it becomes infatuated with a number or a principle, wants to coordinate everything to the object of its infatuation.

God's genius is not so narrow; it knows how to use all means furnished by nature. If the number 24 lends itself to certain harmonies, the numbers 25, 26, 27, and 28 furnish others. They all enhance one another through a universal mechanism. If there exists an exclusive passion for a particular number, a Phalanstery would be very disconcerted if it had to augment or reduce the number of groups devoted to a particular culture or to a particular function; it must be possible to change the system of accords each time that the number of groups in a series changes.

A particular series has agreed upon twenty-six groups of applegrowers, but various associates are fond of a twenty-seventh kind of apple, and want to introduce it into the district. It is necessary to collocate their group in the general series of applegrowers, where perhaps it will be adopted in reserve, or annexed to one of the two octaves which will be richer for the addition of this new element; or perhaps it will be better placed in the octave than one of the groups that is already part of it, and which from then on will be held in reserve or jointly between the two octaves. Perhaps this new group will furnish some means of usefully returning a series to the free order that faltered in the measured order. . . .

The passional mechanism can modulate in the fifth power by twelve tetra-octaves or quadruple octaves; such would be an organ having 144 keys or twelve octaves consecutively, and repeating them on four manuals played in harmony with quadruple tones:

> in direct and inversions, major;
> in direct and inverse, minor.

It can be seen how much more extensive the passional system of the fifth power is than our musical system which includes only seven octaves, and avoids the four nuances that would have to be arranged between accords, by the method of temperament.

The disparity of human character, which has so strongly disoriented science, is nothing else but a mechanism of the fifth power having twelve tetra-octaves forming 576 steps on the scale, backed by 234 steps on the sub-pivot and ambiguous in various degrees. It is fitting to foresee these immense problems, as much to attest to the attention merited by the calculus of the measured series which will explain it, as to point out the pettiness of civilizee theories. Civilizee theories figure domestic accord by the smallest possible combination—the affectionate household with no money which is limited to a loving husband quarreling with his loving wife, and to children asking bread from the father, who gives them the whip. After three thousand years of work to have invented only this pitiful social mechanism! How can one dare to doubt that a great theory concerning the passions remains to be discovered (this study will not be the work of one day), and that in this sense there is a new world to be discovered as unknown as was America before Columbus.

AP, pp. 152–58

III. WORK AND THE ECONOMY

FOURIER'S VOW AGAINST COMMERCE

Bringing to light the underhanded maneuvers of the stock market and the brokers is to undertake a Herculean task. I doubt that the demi-god, cleaning the stables of Augeas, felt as much repugnance as I do in excavating this cesspool of moral filth, this gambling den of stockjobbing, the stock market—a subject that science has not even superficially examined. What is needed, in order to deal with it, is a practitioner brought up in the midst of the commercial sheep-pens, as I was from the age of six. From that time on I noted the opposition which prevails between commerce and truth. I was taught in catechism and at school that one must never lie; then I was taken to the shop to be trained at an early age in the occupation of lying, *the art of selling*. Shocked by the chicanery and fraud that I saw, I proceeded to take aside the merchants who were the victims and to reveal the deception to them. One of them, in complaining, maladroitly gave me away, which cost me a thorough spanking. My parents, seeing that I had a taste for truth, cried out in a tone of reprobation, "That child will never be worth anything in commerce." In fact, I conceived a secret aversion for commerce and at the age of seven I swore the oath which Hannibal had sworn against Rome—I vowed an eternal hatred of commerce.

I was enlisted whether I liked it or not. Lured to Lyon by the promise of a journey, I was taken to the door of the banker

Scherer, where I deserted on the spot and declared that I would
never be a merchant. This was like refusing marriage at the
door of a church. Then I was led back to Rouen, where I deserted a second time. In the end I was broken to the yoke, and
my best years lost in the workshops of falsehood, where from
all sides the sinister augury rang in my ears, "A very honest
boy!" In effect I was duped and robbed in all that I undertook.
But if I am worth nothing in the practice of commerce, I am
worth something when it comes to unmasking commerce's practices.

                                                    AP, pp. 68–70

ON COMMERCIAL CAPITALISM

. . . Let us begin by posing the question in a familiar way.
Is the present system of commerce sensible or absurd? What
must one think of it, judging from the acknowledged results
such as bankruptcy, double-dealing, the proliferation of middlemen, exterior and interior monopoly, stockjobbing, cornering
the market, usury, and other achievements of free competition?
Are all these truly the "perfection of perfectivism," as our modern philosophers claim?

In every mechanism, whether material or political, true economy consists in simplifying the play of cogs and wheels and
reducing the number of machines; in diminishing rather than
increasing the expense and the middlemen. This seems a paltry
truth, since it is so obvious.

Keeping this principle in mind, what would one think of an
industrialist who, seeing a mill in good condition and able to
grind a thousand pounds of grain a day, proposed to replace this
mill by another having ten times as many wheels and grindstones, and requiring ten millers instead of one in order to grind
only the same quantity of grain? Almost anyone would point
out to this industrialist that he is as crazy as a loon to want to
increase the grinding action tenfold, and that, on the contrary,

an effort must be made to reduce the machinery, preferably by simplifying it.

Our savant would answer that by increasing tenfold the number of grindstones, wheels, middlemen, millers, carpenters, stone-cutters, etc., more money will be earned, and that will *give a better living to everyone.* Yes, but this is unproductive work, work done at the expense of the consumers, who still end up supporting the cost of this new investment. But, the industrialist will say, this new mill will be so overloaded with such complicated machinery, so confusedly arranged, that the eye will get lost looking at it; an inexperienced bourgeois will understand nothing of its workings, he will not be able to follow his grain or his wheat in the complicated process, and as a result the miller will be able to steal three or four times the amount of grain that he presently steals, and that will *earn a better living for millers.* Another absurdity! Our response to the industrialist is only to say that we seek to keep from being cheated by millers; we do not seek to give them new means of fleecing us—they do that enough already.

In short, everyone will see that the industrialist's proposal is the height of effrontery, that this man is an impudent rascal, and that to accuse him of lunacy would be giving him too much credit. Anyone would know how to refute his sophistical argument about the advantage of feather-bedding; anyone would be able to point out that *the workers who increase productivity* are those who should be paid for their labor, while the middlemen and the machinery which increase production costs without increasing production must be reduced. This very simple judgment is enough to overturn the theories of all economists whose commercial system has no goal other than to employ ten times as many middlemen and capital than natural, or social, or true economy would require.

One is convinced of this by the proliferation of tradesmen who have cropped up during the last thirty years but whose range of services has not varied or increased. In some cities it is possible to count up to thirty merchants of the same sort, while in 1789 there were only three. Has money therefore increased in value? Have merchants become more honest? Far from it. Extortion and chicanery have increased immeasurably, and this swarm of commercial partisans has become so refined in cunning and the art of selling, that today one is deceived even in buying matches which are now made of fake sulphur and coated in such a way that they no longer light. All other forms of banditry, bankruptcy, monopoly, etc. have been similarly perfected, as I will illustrate presently. It is obvious that the science called political economy, that of free competition, has duped society in every way through the intricacy of its deceit and through the complexity and cost of unproductive middlemen, misappropriated capital, and other losses and wastes which ultimately fall back upon the consumer. It is the consumer who pays for the profits and the fraud of these numerous merchants, not to mention bankruptcy from which the merchant profits at the expense of the public.

When a science is found to bring about such grotesque results, is it not thereby condemned? Is this science not the counterpart of the charlatanism which I just described: of the mill where the number of wheels and middlemen are increased tenfold in order to mill only the same quantity of grain in the same amount of time to facilitate pilfering? Such is the state to which free competition has led us. To praise this proliferation of middlemen and cheating is as if one were to advocate filling in or blocking the canals to give a living to the truckers, wheelwrights, and innkeepers in whose interest it would be to abolish water transport.

Why is the vice of complexity extolled in commerce, while modern administrators are ceaselessly reproached for the same error of multiplying civil servants who are obviously unproductive, since doubling or tripling their number does not even accomplish the same amount of work? Is this proliferation justified by saying that the creation of these parasitic jobs provides a living to many people? Does economy consist in allowing a privileged few to earn a living at the expense of the multitude? It is certain that if one court of law, sufficiently served by twenty judges, is suddenly enlarged to employ sixty judges, all receiving the same salary as that of the original twenty, this tripling will support forty families. But it will be at the expense of the 40,000 families under their jurisdiction, and will add nothing to either the product or the functions useful to the producer.

At the time when the ports of France were blocked, and Marseilles and Rouen were unable to communicate by sea, the inland port of Chalon-sur-Saône was the pivot of a great movement of transport by water and by land. Can it be claimed that the closing of the seaports was an advantage because it gave work to people at Chalon-sur-Saône and along the trade route? The population of a single suburb of Lyon grew to 2000 inhabitants as a result of the profits of that parasitic industry which caused the cost of transportation from Marseilles to Rouen to be ten times more than it was by sea, disregarding the deterioration of the transported goods, much greater in the case of inland transport.

Let us conclude that rather than looking out for the profit of commerce—a true bloodsucker seeking only to pressure producers and consumers, who are a hundred times more numerous than the businessmen—one should look out for the good of the producing class and the consumers, who make up the immense majority and who pay for, in a decrease of profit and an increase of cost, the profits that the traffickers reap in distributing goods and products. This truth can be more succinctly expressed —real economy consists in favoring the services of those who increase the production of goods, and in reducing those services which add to the production cost without augmenting production. Is this thesis not shown to be true by the examples cited above of adopting machinery and filling in canals? If so, by what reasoning have economists been able to persuade us that it was an advantage to triple or to increase tenfold the mass of tradesmen, whose intervention, far from adding to production, introduces into the distribution of goods a horde of evil-doing criminals?

. . . Our century, having given credence to the sophisms of free competition and to the immoderate proliferation of tradesmen, is no longer capable of dealing with questions of natural

economy or the number of non-productive services. With regard
to these questions, our minds are like faulty strings which are
incapable of playing a true note. Commercial influence has truly
distorted all the politicians' minds. Commerce today is comparable to the king's favorite who has invaded every domain of
power and has subordinated all the state ministers to his will.
Even agriculture counts only as an accessory to commerce.
Princes have been seen to pass through a purely agricultural
region ruined by a bad crop and to promise that *commerce will
go well*. But what does it matter to these unfortunate farmers
that there be trafficking and shady dealings in the large cities?
That will not replace the ruined harvests; it will not give them
the revenue to subsist on; this does not any less reduce them to
living for the next six months on wild grass and nettles. Nevertheless one pretends to bring help to a starving village by praising
the benefits of speculation from which it will not gain a farthing.
Princes are led to believe that all is going for the best when
speculators flock to the stockmarket. But ideas are so embroiled
on this point that there is no end to the confusion. The fashionable word *commerce* designates all the branches of industry.
All have been named when commerce has been named. Thus
commerce profits from this infatuation by deriving advantages
from all the political favors which the government thinks it is
bestowing upon productive industry.

It will not be an easy task to dispel these misconceptions.
They are to be seen in political and in economic illusions.

. . . The political illusions can be reduced to one fundamental error, that of wanting to enrich nations instead of individuals. Calculations and balance sheets show us that a certain nation, England for example, is colossally wealthy, and yet
her cities swarm with beggars. I cannot repeat too often that
London, from whence come schools of political economy that
teach nations the art of becoming rich, that this same city contains 115,000 beggars, tramps, etc. And so it is in all England's
cities. Could not one say to the English, by way of common
sense, you have become a rich nation whose soil is covered with

the poor; try rather to become a poor nation whose soil is covered with the rich.

Our best minds know how, if necessary, to prove that pain is not an evil, that gout and stones cause no suffering; all of them know how to show us public wealth amid heaps of beggars. They all have the talent of an alchemist who teaches the art of making gold, while they make you spend your gold in pure loss. Good sense requires that the growth of public wealth be judged by that of each individual. The sovereigns, the notables, and the financial tycoons will always have more than enough; it is thus the masses and not the notables who must be enriched. Such is the problem that eludes the learned; they pacify us with commercial illusions about the wealth of nations to mask the poverty of individuals and the absurdity of our system of distribution.

Of what importance is the prestige of colonial monopoly, the balance of trade, and the encroachment of industry that lead only to the production of a huge majority of poor as is seen in England, Switzerland, France, and in all of civilization? Our economists never take into account the suffering of the people, or the disaster of wars caused by ambitious speculation. Such a state, like the Old Regime of France, presents showy pictures of colonial profit and says nothing about commercial wars, irresponsible borrowing, and other calamities caused by colonial adventures. Neither do they mention the revolutions provoked by colonial pretensions. Was it not jealousy over sugar and coffee that caused England to provoke the revolution that led Louis XVI and the French elite to the scaffold, that took 4 million French lives, and cost 4 billion [sic] lives from among the clergy alone? Our economists take account of none of these scourges; they only see their account books balanced to the last penny.

After dispelling the political illusions we will do the same for the economic illusions, the erroneous notions about the commercial machine which prohibit us from distinguishing productive from nonproductive functions, and from distinguishing parasitic services that should be eliminated, like useless stockjobbing, from indispensable services worthy of protection, such as transportation. All this is confused under the title of com-

merce—the good of commerce, the friends of commerce. This
confusion must be eliminated.

AP, pp. 70–77

THE PLACE OF BOURGEOIS SOCIETY
IN HUMAN EVOLUTION

We have examined one of the most ancient themes of controversy, that of liberty; we will now treat of the most recent—
the question of commerce, which has become the absorbing subject of interest in modern times.

The present system of commerce, based on anarchical competition, will furnish us a fine occasion for censuring science,
which has not discovered that in commerce, as in any other
branch of relations, *simple* liberty is a source of discord and
disorder; that all liberty should be sustained by guarantees and
counterpoises; in fine, that liberty should be *compound* and not
simple, like that of the merchants, against whose frauds the
social body has no guarantee.

The merchants at present are free, but the social body is not
so in its relations with them, for people are obliged to make
purchases; they cannot dispense with food and clothing, which
can be obtained only by buying; they are then dependent on
the seller, to whose extortions they must submit.

Such a mechanism is only *simple,* and not *compound* liberty;
the liberty is all on the side of the seller, of whom the consumer
is the dupe, and against whom he has no guarantee. To raise
the commercial system to *compound* or *reciprocal* liberty, it was
necessary to discover and introduce this guarantee.

Strange oversight, that after a hundred years of mercantile
controversy it has not been observed that civilized commerce
is of the simple and not of the compound mode; that it insures
liberty and proper guarantees to but one of the contracting parties—to the *seller, and not the buyer*.

This truth is as new as was that announced by Copernicus,
when he declared that it was the earth which turned and not
the sun. But since the study of commerce dates back only a

century, ought we to be surprised at the errors which have been committed in regard to it, when on so many other subjects, especially that of liberty, we see errors lasting for centuries?

It is not surprising, then, that the mercantile controversy which is of comparatively recent date, should still occupy itself with the simple method, which is always the first tendency of the human mind. No one is to be blamed for being a *simplist* in a study which is only at its commencement; but after a hundred years of experience, is there any excuse for not perceiving that we are on the wrong track, that we are speculating on the simple mode, which is without guarantees? Is an age which talks so much of checks and balances, and of guarantees and equilibria, pardonable for having failed to recognize that there is not a shadow of guarantee, check, or balance in our commercial system?

There exists, nevertheless, in the present order a fine germ of truth supported by proper guarantees; men in earnest pursuit of the truth should not have failed to discover it in the monetary system. We shall point out in this system a clue to discoveries which have been shamefully missed by our economic sciences, which, in this matter, deserve censure.

Whoever seeks for real discoveries should know that he who proposes anything new is obliged to disregard the opinions of his age, and give a denial to its dominant prejudices. Could Kepler, when demonstrating that the earth turned on its axis, compliment his contemporaries who believed it immovable? I am in the same position—I bring a theory whence will spring riches, truth, and social unity; can I felicitate the age for having, under the auspices of its mercantile doctrines, fallen into the slough of indigence, fraud, and duplicity of action? As well compliment the goat for having been left by the fox at the bottom of the well. Men are blinded in respect to these enormities by the incense of the sophists who delude them with their flattering theories of progress and perfectibility; they would receive the same delusive flatteries from discoverers. But let no one be deceived in this—where there is incense for the age, there are no new ideas. If we sincerely desire new truths and real discoveries, we must not demand flattery from him who brings them.

Commerce being the link or tie of the industrial system—being for the social world what the blood is for the body, it was in commerce that the attempt should have been made to introduce practical truth in place of that chaos of vices and frauds. Had the philosophers sought to reform the commercial system, they could have rendered a real service both to governments and peoples; instead of disorganizing the social world by their mania for overthrowing governments, they would have put it on the track of practical reforms.

In antiquity, commerce appeared contemptible to the philosophers, who looked upon it as the domain of falsehood and fraud; but since they have seen it grow to colossal dimensions by means of the invention of the compass and the discovery of the two Indies, they at least determined to study it.

The first thing which should have been remarked by men who were seeking for truth, was that it is wholly banished from commerce.

Another important observation which the examination of commerce should have suggested, was that in it are to be found the germs of various kinds of association.

Political science had then two problems to solve in the study of the commercial mechanism; the one positive, which consisted in developing the germs of association—the source of all economy—and in introducing it into agriculture; the other negative, which was to banish from the commercial system the fraud and falsity which pervade it generally, and which are the greatest obstacles to the activity of industrial relations.

These two problems were intimately connected, and the solution of the one would have led to the solution of the other; for guarantees of truth cannot be introduced into commerce without the aid of association, and the associative principle cannot be extended without discovering the guarantees of truth.

A fine and noble career was here opened to science. Governments and learned bodies should have united in encouraging the study, and, if necessary, in making it obligatory; with the

least success, it would have led the social world to the sixth
society, called guarantism, which is a very happy state in comparison with civilization.

Political economists, to whom the analysis of commerce properly belongs, have made of it as of other branches of study an
arena of controversy; they have basely bowed before the golden
calf, and extolled the whole array of mercantile duplicities, the
attack upon which should have been the first work of men sincerely seeking for truth. They could not have been ignorant
that commerce in its present state of entire liberty is a sink of
abominations, such as bankruptcy, forestalling, extortion, speculation, usury, monopoly, fraud, adulteration, and the like. These
characteristics offered a collection of vices hideous enough to
have stimulated the friends of truth; the scandalous fortunes
of speculators, monopolists and commercial operators of all
kinds, showed plainly enough that commerce is the vulture of
productive industry; that under the pretext of serving, it audaciously spoliates it.

All these enormities have been without power to arouse the
economists or any other class of philosophers. They who would
carry reform into so many departments have not dared to attempt it in those relations where it was as easy as it would have
been honorable to introduce it, and where they could have
operated without causing either trouble or distrust; for no one
is an advocate of commercial frauds which are as onerous to
governments as to the producing classes. Had the philosophers
sought to discover a method of true and equitable commerce,
and declared open war against the system of falsehood, extortion,
and complication which, under the name of free competition,
reigns in commercial relations, they would have secured the
thanks and approval of all classes.

In this examination, I accuse not so much the philosophers
as the whole system of civilization which encourages corruption.
If an age upholds a vice, writers who seek popularity will not
fail to extol it. But in analyzing this labyrinth of corruption,
I will commence with the errors of the philosophers in com-

mercial studies; we will then pass to those committed by nations.

The manner in which the philosophers have treated commerce proves clearly that the sacred fire is indeed extinct among them. Let us examine the opinions which an intelligent and honorable body of men would have entertained, and how they would have acted.

Nature is never at fault in the *collective* impulses which she gives to the human race. When a profession excites universal contempt, be sure that it conceals some latent vice. We find no nation despising government, the sacerdotal order, the judiciary, or the military profession. These functions enjoy everywhere general consideration; they enjoyed it before any philosophical theories existed. Whereas commerce has excited among all primitive nations a well-merited contempt.

There have been cited as an exception to this rule certain ancient states which were devoted to commerce, as for instance, Tyre and Athens. But these states had no extended territory—the famous republic of Athens was not the hundredth part the size of France. A people without territory like the Athenians, or living on an ungrateful soil like the Hollanders, form an exception to the general rule; they devote themselves to parasite industry; they become industrial corsairs, monopolists, and traffickers. They may well tolerate the mercantile profession, which is their only resource, and by the aid of which they spoliate the producing nations.

It is nevertheless certain that all nations, with some rare exceptions which confirm the general rule, have exhibited an innate contempt for commerce. The Gospel makes no distinction between traffickers and thieves. Christ scourged the former and drove them from the temple, of which, says the evangelist, they had made a den of thieves.

At that epoch men and things were called by their right names. Hence Christ called the civilizees a race of vipers, and the traffickers a band of robbers. This was the frankness characteristic of the olden time. The merchants and financiers of antiquity were rogues on but a small scale; they did not devour millions as at the present day. Now civilization being in the habit of sending small rogues to the gallows and extolling great ones, it was natural that the mercantile class should be despised, so long as it robbed in a small way. Horace and other writers of classic antiquity amused themselves at its expense, and openly ridiculed the arts of money-getting held in such high estimation in our days.

All this has changed since the discovery and conquest of the two Indies; the quantity of industrial products has increased tenfold, and as a consequence the profits of the merchants, thirtyfold; for to the regular profits of commerce must be added those of usury, stockjobbing, and monopoly. In a word the merchants of our days are no longer petty rogues like those which Christ scourged and Horace satirized. A stockjobber or a great speculator makes at the present day in a single year more than ten monarchs. It is stated that a house in London made the sum of sixteen millions of dollars in one year on French loans. Now where is the sovereign in Europe who could lay aside, not in one year but ten, sixteen millions after paying the expenses of his household? It is doubtful whether the sovereigns of Austria and of France, after deducting the expenses of the court and household, have at the end of the fiscal year a million left; neither of them then could save as much in ten years, as a great financial operator makes in one.

This gigantic development of mercantile industry has bewildered the philosophers; they have turned toward the rising sun and prostrated themselves before the god of speculation and stockjobbing. Their science did not cringe so low before the commercial and financial interests a century ago. This independence of opinion no longer exists; we see only insolent pretensions on the one hand, and the degrading humiliation of science on the other; the mercantile vampires call for incense, and obsequious science proclaims that such incense is their due; it teaches the nations respect for them and all their nefarious plots of monopoly and speculation.[1]

[1] The term which Fourier uses in French is *agiotage*; there is no one word in English which expresses it fully. Agiotage signifies the

With a public sentiment thus corrupted, it was not surprising that no discoveries have been made which would have led to reform in the commercial system. The ancients were excusable for sneering at the commercial power while yet in its infancy, but at the present day the whelp has become the lion; it is a new power which disputes authority even with governments themselves. We have seen the civil power contend against the colossal influence of the clergy in the Middle Ages, but now when a new tyranny—that of the strong box and the monied interest, the worst of all tyrannies—would seize in its grasp kings and peoples, we see the whole scientific corps prostrating itself before the mercantile colossus, that parasite which, without producing anything, appropriates to himself the wealth of nations, and forms in the industrial system a new influence, more potent than that of potentates themselves, a vampire which, without legal sanction, enters into competition with the legal authorities, and arrogates to itself the lion's share.

The division is the more unequal from the fact that government levies its taxes in the *simple* mode, while commerce and banking reap their profits in the *compound;* that is, the former levies only on the products of its own country, while the latter levy indifferently upon those of all countries. Certain bankers, who are neither French, Austrian, nor Spanish, have, perhaps, at the end of the year levied from the imposts of France, Austria, and Spain, in the form of dividends on the national debts, a share larger than that of the governments themselves, from which must be deducted the expenses of the civil list; these deductions made, there remains much less to the governments from the product of the taxes than to the bankers who negotiate the national loans. After meeting the expenses of the different branches of the public service—war, marine, etc.—the sur-

manoeuvres of financial and commercial operators to raise or lower the price of government and other stocks, and merchandise of all kinds, by means of combinations of capital, monopoly, financial contractions, plots, panics, etc. It comprises, consequently, stock-gambling, monopoly, and speculation, and in general all schemes for producing an artificial rise or fall in the market.—Note of A.B.

plus goes not into the hands of the administration, but falls to usurers and stock-operators.

Civilized states at present are in the position of embarrassed landholders, who find the usurer drawing from their domains much more than they themselves who cultivate them. And as national debts go on increasing, the mercantile power which shares in the authority of governments tends to become their superior, and to bring them under its influence, or at least to maintain an equal sway with them. Never was duplicity of action more evident.

The strong box is in civilization all-powerful; thus we have seen the Congress of Aix-la-Chapelle hesitating to decide upon anything till the arrival of two great bankers. When a political emergency places the revenues of a country at the mercy of a class of money-lenders, they become, from this fact, the rivals and competitors of the government; this is the case at the present day with the financiers who manage national loans, and who see ministers at their feet. These *devourers of the future* give tone to public opinion and to the theories of the philosophers, and rule rulers themselves. So true is this, that any ministry wishing to thwart the machinations of the money-lenders and leaders of finance fails completely, and will continue to fail, until there shall be discovered a true and equitable system of commerce by which speculation, stockjobbing, usury, fraud, monopoly, and all other mercantile artifices lauded by the political economists, shall be abolished.

This state of things should have attracted the attention of science. It is clear that civilization has changed its character, and that monopoly and stockjobbing, which are two commercial characteristics, have overthrown the old order of things. Is this a subject of congratulation or of alarm? What is the final *result foreshadowed by this monstrous irruption of the mercantile power, whose encroachments are constantly on the increase?*

This is a question which should have occupied the attention of our learned bodies in connection with the two problems already stated, namely,

—To develop the germs of commercial association, and give the principle universal application.

—To combat the fraudulent system of commerce by the discovery of the true or equitable system.

These problems opened to genius a brilliant career, which it has entirely neglected.

The dependency of governments is constantly increasing, and the ascendency of stockjobbers and bankers has attained such a height that the operations of the Exchange have become the index of public opinion. If the funds fall, it is an infallible sign that the administration is pursuing a wrong policy; this fall is often the effect of the intrigues of stock-gamblers who are more powerful than the ministry.

As soon as a cabal can put into operation this engine of political commotions—this fall in the public funds produced by intrigue—the public join in chorus against the policy of the administration. Nothing more is necessary to bring undeserved disgrace upon a ministry, and often to compromise the welfare of an empire through the intrigues of stock-gamblers and speculators. Was ever bondage more thoroughly established? And can any government doubt that it is under the rod of these lords of finance whenever the State is in debt? that is, in every civilized nation, since national debts are a disease especially characteristic of the third phase of civilization.

Our philosophers, with their pretensions to profound analysis, know not how to analyze this monstrosity, and do not perceive in it a transition of the civilized order from the third to the fourth phase, according to the following table.

TABLE OF THE PROGRESSIVE MOVEMENT OF CIVILIZATION.

Characteristics of the Entire Period and of each Phase.

PIVOTS OF THE WHOLE PERIOD.		
	Individual Characteristic.	SELFISHNESS.
	Collective Characteristic.	DUPLICITY OF ACTION.

INFANCY, OR FIRST PHASE.

ASCENDING VIBRATION.

Simple Germ.   Exclusive Marriage, or Monogamy.
Compound Germ.   Baronial or Military Feudalism.

  PIVOT.   CIVIL RIGHTS OF THE WIFE.

Counterpoise.   Federation of the Great Barons.
Tone.   Illusions in respect to Chivalry.

ADOLESCENCE, OR SECOND PHASE.

Simple Germ.   Communal Privileges.
Compound Germ.   Cultivation of the Arts and Sciences.

  PIVOT.   EMANCIPATION OF THE SERFS.

Counterpoise.   Representative System.
Tone.   Illusions in respect to Liberty.

APOGEE, OR MATURITY.

Germs.   NAUTICAL ART; EXPERIMENTAL
                        CHEMISTRY.
Characteristics.   DESTRUCTION OF FORESTS; NA-
                        TIONAL DEBTS.

VIRILITY, OR THIRD PHASE.

Simple Germ.   Mercantile and Financial Spirit.
Compound Germ.   Joint-stock Companies.

  PIVOT.   MARITIME MONOPOLY.

Counterpoise.   Anarchical Commerce.
Tone.   Illusions in Political Economy.

DECLINE, OR FOURTH PHASE.

DESCENDING VIBRATION.

Simple Germ.   Trust or Loaning Companies.
Compound Germ.   Trades monopolized and controlled
                        by Capital.

  PIVOT.   INDUSTRIAL FEUDALISM.

Counterpoise.   Contractors and Managers of the
                        Feudal Monopolies.
Tone.   Illusions in Association.

Ascension or Growth. The two phases of ascending vibration or movement effect the abolition of personal or direct servitude.

Declension. The two phases of descending movement effect the increase of collective or indirect servitude.

The APOGEE is the epoch in which civilization assumes forms the least ignoble; I do not say the most noble, because this society is always ignoble, and varies in its four phases only by shades of *selfishness and duplicity,* which are always dominant because they are the pivots of the civilized mechanism.

Experimental chemistry and the nautical art are characteristics of the apogee; on these two branches of knowledge depend the perfection of industry, and the facility of communications.

As soon as the civilized period is provided with these two levers, it is ripe for passing to the next higher social period, and any delay becomes prejudicial, since it engenders the four characteristics of the descending movement or vibration. In that case, scientific achievements become an evil rather than a good. Many of the sciences become injurious and dangerous to the civilizees from the moment they have entered the third phase. Once possessed of the two characteristics of the apogee, this period is like a ripe fruit which thereafter can only deteriorate. Thus the increase of knowledge is desirable in civilization only as maturity is desirable for a fruit; as soon as it has arrived at the ripe state, it should be put to some use.

Now what is the use or function of civilization in the social movement or the progress by the human race? It is to advance the race to the sixth period or guarantism. As soon as it has acquired all the means necessary, *it should escape from itself;* it should seek for an issue, and enter upon guarantism. If it delays this necessary step, its scientific acquisitions are only a burden to it; it grasps more than it can carry.

As a proof of this, do we not see that the nautical art, one of the finest achievements of human genius, has already engendered two characteristics of the third phase—*mercantile spirit and maritime monopoly*—together with other calamities which would have had no existence in the sixth period. The excess of knowledge and of industrial improvements has become detrimental to us in the same way that the most wholesome food becomes deleterious when taken in improper quantities; and it is to exceed the proper measure to *remain civilizees* after we are provided with the levers of the sixth period. When we have attained the degree of social development which characterizes the *apogee of civilization*, we may be compared to the silk-worm which, having reached a certain stage of growth, has need to change its form and pass to the chrysalis state.

We had arrived at this industrial maturity as early as the middle of the eighteenth century. We then possessed the two characteristics of the apogee, and an issue from civilization should have been sought without delay.

The genius necessary to discover this issue, however, was wanting, and our sciences have become to us more pernicious than useful; they have produced only the germs of social convulsions and of political and moral corruption. In brief, we have traversed the third phase, and are about to enter the fourth or the decline of civilization.

Each one of the four phases has its point of plenitude or apogee like the entire society itself. It is evident that the third phase of civilization has passed the apogee, since we see the predominance of the two essential characteristics which distinguish it.

Let us remark that during the three phases of civilization already passed through, philosophy has never cooperated in social improvements, though it arrogates to itself that slight honor; it has always been *passive* in respect to the social movement. I have already offered some suggestions on this point, which I will state anew.

1ST PHASE. This phase arrives at its full by the concession of civil rights to the wife. This is something with which the ancient philosophers, like Confucius and those of Egypt and Hindostan, never troubled themselves; they did not even manifest an intention to ameliorate the condition of woman. The women of antiquity had even less liberty than those of the present day; they did not share in the various amatory rights, such as that of divorce, and the moralists were indifferent as now to their welfare.

2D PHASE. Civilization entered upon this phase by the amelioration of the system of servitude. This improvement was the effect of the feudal system; slavery was first transformed into serfdom, and then the serf population was furnished with the means of collective and gradual emancipation. By attaching this class of bondsmen to the soil instead of to the individual, it turned to their advantage the benevolence or the selfishness of each feudal lord; and the *community* being able to obtain in one case a concession from the avarice of a father, in another a concession from the generosity of a son, advanced step by step toward liberty. This is a process of which the ancient philosophers had no idea.

3D PHASE. This phase is developed by the influence of the commercial policy, originating in colonial monopoly. This influence was not foreseen by the philosophers, and they have discovered no means of counterbalancing it, nor even of attacking it in its most oppressive form, that of insular monopoly. They have treated the subject of commercial policy only to extol its defects and vices, instead of combating them, as they should have done.

4TH PHASE. Civilization is tending toward this phase by the influence of powerful joint-stock companies, which, by forming combinations and securing special privileges, will control industrial relations and regulate the conditions of labor. These companies conceal the germ of a vast feudal confederacy, which will soon obtain control of the whole industrial and financial system, and will give rise to a vast COMMERCIAL FEUDALISM. This the philosophers have not foreseen, and while they are all infatuated with the mercantile spirit, the influence and tendencies of which they have so little understood, events are in preparation which are to change the existing state of things, and cause civilization to decline into its fourth phase.

But the philosophers do not trouble themselves with providing against future storms; they consider the social movement only in a retrograde sense, and occupy themselves with the past and the present alone. Now that the commercial spirit is dominant, they will decide according to their custom that the present condition of things is the highest state of social development. They will restrict themselves to glorifying what they see before them, without presuming that the civilized order may assume new forms.

And when civilization shall have arrived at its fourth phase, when the commercial feudalism shall be fully established, we shall see the philosophers coming in after the change has taken place, and broaching new theories on the subject. We shall see them lauding the fourth phase with its vices, and writing volumes on the new order, in which they will then see the ultimate of human progress as they see it at present in the third phase with its commercial spirit.

We shall consider the foregoing table again, and go into an examination of the special characteristics of each phase. It is evident that civilization is tending to the fourth. The absorbing predominance of the commercial spirit and power denotes a speedy downfall into commercial feudalism or a universal monopoly of commercial relations, an alliance between the monied classes and the nobility or great landed proprietors, and a regular division of prerogatives and privileges between these two parties already united in interest.

When we see civilization elated with this declining and decrepit phase of its career, we are reminded of a faded belle who, boasting of her attractions in her fiftieth year, excites at once the remark that she was fairer at twenty-five. So it is with civilization, which, dreaming of perfection and progress, is constantly deteriorating, and which will find but too soon in its industrial achievements new sources of political oppression, crimes, and commotions. Commerce is tending to a participation in the functions of government, the policy of which is already subject to the *sanction* or the *veto* of the great bankers and capitalists. Theorizers, with their checks and balances, think they see in this unnatural alliance a political counterpoise; but it is only a league against the producing interests. Combinations like these for the purpose of acquiring power are not political counterpoises; such counterpoises should be two-fold or compound in their action, like that of our gold and silver coin which, from the compound influence of foreign exchanges and the value of bullion, obliges government to keep it at its standard weight and fineness.

There is no real equilibrium of this kind in the present system of commerce; on the contrary, it is an abyss of fraud, rapine, and anarchy; it is an industrial corsair which should be muzzled by some kind of restraint. Instead of seeking for a remedy for this state of things, the age has become infatuated with all its excesses and abominations, under the impression that commerce is necessary.

Ten times the amount of commercial transactions will be necessary on the establishment of association, in which production will be three-fold and the amount of sales ten-fold greater than at present; for the demand for foreign commodities will extend to the whole mass of the laboring population in all the zones. But however great may be the development of the commercial system which shall be then in operation, it will not be carried on by fraud and deception.

Let me define more exactly the charges to be brought against the present system of commerce. It is a dishonest agent which produces *one,* and embezzles *ten.* It is a valet whose services are worth *ten* crowns, and whose thefts amount to a *thousand.* This will appear evident when I come to enumerate the special characteristics of the commercial mechanism.

Its first spoliation is to employ a *hundred* agents, when *ten* would suffice in a true system; the labor of ninety individuals is thus absorbed in functions which are parasitic, *compared with those of a true system of commerce.*

The plan of such a system was the problem to be solved; and the sciences should have been held to make an investigation of the true commercial method.

But did not honor oblige scientific men to denounce that system of commerce which constantly tended to engross the control of productive industry? Should they not at least have proposed some remedy against its encroachments, when the search for such a remedy would have been attended with results so highly advantageous?

In conformity with a maxim of the philosophers—to proceed in the study of all intricate problems *by analysis and synthesis*—the science of political economy should have furnished an exact analysis of the characteristics of commerce; doubtless it lacked the courage to attempt it, for the portrait would not have been very flattering to the golden calf. It is an omission which I shall repair in this work; and as nothing is more important than to enlighten governments and the producing classes as to the enormity of mercantile extortions, I will present a brief analysis in tabular form of the present system of commerce.

First I will remark, that we find, among the most intelligent classes, men who are in entire ignorance as to the real nature of commerce. In a recent discussion in the public press on the subject, I remarked a mass of errors, one of which was to confound commerce with manufactures. To extol the former, it was stated that the Emperor Napoleon, on visiting the vast manufacturing establishment of M. Oberkampf, was so highly pleased that he took the cross of the Legion of Honor from his own breast to bestow it upon him. But what had this to do with the question of the commercial system? M. Oberkampf was a very useful manufacturer, and so great a stranger to commercial intrigues that two years afterwards he returned the decoration to the Emperor, declaring that he could no longer struggle against the machinations of commerce, which had raised the price of raw materials so high that manufacturers were obliged to close their factories and dismiss thousands of operatives, leaving them without work.

In this, M. Oberkampf was only the echo of daily complaints made by manufacturers who are constantly embarrassed by the schemes of speculators and monopolists.

Commerce is the natural enemy of manufactures; while feigning a solicitude to supply them with raw materials, it in fact labors only to spoliate and render them dependent. So in most of the manufacturing towns, it is well known that the manufacturer of small means works only for the dealer in raw materials, just as the small farmer often works only for the usurer, and as the humble attic student toils for the distinguished academician, who stoops to publish under his own name the fruit of the vigils of some poor and hired assistant.

In a word, the merchant is an industrial corsair, living at the expense of the manufacturer and the producer. To confound the functions of the merchant with those of the manufacturer is to ignore the alphabet of economic science.

Whence comes this extreme ignorance in respect to the commercial mechanism? Evidently from the fact that no one has ever made an analysis of commerce, and that men, in disputing on the subject, have had no real knowledge of it. A general idea of the question may be obtained by consulting the two following tables:

SCALE OF COMMERCIAL METHODS AS THEY EXIST IN THE DIFFERENT SOCIAL PERIODS.

In the primitive state,	1. Payments anticipated.
In the savage state,	2. Barter or direct exchange.
In the patriarchal state,	3. Traffic or indirect exchange.
In the barbaric state.	4. Government monopolies, established valuations.
In civilization,	5. Individual competition.
In guarantism,	6. Collective and combined competition.
In simple association,	7. Continuous consignments.
In compound association,	{ Anterior valuations, Compensations by arbitration.

In conformity with the above table, we must analyze individual competition, the fifth or civilized method, which is a system of fraud and complication, and point out the errors which have prevented the human mind from discovering the sixth method—that of guarantism—with its system of combined, direct and equitable exchanges.

This study will require an analysis of the characteristics of the present or fifth method. The following is a table of them.

SYNOPTICAL TABLE OF THE CHARACTERISTICS OF CIVILIZED COMMERCE

DISTRIBUTED IN A MIXED SERIES.

PIVOTS. { Direct. COLLECTIVE INTEREST SACRIFICED TO THE INDIVIDUAL.

Inverse. INTERMEDIATE PROPERTY.

1. Duplicity of Action.
2. *Arbitrary Valuation.*
3. *Tolerated Fraud.*
    4. Absence of Concert and Combination.
    5. Withdrawal of Capital.
    6. Decreasing Salaries and Wages.
7. *Artificial Gluts or Over-supplies.*
8. *Depressive Abundance.*
9. *Inverse Encroachment.*
10. *Policy of Competitive Exclusion.*
    11. Stoppage of Circulation, or Want of Credit.
    12. Artificial Money.
    13. Fiscal Complication.
    14. Fraud and Vice rendered Epidemic.
    15. Obscurantism.
16. *Parasitism.*
17. *Forestalling.*
18. *Speculation and Stockjobbing* (agiotage).
19. *Usury.*
20. *Fruitless Labor.*
21. *Industrial Lotteries.*
    22. Corporate Monopoly.
    23. Fiscal or Governmental Monopoly.
    24. Exotic or Colonial Monopoly.
    25. Simple or Maritime Monopoly.
    26. Feudal Monopoly.

   27. *Provocation to Fraud.*
   28. *Waste and Depreciation.*
   29. *Adulteration.*
   30. *Sanitary Lesion.*
      31. Bankruptcy.
      32. Smuggling.
      33. Piracy.
   34. *Maximations, Forced Levies.*
   35. *Speculation in Slavery.*
      36. Universal Selfishness.

Quadruple Transition, Direct and Inverse, and in Simple and Compound Modes.

   COMMERCIAL CORPORATIONS.
   COLLECTIVE AND REDUCTIVE COMPETITION.
   SIMPLE INTEGRAL MONOPOLY.
   COMPOUND INTEGRAL MONOPOLY.

The number of frauds and vices in this table could be greatly augmented. I should extend it to *sixty* in a regular treatise on commerce.

Among the *thirty-six* characteristics, several are already known; for example, speculation, usury, and bankruptcy.

But can we find in the voluminous writings of the political economists a single definition of either of these three characteristics; that is to say, a description of

   All kinds of bankrupts?

   All kinds of usurers?

   All kinds of monopolists and speculators (agioteurs)?

We find nothing of the kind, which is a proof that in all the treatises on commerce, the first step has not yet been taken, namely, that of analysis and definition. A singular omission this on the part of men who lay it down as a maxim to proceed by analytic methods.

The same course has been pursued in respect to all the branches of science which have occupied the attention of speculative philosophy. Its authors do not analyze even the subjects upon which they treat, so that, in fact, they have no clear conception of the problems they discuss. I have shown this in a preceding chapter in respect to liberty, an elementary analysis of which has not been made, that is, an analysis of its three modes, and of the seven natural rights and their pivots; nevertheless, how many volumes have been written on the subject of liberty, without the first condition being fulfilled or the first step taken required by philosophy itself, which enjoins on us to proceed by analysis and synthesis.

This should have been the first work of our modern economists when they began the study of commerce; and after this analytic dissection of the monster, their next step was to proceed to the countersynthesis, that is, to the construction of a commercial mechanism which would guarantee the extirpation of the thirty-six characteristics of false commerce, or individual and anarchical competition.

A regular study of commerce, then, like that of liberty, would have led to the conclusion that real and efficient guarantees should exist in all branches of the social mechanism—branches of which the civilized social order is wholly destitute. This need being recognized, it would have led to researches for a system of general guarantees, which constitutes the sixth period. It was to this point that the human mind should have been led; it should have been convinced that civilization is in no sense the ultimate social condition which it demands, since it calls everywhere for justice, based on guarantees which that order cannot secure.

The analysis of commerce would also have led men to speculate on the means of extending the germs of association, which we see springing up through the economic instinct of the merchants. A study of the development of these germs might have led to important discoveries in association. Thus a methodical analysis of commerce would have opened to the world several avenues of social progress.

Not only no positive knowledge has been acquired in respect to this subject, as I have shown by the two tables of methods and characteristics, which should have been the first in a regular analysis, but the question has been obscured to the extent of confounding commerce with manufactures, of which it is the natural enemy, and of subordinating the latter to the various interests of the former. We see our manufacturers systematically sacrificed to the machinations of monopoly and speculation.

So long as a false system is popular and universally upheld, no one seeks to correct it; and this explains why it is that it has not occurred to our age to undertake a reform of our fraudulent commercial system. Governments and religion have been assailed, while the remedy for our social evils was to be found in a reform of commerce, an agency which has secured to itself the respect even of sovereigns, though it is their greatest enemy, since it leads them into national loans, which are the most fruitful cause of revolution; it is to them what the usurer is to a young man of family.

Commerce is the weak side of civilization, the point at which it should have been attacked. It is secretly hated by rulers and peoples; in no country does the class of landed proprietors and producers look with a favorable eye upon the parvenus who, entering our cities barefoot, soon make their hundreds of thousands. The honest landholder cannot understand this sudden accumulation of wealth; whatever care he may give to the management of his estate, he succeeds with difficulty in adding a few hundred dollars to his income; the profits of speculators and stockjobbers amaze him; he would give utterance to his astonishment, and express his suspicions of the whole system, but he is silenced by the political economists who hurl their anathemas against any one who dares to criticize *le commerce immense et l'immense commerce*.

Some governments have endeavored by coercive measures to put a stop to the excesses of commercial speculation and stockjobbing. But they failed. It is not by force that the mercantile hydra is to be overthrown; it is a serpent which has coiled itself around civilization, and resistance only causes it to contract its folds closer than before. There was but one means of opposing commercial rapine, and that was the discovery of a true and equitable system of commerce; a discovery of the highest importance, as it would have greatly increased the resources of governments, while doubling at the same time the profits of productive industry. For the sixth society, that of guarantism, yields a product double that of civilization, and we enter upon guarantism from the moment that we organize equitable commerce in the place of free competition, which is only a compound of fraud and complication.

The present system of commerce—the false and fraudulent system—was the growth of circumstances and accident. It is not a work of design, but the result of a rude and simple impulse—the tendency of the individual seller to defraud as much as possible for his own interest.

Never did a system better deserve condemnation as being vicious and corrupt; and it is clear that it should be counterbalanced by some means of guarantee against individual frauds, by some agency organized in such a manner as to unmask and prevent its extortions. With such a guarantee the commercial system would be changed from simple to compound; it would become what the grafted is to the wild fruit.

Now what is the power by the intervention of which commercial frauds can be repressed? It is the government. . . .

I am aware that in the present order it is not admissible—that if the government should interfere with the system of *simple* or fraudulent commerce, the effect upon general industry would be pernicious. But under the *compound* system, if the government should cease a moment to intervene for the guarantee of truth, everything would be thrown into disorder; just as false weights and measures would become general, if the administration should for a moment relax its strict supervision.

How should this intervention be exercised? What should be the mode? We have an example of the true mode under our eyes in weights, measures, and the metallic currency; these are the only branches of our commercial relations in which there exists practical truth; and yet they are under the exclusive regulation of the government—which is a very different thing from that fraudulent license that reigns in commerce, and produces

only fraud, anarchy, and the multiplication of parasitic agents
to ten times the number necessary.

If the economists were really in pursuit of the truth, they
should study to assimilate the commercial to the monetary system; the latter is not a simple government monopoly, like that
of tobacco, for example, in France, but a system counterbalanced
by the double check of commercial exchange and the value of
bullion, which, as I have said, obliges the mint to maintain the
coinage at a standard fineness. The gold and silver currency is,
then, a compound fiscal monopoly, which, as in all operations
of the compound order, insures practical truth.

Reformers who recommend us to proceed from the known
to the unknown had here before them a fine guide; they might
have made an application of the system by organizing commerce
also as a counterbalanced monopoly, controlled like the coinage
by the State. This would have been the means of realizing commercial truth, which would have led by degrees to association.

A sense of honor should have induced men of science to undertake this study. They are now openly sneered at by the merchants; with the banker and stockjobber, the name of savant
is an object of derision. Hence science, to defend its honor
against the outrages of this tribe of parvenus, as well as to establish the reign of truth, should have sought for means to correct the commercial system which it secretly despises, and to
raise it from the simple and fraudulent mode to the compound
and equitable. It would have found in this discovery an avenue
to fortune for governments, for the people, and for men of science themselves. It has preferred the policy of truckling; it has
servilely flattered traffic and stock-gambling, and has extolled their
frauds and speculation, and has made the interests of commerce
the rule of practical action. In thus neglecting a study which
honor and the love of truth alike imposed upon it, it has failed
in discovering the most direct issue from civilization; it has misled the social world, and lost itself.

In execution of the plan I proposed to myself in developing
the Theory of the Combined Order, it was necessary to proceed

by successive steps, to give first a mere outline of the subject treated, then abridged essays on the same, and last, a full treatise.

In conformity with this method, I have limited myself in treating the questions of liberty and commerce to a summary exposition of the errors prevalent on these subjects. If I had gone more into details, I should have violated the plan which I had decided to follow.

The more especial object of these sketches was to prove the error of the prevalent opinion that the secrets of nature are impenetrable mysteries, and to show that the *most valuable scientific discoveries were more frequently the result of chance than of the diligent efforts of genius.* If our men of science will not undertake a methodical study of the LAWS OF NATURE, she certainly is under no obligation to reveal them, any more than she is bound to bestow harvests on the cultivator who will not plough or sow.

TSO, I, pp. 89–110

WORK IN THE PHALANSTERY

It is not in the material organization of the series that any serious difficulty is to be apprehended. The obstacle to be feared will be found in the play or action of certain passions, which our moral theories would lead us to repress. And yet a series, the most regularly organized, would lose all its properties, such as industrial attraction, direct accord of inequalities, indirect accord of antipathies, etc., if the three forces, which I have termed the distributive or regulative passions, were not developed and called into action. If, in a series, but one of the three is thwarted in its action, the series becomes deranged, its accords weakened, its enthusiasm and emulation reduced to a mere semblance, and its harmony and equilibrium destroyed, especially in the important problem of the division of profits.

We will now explain briefly the nature of the three regulative passions.

I will commence with the *alternating passion*. It is the desire felt by the soul of periodical variety, of changes of scene and occupations, of contrasted situations, of incidents and novelties calculated to excite charm, and to stimulate at the same time the senses and the soul.

This want is felt moderately from hour to hour, and strongly after an interval of two hours. If it is not satisfied, man falls into a state of ennui and apathy.

By means of short occupations or short industrial sessions of an hour and a half, or two hours at the most, every one will be enabled, during the course of the day, to take part in seven or eight different attractive pursuits, to vary them the following day, and join other groups. This system is the desire of the eleventh passion—the *alternating*—which tends to fly from one occupation or pleasure to another, and to avoid the excesses now committed by the civilizees, who prolong a party or fête for six hours, a labor for ten or twelve, a ball all night at the expense of sleep and health.

Our pleasures have at present no connection with industry, and are consequently unproductive; whereas in the combined order they will be connected with productive industry, which will itself be a succession of pleasures, when rendered attractive.

To facilitate the frequent changes of occupation which will be necessary, a spacious and elegant gallery, warmed in winter and ventilated in summer, will extend along one front of the palace of the association; passages on columns will connect the different ranges of buildings, and underground passages will lead to the stables. By this architectural arrangement, the residents can communicate with all parts of the edifice, with its public halls, dining-rooms, workshops, and the outhouses, without being exposed to changes of temperature, to the rain or wet. In the fields, large wagons for fifteen or eighteen persons will be employed to transport the groups.

Some persons will pretend that these arrangements will be very expensive; they will cost much less than the outer clothing and carriages which are rendered necessary by exposure to the cold and wet, without taking into the account the colds, inflammations, and fevers caused by sudden changes of temperature.

It will also be asserted that the frequent changes of occupation will consume a great deal of time; they will require from five to fifteen minutes—less than a quarter of an hour on an average in agricultural pursuits, and half that time in in-door labors. They, who regret this loss of time, might regret also that devoted to sleep, and propose to suppress it. They do not know that activity and energy in labor are increased by brief periods of repose; the attractive industry of the future, prosecuted from passion, will be ardent; men will do more in one hour than is now accomplished in three by our hired laborers, who are slow, awkward, and without interest in their work, idling whenever an opportunity presents. In the combined order, the ardor of people in industry would become hurtful were it not frequently tempered by the suspensions which a change of occupation requires. I say this in answer to critics, who judge of the operations of association by the habits and methods of civilization.

I now pass to the examination of the two other regulative passions.

The emulative and the composite are in perfect contrast—the first is calculating and speculative in its character and action; the second, exhilarating, productive of enthusiasm, of exaltation, and of blind zeal and devotion.

The emulative gives rise to party spirit, to the love of management, diplomacy, and intrigue; it is strong, for example, with the ambitious, with courtiers, corporate bodies, and the commercial classes. Its distinctive feature is to combine calculation with passion. With the diplomatist or intriguer, all is calculation; every act, however trifling, is performed with reflection, and at the same time with celerity. The ardor of this passion then is controlled by reflection, forming a contrast with the unreflecting ardor and enthusiasm which are characteristic of the composite. They stimulate the groups of an industrial series by two contrasted impulses.

The love of intrigue is so imperious a want in man that in the absence of real intrigues it seeks for artificial ones, in games of chance, in theatrical representations, and in works of fiction. If a company is assembled, means must be provided for satisfying this passion—by putting cards in their hands, or by some other device. There is not a more unhappy being than a courtier, exiled to a provincial town, where his love of intrigue finds no field of action. A rich merchant who, retiring from business, suddenly withdraws from commercial schemes and speculations, which are active and exciting, becomes often, in spite of his fortune, the most melancholy of men.

The principal function of the passion, in the serial mechanism, is to excite rivalry, create dissonance between groups so nearly alike as to dispute the palm of excellence, and balance suffrages. We shall not see three groups, cultivating three varieties of the butter pear, form an accord; on the contrary, these groups, occupied with contiguous varieties, are in rivalry and discord; it is the same with three groups cultivating the yellow, gray and green pippin.

Discord between contiguous shades or varieties is a general law of nature; in colors, scarlet does not harmonize with its contiguous tints, cherry red, pale red and orange red, but it harmonizes with its opposites, dark blue, dark green, black and white. In music, the note D does not accord with C sharp, or E flat, which are contiguous to it, nor with C and E natural, which are sub-contiguous. We repeat, in social harmony, discords are as necessary as accords.

But discords can not take place between groups, occupied with distinct varieties, like those cultivating the peal-pear and the orange-pear. There exists between these two little pears a difference too striking to admit of hesitation on the part of judges; they will say that they are both good, but too little alike to allow of comparison. As a consequence, rivalry and party spirit can not be excited between the two groups which cultivate them; the emulative finds no field of action.

We must then, in every series, whether of an industrial or other character, form a scale of functions or varieties nearly alike—the *compact scale* as I have elsewhere called it. It is the means of securing a free development and action to the passion of emulation, of exciting great ardor in all works, a close intimacy among the members of each group, and of giving to every product the highest degree of perfection.

We should fail, however, in securing this latter result if, on the part of consumers as well as of producers, great refinement of taste were not cultivated. Of what use would it be to perfect to the highest possible degree every variety of product, if the population of the combined order was uniform in its tastes, indifferent as to what it consumed, eating only to satisfy the appetite, and interdicting itself out of deference to moral precepts, all pleasures of the senses? Under such circumstances, general perfection in industry would fail for want of appreciation; the emulative spirit would lose its activity among the groups of producers and preparers; agriculture would sink back into the rude state in which we see it in civilization, where, out of a hundred persons, scarcely one is found capable of judging of the excellence of products; hence it is that so little care and attention are given to perfecting qualities, and that most articles of consumption are now of so inferior a kind.

The serial system must be applied to consumption as well as to production; it would fail if it were not. It is very easy to introduce it into the former; it is only necessary to establish two scales or series of tastes, one operating on the different modes of preparation, the other, on the different qualities. Groups will be formed, each with an inclination for some special mode of preparation or some particular quality; and the series, both in the kitchens and at the tables, will be organized.

We come now to the third of the regulative passions, the *composite*, which establishes accords and sympathies between groups and the members of groups, and creates enthusiasm and exaltation. The passion we have described, the emulative or party spirit, is not alone sufficient to stimulate the groups in their works; we must put in play the opposite force or motor, the composite, with its sympathetic leagues and enthusiastic zeal— the most romantic of the passions, the enemy of calculation and of reflection. This passion will be called into action and applied to the industry of the combined order; it will find there

a field for its play and development; it will be one of the stimu-
lants that will render industry attractive. Together with the emulative, it will replace the low incentives, such as the fear of
want or starvation, the necessity of feeding helpless children,
the dread of the poorhouse, which, in civilization, impel the
masses to labor.

Instead of such abject incentives, the combined order will,
by the constant employment of the three regulative passions,
stimulate the industrial groups by a four-fold charm—two of the
senses, and two of the soul, thus creating four kinds of sympathy
between the members of a group.

The two sympathies of the soul will consist in the accords
of identity and of contrast.

There will be sympathy or accord of identity between the
members of a group, for the reason that they will be necessarily
identical in opinion and feeling in respect to a pursuit which
they have chosen from passion, and which they can quit when
they desire. The accord of identity becomes a potent charm
with one who sees himself aided by a group of zealous cooperators, intelligent and affable; it is as agreeable as the association
with the coarse, mercenary, and awkward hirelings of civilization is repulsive. Cooperation between polite and friendly persons excites ardor in the work or function with which they are
engaged, a desire to renew the work, and to meet at repasts of
the group at times when industrial operations are suspended.

The second charm of the soul is that derived from accords
of contrast. I have said that to create it among the groups of a
series, the groups must be distributed in a compact scale, and
occupied with consecutive and contiguous shades or varieties;
this distribution gives rise to accords and friendly leagues between groups of a different character, as it does to discord or
rivalry between contiguous groups.

Besides these two sympathies of the soul, one of identity, the
other of contrast, an industrial group must be stimulated by two
other motives which charm the senses—the first, the excellence
and perfection of its products, eliciting the praises of judges;

the second, the charm caused by the display, the elegance and refinement that exist in the entire series.

To sum up, if the three distributive, combining, and classifying passions, which are the organic forces of the series, are not developed combinedly, industrial attraction will not be created, or if it appears, it will die out by degrees and cease.

Thus, to render industry attractive, the condition to be fulfilled is to form series of groups, subordinated to the play of the three distributive passions. They must be—

RIVALIZED by the *emulative*, which creates discords, generous rivalry and competition between contiguous groups, provided the groups are distributed in a compact scale, or scale formed of tastes and functions very closely allied.

EXALTED by the *composite*, which creates accords and sympathies that charm both the senses and the soul, and generates enthusiasm and devotion among the members of a group.

CONNECTED or interlinked by the *alternating or modulating passion*, which is the support of the two others, as it maintains their activity by means of short occupations, and the choice of pursuits and pleasures, thus preventing satiety and lukewarmness.

I insist on the importance of this latter passion, the most proscribed of the three—on the necessity of short and varied occupation, the absence of which in our civilized system of industry is its condemnation; let us observe its effects in a material and a passional sense.

In a material sense, it conduces to health and vigor. Health necessarily suffers if a uniform labor, like weaving, sewing or writing, which does not exercise successively all parts of the body, is prosecuted the entire day through. Even active occupations, like those of agriculture, are injurious when thus prolonged ten or twelve hours a day. One exhausts the members and viscera, the other vitiates the solids and fluids.

The evil is increased if the labor, whether active or passive, is continued for months and years. In some branches of industry, we see the working classes afflicted by special diseases, caused by the nature of their labors; while other branches, such as the manufacture of various chemical products, are the death of the workman, and from the simple fact of prolonged application; he would be exempt from danger if the system of short periods of labor, say of two hours' duration, was introduced, and the labor repeated but two or three times a week.

The wealthy classes, for want of this system, are subject to other diseases, such as apoplexy, rheumatism and the gout. Obesity, which is common among the rich, denotes a radical defect in the equilibrium of the system, and a mode of life, which, in occupations and pleasures, is contrary to nature. Perfect health is only to be attained by this continual alternation of occupations, which, exercising successively every part of the body and every faculty of the mind, maintains both in activity and equilibrium.

In a passional sense, the alternating passion produces accord and agreement between characters, even of an opposite nature. For example, A and B are two persons of entirely dissimilar dispositions; but it happens that among the groups to which A belongs, there is a third in which his interests coincide with those of B, and in which he derives advantages of various kinds from the tastes of B, although the opposite of his own. It is the same with the tastes of B as regards A. As a consequence, without a real friendship existing between them, there is esteem, and an exchange of good offices.

Thus interest, which separates friends in civilization, may be made to unite enemies even in the combined order; antipathetic characters are conciliated by indirect cooperation, resulting from the connection and alternation of pursuits, which is the effect of short occupations.

These short periods enable a series, if composed only of thirty persons, to introduce its members into a hundred other series, and form with them ties of friendship and of interest. We shall see that this connection is indispensable to the solution of two important problems—first, the equitable division of profits according to labor, capital and talent; and second, perfect agreement in matters of collective interest, effected through self interest, which at present is the most fruitful source of discord.

It is, then, by means of one of the passions the most sharply criticized by the moralists and philosophers—the love of change and variety—that we shall solve so many problems in which they have failed.

Like the moralists, one must be the enemy of nature to deny this want of variety, the necessity of which in material matters is clearly evident. Any enjoyment, for example, which is long continued, becomes an excess, dulls the senses, and destroys the pleasure; a repast of four hours degenerates into an abuse; an opera of four hours wearies the spectator. As regards change and variety, the soul is as exacting as the body; all the affections, even love, are subject to the law of alternation.

The animal and vegetable kingdoms require changes and crossings; without them, they degenerate. Our stomachs, in like manner, require change; an habitual variety of food facilitates digestion and promotes health; the stomach will soon repel the most delicate dish, if presented to it daily.

The mind, in like manner, becomes fatigued by the long continued exercise of one faculty; characters, in which the ALTERNANT is predominant, require the exercise of two or three passions at the same time, to read cumulatively two or three works, to be engaged in two or three studies.

The earth itself needs alternations of crops and modes of culture; the vegetable creations need to be reproduced by changes of seed, shoots and other means; the soil requires changes of manures. All nature seeks variety; it is only the moralists and the Chinese that desire monotony and uniformity; as a consequence, the Chinese are, from their habits of stagnation, the most perverted of races and the farthest removed from the paths of nature.

The three regulative passions, being the most strongly condemned by our moral theories which are in every way opposed to attraction, play as we may presume an important part in the social system designed by nature; they hold the rudder, for it is they which direct the series. A series is imperfect in which they do not act combinedly and freely.

They form, in the scale of the twelve passions of the soul, the neutral principle.

The active principle—the four affectional or social passions.

The passive principle—the five sensitive or sensuous passions.

The neutral principle—the three distributive passions.

The latter are neutral, because they are but the result of the play of some of the nine others; each one of the three can only act or be developed by calling into action at least two of the nine others. It is for this reason that they have escaped the observation of analysts, and that their existence has been overlooked. I was led to their discovery by calculations on the neutral principle which we find in all departments of nature, a principle not admitted by the moderns, but suspected by the ancients.

Let us observe that the three neutral passions lead to the great end to be attained—the harmony and equilibrium of the passions, and by means of which our moral theories are ignorant; we shall see that this harmony and equilibrium, so vainly sought, results from the action of the alternating passion, which prevents excesses by varying occupations and pleasures before they are carried to an extreme. It thus establishes balance and equilibrium in the action of the passions by a great variety of pursuits and pleasures, and not by a calculated moderation, inasmuch as it operates in conjunction with two impulses—the emulative and the composite—both of which tend to extremes, even in virtue, and would lead to excesses, were they not tempered by the influence of alternation, or periodical change.

Thus the industrial series will be actuated by three motors—by two contrasted impulses, tempered by inconstancy. Such is the secret of the equilibrium of the passions; it is attained by means the very opposite of our visionary theories of moderation and of frigid reason, that is, by their free and full development in an order suited to them.

Let me here remark that nothing is so well calculated as the theory of the passions to confound all our moral and philosophic doctrines, which hold that these springs of action, these motors in man were created at random, and that God has had to leave to legislators and moralists the task of regulating and harmonizing them. The passions may, in the social mechanism, be compared to an orchestra of sixteen hundred and twenty instruments: our social guides in wishing to direct them resemble a band of children who, gaining access to the orchestra of an opera, and laying hold of the instruments, should produce a frightful charivari. Are we to conclude from this that music is the enemy of man, that we should suppress the violins, stop the bass-viols, and smother the flutes? Not at all; we must drive away these little intruders, and place the instruments in the hands of expert musicians. In like manner the passions are no more the enemies of man than are musical instruments; man has no enemy but our ignorant moral and philosophic guides, who wish to control the passions without possessing the least knowledge of the mode of action assigned to them by nature, and of the social mechanism to which they are adapted. When this social mechanism shall be tested, it will be seen that the passions are all good as God created them, and that when normally developed, they tend to social unity and harmony.

TSO, II, pp. 52–60

THE EFFECT OF ASSOCIATION ON THE PASSIONS

Our century felt this and has thus experimented with associative orders that choose the mass rather than the family as the pivot; orders that subordinate the harmony of the family to the harmony of the collective.

These associative and colonial experiments have all failed in Europe; Robert Owen, Van den Bosch and Aracktchejew have fallen. I do not speak of the Moravians who are industrial monks, given to monstrosities like placing women in lotteries.

Neither do I cite in the list of experiments the Saint-Simonians, who had neither the knowledge nor the desire to attempt associative experiment even though it would have been easy at the time of their vogue to obtain contributions totaling a million. But this was not their secret objective. By means of association they wanted to exploit the world. They wanted to use this as a steppingstone to found a religion and to grant themselves prelacies in order to lay their hands on donations, heritages, and fortunes.

Lastly Francia, an audacious and quite ingenious daredevil, took a remarkable step in the art of associating in America. He sensed that the objective was to affect the solidarity of the masses in order to help the individual. But he bullied the problem instead of solving it. He went directly to the goal, but by the wrong means. He used a coercive and semi-monastic method, and created an ambiguous community without sufficient gradation of classes and thus stamped out liberty.

Now it is a matter of correcting that defective initiative which was devoid of truly attractive means. Francia partially knew how to get out of the rut of civilization, but he did not know how to innovate, or how to operate by the scales of inequality and the principle of attractive industry.

The problem is to *change the direction* of passion rather than to change or repress the passions and instincts. What are germs of evil today must be transformed into propitiary germs, like cupidity which forces the lower class into the role of petty thieves, and the higher class into the role of great thieves who hang the little ones.

Let us give an example of this metamorphosis applied to petty thieves, because the great ones merit respect.

In our society people steal for two reasons; because they lack what they need, and because they are able to get rid of the stolen goods. In the combined order these two motives will no longer exist. The people will enjoy abundance, and they will not be able to sell stolen objects. Furthermore they would be dishonored, ruined, exiled, and even banished. Let us look more closely.

Bastien is a skillful fisherman, a practicing officer in the series of groups which take care of the fish preserves and rivers. (I say practicing officer because each industrial series has two groups of officers, those of theoretical and practical production, and those of etiquette chosen from among the rich sectarians. The latter have a ceremonial function; they preside at meetings and celebrations, and they give luster and embellishments to their group and to their series. It is similar to the French Academy, where there are two kinds of academicians, those of talent and those of the Protectorate.)

If Bastien were a fish warden for a civilizee preserve he would steal as many fish as he could. But he will not even dream of stealing fish in harmony where the passion for thievery, so common in the contemporary era, will find free and attractive *grafting* and *counterpoints*.

Negative counterpoints. Bastien would not be able either to eat or to sell the stolen fish; he has no household and he has a subscription for the tables of the third order. He could only take the fish to the kitchens of his Phalanstery where he would be told that fishing is not in season, and would be asked for what reunion he had gotten the fish. Bastien would have no order to show and the theft would be known.

Will he take it to market in the next town? He would be seen leaving his Phalanstery and asked about the fish he carried. Once arrived in town how would he sell it? The chances of stealing, of receiving and selling stolen objects that exist in the family system will not exist in urban Phalansteries. When the fishing season is open, fish will be ordered in assorted lots by the weight of two or three hectograms. Out of season fish will be ordered and delivered, and the order will be put on a running account and paid each month. In twenty other cases too lengthy to consider, Bastien would not be able to turn his fish into money, and the theft would be discovered.

The impossibility of placing stolen goods is a very powerful counterpoint to theft. The only exception would be liquid cash, but money will be rarely lost because it will not be carried about except when travelling.

Positive counterpoints. The risk of disgrace. If the theft is recognized Bastien is dishonored, ruined. His worker's shares of stock would fall in value so that they would render only 12 per cent instead of 18 per cent, 24 per cent and 30 per cent; his ranks in the groups and series would be forfeited; he would be eliminated from various testaments where he has legacies by virtue of industrial inheritance; he would be excluded from all reunions of pleasure. He would be a man lost for having merely attempted a petty theft. Big thefts like the theft of a wagonload of fish, game, or fruit, are impossible.

Vice is already quite prevented by these two curbs or counterpoints, the first of which is *imposed*, and compulsory and consists of material obstacles; the second is attractive and consists of opposing large profit, well-being, consideration, and advancement to the mediocre chance of a little theft which, promising little money, would expose the thief to frightful disgraces.

Let us pass from counterpoints to grafting, which operates through egoism opposed to itself in the double mode.

Simple egoism is the crude impulsion that brings about theft through need or cupidity: this need does not exist in harmony as even the poor enjoy a happy existence. But the civilizee is insatiable, he wants to enrich himself at the expense of the mass. In the contemporary era Bastien would steal fish if he ran no risk of being caught. But in the new order he will not steal, even without the risk of being caught. He will be restrained by:

Composed egoism, or the concurrence of various greedy impulses. Bastien will be actively interested in there being no theft in any branch of cultivation or fabrication because he has interests in and co-operates in thirty functions to varying degrees with superior, average, or inferior talent. If theft were introduced into his Phalanstery, Bastien, stealing from two or three functions in which he might succeed, would run the risk of losing in twenty-seven others. It follows that the harmonians, through composed cupidity and potential gain from all sides, will guard against theft. Theft will be prevented without recourse to the police, and punished without recourse to a judicial system, as we have already seen.

Thus egoism and cupidity (so defamed by philosophers who know nothing of the causes and subtleties of passion) become a source of virtue when they are grafted upon themselves; when to simple impulse is joined a composed impulse born of thirty coinciding interests. This grafting is not practicable in civilization, as it encounters three obstacles—first, the solitary nature of duties; second, the lengthy sessions which hinder the individual from being initiated in many kinds of work at an early age; and third, the separation of the work of cultivation, fabrication, housekeeping, and teaching, which are all united in a rural Phalanstery.

Let us note that the example given includes only mediocre nuances of positive counterpoints and composed egoism. Many more beautiful ones are to be seen in the mechanism of equilibrated distribution, where the noblest passions, honor, friendship, and love simultaneously intervene to ennoble all egoism and all branches of cupidity. These number about eighty for each individual, and they all coincide with strict justice, through the impulse of calculated cupidity.

It is thus that our passions, so degraded by ignorant philosophy, become beacons of virtue when they are developed in the order desired by the creator; when they are submitted to the grafting of simple egoism upon composed egoism, and to the concurrence of double counterpoints, at least some of which must be based upon attraction.

To get a sense of the harmonians' disdain for the idea of domestic theft, and of the amicable bonds created by each branch of industry among the co-operators, it will suffice to glance at the branch with which we have already dealt. Fishing is scorned today in favor of hunting because everything works backward in civilization, pleasures as well as interests.

Unitarian fishing, or fishing in a combined regime, intimately rallies the three classes—rich, middle, and poor—of both sexes and of all ages. All find pleasure in it, first because of the abundant catch which will enable many fish to be given to the poorer classes, while reserving the most beautiful for the tables of the first order and for orders placed in advance. The small well-stocked rivers will increase today's catch tenfold, and an abundance of pike will be guaranteed by diminishing and selecting the small fry, according to connoisseurs.

Another tenfold increase will be had by virtue of fish preserves which will be closed off by a grill to guard against flood and otters, which will be quickly destroyed. Thus there will be fish for all the people, who today do not eat even the wheat they cultivate, much less taste fine fish.

All classes will arrive at this work with pleasure especially the women and children who feed the fish. Each fish preserve is differentiated by species and is renewed by a running stream.

The short sessions at the fish preserves are very agreeable because the well-off class will come by omnibus if they come from far away. The work is done under a parasol or a cloth canopy carried upon twelve, fifteen, or twenty posts, and transported as the work requires, as during harvests. On fishing days nothing is more pleasurable than to catch an abundance of fish with no great hardship. This kind of work has even more prestige as the fish nourish themselves in part on their own species and devastate nothing, whereas game devastates much, if it is very abundant. The harmonians, however, will fence in all the forests.

For every other kind of work I could cite various charms unknown in the contemporary order which would prove that our moralists are very ill-advised when they seek gentle fraternity, love of work, and social virtue in familial and fragmented industry. These advantages can only be born of combined industry; by developing each passion through grafting and real counterpoints, rather than the imaginary ones of morality. The morality of civilization gives us the scaffold and hell; sovereignty with neither bread nor work; pride in the fine name of free man without fortune; the happiness of living under a bestowed charter; and of obeying Seneca, the hypocrite, who preaches the scorn of riches and amasses through pillage a fortune of one hundred and twenty million francs in today's currency. These are civilization's counterpoints.

When a century gives the pompous title *love of wisdom,* of *philosophy,* to these scientific jugglings it is not surprising that it calls the opposite science folly. The latter comes with arithmetic book in hand to expose the regular calculations of grafting, balance, and counterpoint of the passions which are developed in series like quantities in mathematics. The former is a

science backed up by its counterproof, the calculation of re-
cuperated movement or the recurrence of the passions, com-
pressed by the mechanism of the family and fragmented industry.

Associative industry was believed to be impossible: the prestige of this idea has already been dispelled by Francia, who organized 300,000 Paraguayans into crude, formless combination,
without knowledge of the system of distribution, or of the scale
of premiums, and of many other associative procedures described
in my treatises.

The champions of impossibility are already reduced to silence.
It is not impossible to associate, since Francia was able to found
200 societies of 1500 people each, and managed to unite them in
the work of cultivation, fabrication, and housekeeping.

The champions of false progress, who only desire verbal progress, remain to be confounded. They must be shown that
Francia's unpolished work is susceptible to immense progress;
that it can be elevated from a mode of constraint to a mode of
attraction. A small experiment with 300 or 400 children will
give this proof and will change the fate of humanity in six
weeks.

If Francia, without theory, knew how to found 200 large
associative colonies whose number augments each year by
swarms, will France, the heretofore great nation, not dare to
found a quarter of a colony? Does she want to justify the nick-
name that Kotzebue gave her? Those little Frenchmen!

OC, VIII, pp. 202–10

ON POPULATION EQUILIBRIUM

Among the inconsistencies and neglects of modern politics,
there is none more shocking than the failure to pass judgment
upon population equilibrium, upon the proportion of consumers to the forces of production. In vain would one discover the
means of increasing productivity four times or even a hundred
times, if mankind is condemned to proliferate as today, to ac-

cumulate a mass of people triple or quadruple the number at which population should be fixed in order to maintain progressive material well-being among the various classes.

Population equilibrium has always been one of the stumbling blocks of civilized politics. Even the Greeks and Romans, surrounded by so many uncultivated regions suitable for colonization, saw no other remedy for overpopulation than to tolerate infanticide and the throat-cutting of superfluous slaves, as did the virtuous Spartans, or to send them to their death in the arena for the amusement of the rabble who, though proud of the title of free men, were far from the role of just men.

In more recent times modern politicians have admitted their discomfiture concerning the problem of population equilibrium. I have cited Stewart, Wallace, and Malthus, the only writers worth consulting on this subject because they confess to the incapacity of science. Their wise opinions about the vicious circle of population are smothered by the juggling economists who brush aside this problem, as they do so many others.

Stewart, the more honest, has treated it very well in his hypothesis of a well-cultivated island, an island that could easily nourish inhabitants of various levels of wealth; but, he says, if this population rose to 3000 or 4000, to 20,000 and 40,000, how could it be fed?

It is answered that one must colonize, send out multitudes; but that is to skirt the question. If the entire globe were peopled, the population carried to its highest number, where could one set up colonies?

Sophists answer that the globe is not and will not be so quickly populated. This is one of the subterfuges of Owen's school, a school that promises happiness but eludes the problem of population equilibrium, saying that the globe will not be full for another 300 years. They are wrong. It will only take 150 years. But in any case putting off the solution 300 years is to lose ground on a problem without guaranteeing that it will be solved even then. If it takes 300 years for the globe to reach maximum population, at the end of 300 years this theory of happiness, or supposed happiness, will still be very defective and will fail as a result of a lack of social politics, and of an overabundance of population.

But as it is certain that this calamity will not be 300 years but rather 150 years in coming, given the universal peace and general abundance provided by the era of association, the theory of this new order must furnish very efficacious means for preventing population excess, and for reducing the number of inhabitants on the globe to about five billion, to a sound proportion of means and needs, so as not to risk a population of six, seven, eight, ten, twelve billion, a superabundance which would be inevitable if the globe were subject to civilization.

Counting on five billion wealthy and happy inhabitants, I assume a reestablishment of temperature which would disengage the Arctic Pole from its polar cap; failing this, the globe would not be able to opulently nourish more than three billion inhabitants. What means will be used to disengage and to fecundate the Pole? I am waiting to make these means known when the time is right and when they are seriously wanted. Without becoming involved in the details, let us restrict ourselves to the heart of the question, to the problem of maintaining a mass of inhabitants in high comfort by preserving the globe from an excess of population that is one of the dangers of the civilized system.

These means depend in part upon the customs of free love which will only begin to be established in about sixty years' time, after the race of civilizees is completely extinct. There is no disadvantage in making these means known, since the need for them will be felt only after a hundred years, when the globe will reach maximum population. In the meantime it must be proved that the theory of association is not at fault either on this point or on any other; and this theory must not be confused with those which sidestep offhand the most important problems such as population equilibrium, basic minimum, etc.

In the associative state nature throws up four barriers to oppose overpopulation—

      1. The vigor of women

      2. The gastrosophic regime

3. The phanerogamic morals
4. The integral exercises

First, *vigor*—We already see the influences among city women; three out of every four sterile women are robust, whereas delicate women are exaggeratedly and regrettably fertile. Sterile women are usually those that one would have thought the most suited to procreation. It will be replied that in the country robust women are not at all sterile; I know, it is one more proof in favor of the natural method, which should operate by the sequence of the four means applied in combination, and not by the isolated use of any one of the four.

Second, *the gastrosophic regime*—Where does this difference in fecundity in favor of robust peasant women come from? It is the effect of a sober life, and of a simple diet limited to vegetables. Women living in cities eat refined foods, which is a means to sterility that will become more frequent in harmony where everyone is a polished gastronome. Hence by combining the extreme vigor of the harmonian ladies with the delicate nourishment which they will enjoy, there will already be two paths toward sterility. I pass briefly over the objections whose examination would fill a longer article than this one; it must be kept in mind that this is a summary.

Third, *the phanerogamic[2] morals*. . . .

Fourth, *integral exercise*—distributed over all parts of the body, by means of short sessions alternating in function. The effects produced upon puberty and fecundity through a change in corporal exercise have never been observed; the contrasts on this point are striking. Villagers attain puberty much later than children living in cities or rich children living in the country. Fecundity is similarly subordinated to the influence of gymnastics. If corporal exercise is integral, including all parts of the body alternatively and proportionately, the genital organs develop later; the proof is to be seen in the case of the children of princes who marry at fourteen to sixteen years, while young villagers are often not nubile until sixteen years. This delay is

[2] Meaning the morality of polygamy. Fourier omitted an explanation in his manuscript.—Ed. note.

due to the difference in corporal and spiritual exercise, which operate inversely in the case of the two classes. (The precocious nubility of princes cannot be attributed to the kind of nourishment they receive, since their diet is very plain.)

Children of noble lineage are given more to exercises of the spirit and much less to those of the body. The result is that their physical and vital faculties, very obstructed, cause the sexual organs to blossom early, and puberty to burst forth prematurely. In harmony the opposite will occur; harmonians will reach puberty later than civilizee peasants because the continual and alternative exercise of all their members will absorb the vital fluids and will retard the moment when, as a result of overabundance and lack of absorption, they will cause puberty to arrive before the time set by nature. Children raised in harmony will not be pubescent until the age of sixteen years for men, and fifteen years for women; and after three centuries this delay will extend to seventeen or eighteen years, even in the tropical zone.

The influence of integral gymnastics upon fecundity will be similar. Fecundity will be so strongly hampered that in order for a harmonian woman to become fertile she will have to prepare herself by observing a calm life style and a special diet for three months so that her body fluids, less absorbed by integral exercise and by the active use of all the parts of her body, will rush to the reproductive organs. Among the class of wealthy city dwellers these fluids are strongly attracted to the reproductive organs when they are not counterbalanced by the intervention of all other parts of the body employed in active work.

When it is known how to employ in combination the four means set forth above, the chances of fecundity and sterility will be the reverse of what they are today. That is to say that a deficit of population will be feared rather than an excess, and measures will be taken to stimulate that very fecundity feared today by every prudent man. The sensible man wants to have only a small number of children in order to assure them the wealth without which there is no happiness. The unreasonable and purely carnal man produces children by the dozen, like Feth-Ali, Shah of Persia, excusing himself since "it is God who sends them, and there cannot be too many honest people in the world." But God, on the contrary, wants to limit the number of children in proportion to the means of subsistence. Social man reduces himself to the level of an insect when he creates heaps of children who will be reduced to devouring one another because of their number. They will not eat one another bodily like insects, fish, and wild beasts, but they will devour one another politically in plunder, wars, and the perfidies of imperfect civilization.

What good is this overpopulation when it is proven that the civilized order, no matter how populous, will never be able to cultivate all its land? More than one-third of France's territory lies fallow; in China there are vast wildernesses four leagues from Peking; and I wager that in Ireland, the most underdeveloped country in Europe, there is much uncultivated land. (I do not call Ireland "populated"; Flanders is populous, Ireland is underdeveloped.)

When right-thinking men, like the Swede Herrenschwand, raised their voices against the double scourge of overpopulation and indigence, when they proclaimed that politics had failed to take ameliorative steps, their voices were smothered and they were accused of madness. Their philippics were weak in that they denounced the evil before discovering the remedy. The obscurantists, known as philosophers, answered that the necessary evils of perfectible civilization must be overlooked; thus even in England indigence has not ceased to increase in spite of the excess of industry and an annual tax of 200,000 pounds for the poor. Confused by these results, philosophy takes refuge behind the odious principle "there must be many poor, in order that a few may be rich." In the exposition of the mechanism of harmony, we have seen the merit of this opinion, as well as that of all our political aphorisms for which we will soon blush, namely those that encourage the heaping up of anthills of people before seeing that they be assured a decent minimum living.

OC, VI, pp. 335–39

IV. THE FAMILY

THE BOURGEOIS HOUSEHOLD

If one reflects upon the many disadvantages associated with permanent marriage and family life, one is astonished at the gullibility of the masculine sex; astonished that man has never envisioned a way to emancipate himself from this sort of life. Aside from the wealthy, it seems to me that domestic life is much less than pleasant for the spouses. I will list eight from among many discomforts that distress every husband to some degree, and which will disappear in the progressive household.

1. *Risk of Unhappiness.* Is there a game of chance more frightful than the drawing of lots to determine the outcome of a life of permanent bondage to one who may be incompatible?

2. *Expense.* The expense is enormous in the present system compared to the great savings which will result from the progressive family.

3. *Vigilance.* The obligation to keep watch over the details of a household, in which it is not prudent to blindly trust the wife.

4. *Monotony.* The monotony must be great in our isolated households since husbands, in spite of the distraction of their work, run in hordes to public places, coffeehouses, clubs, theaters, etc. to divert themselves from the proverbial satiety of *always eating from the same dish.* This monotony is even worse for wives.

5. *Sterility*. Sterility threatens to undo all plans for happiness and disconcerts both the spouses and their parents; it delivers their inheritance to other relatives whose overt or covert avidity and ingratitude are the despair of the rightful legatees; and it inspires in the husband an aversion to his sterile wife and to the conjugal knot which has made impossible his hopes of inheritance.

6. *Widowerhood*. It reduces the husband to the role of prisoner, much worse than the small annoyances of bachelorhood. If the husband precedes his wife to the grave he is dogged by bitter anxiety until the moment of death—his children may be delivered into mercenary hands; ruin may await his young family.

7. *Family Alliance*. The disadvantage of allying oneself with a family that rarely yields the profit or pleasure that one would expect based on kinship and past conduct.

8. *Cuckoldom*. Lastly, cuckoldom, which is doubtless the most unfortunate and exhausting accident, since the husband is certain to suffer the same fate to which he subjected others before marrying.

Seeing the numerous disgraces associated with marriage and the isolated family, how can men have failed to seek an end to their servitude? Why have they neglected to demand domestic innovation which could never produce anything more unhappy than present family life?

It is said that in political affairs the most powerful make the laws. It is not the same in domestic affairs. The masculine sex, although stronger, has not made the law to its advantage in establishing isolated households and permanent marriage. It might be said that such a system is the work of a third sex who wanted to condemn the other two to boredom and vexation. Could a better system have been invented to insure the languor, the venality, and the falseness which pervade our isolated families; a system more harmful to a relationship of love and pleasure?

Marriage seems an invention to reward perversity—the more cunning and seductive a man is, the more easily he can attain opulence and public esteem through marriage. It is the same for women. Let a man put into play the most infamous motives to obtain a rich match; as soon as he finds himself married he has become a saint, a tender husband, a model of virtue. Exploiting a young lady to suddenly attain an immense fortune is an end so agreeable that public opinion pardons all for the gay dog who knows how to bring off the match. He is declared by all to be a good husband, a good son, a good father, a good brother, a good son-in-law, a good relative, a good friend, a good neighbor, a good citizen, a good republican. The style of the apologists is such that they wouldn't know how to praise a fellow without declaring him good from head to toe. Opinion reacts similarly in regard to a business tycoon who manages to wed a large sum of money. A wealthy marriage is comparable to baptism in that both promptly wash out all prior stain. Mothers and fathers in our civilization thus have no choice other than to encourage their children to try all methods, good and bad, to land a wealthy marriage partner. Marriage, true civil baptism, effaces all sin. But public opinion is not as indulgent for other parvenus, reminding them for a long time of the turpitudes that led them to fortune.

For one who attains happiness through a rich marriage, how many others find nothing but the torment of their lives! The unhappy are able to recognize that the enslavement of women is hardly to man's advantage. What dupes men are that they have compelled themselves to wear a dreadful chain; what punishment they endure for having reduced women to bondage.

If married life can guarantee against some of the inconveniences of celibacy, it gives *no positive happiness whatsoever*,[1] not even in the case of a perfect accord between spouses. For if

[1] I make exception of the case where one acquires a great fortune in marriage. But in the state of liberty and in the progressive household there are also ways to elevate oneself to fortune through love alliances. As for other pleasures, marriage offers none which are not more easily obtainable in this new order of society. Here even the oldest may freely show their affection without exposing themselves to the falseness and ridicule which hounds the civilizees in middle age and finally throws the old into absolute indifference.—Fourier.

their characters are eminently well suited to one another nothing will hinder them from living together in a differently organized domestic system where love would be free. We will see
after examining the picture of new domestic order that marriage presents not a single chance of happiness that the spouses
could not find in a situation of total liberty.

In order to numb us to the obvious impropriety of aligning
passion and marriage, philosophy preaches fatalism to us, telling
us that in this life we are destined to tribulation, that we must
learn to resign ourselves, etc. Not at all! All we must do is
invent a new mode of domestic society accommodated to the
expression of passion, which is precisely what we have neither
looked for nor created. I intend to help you envision this
new mode of private life whose invention was so easy.

Let us continue to discuss the inconveniences of the system
of isolated households and permanent marriage which estranges
us in every way from *positive happiness* and real pleasure. Freedom in love, joy and good will, insouciance, and more, are not
even dreamed of because philosophy habituates us to regard the
desire for true good as vice.

In spite of all that philosophy does to prepare us and wheedle
us into marriage (as one cajoles a child before administering
medicine), and in spite of philosophers' benign and sugar-
coated insinuations about the happiness of marriage, men are
nevertheless terrified at the prospect. The conjugal knot must be
very formidable since before tying it men shiver several years in
advance. I am not speaking of unions between the rich; all is
rose-colored in a marriage that begins with a good revenue.
Even so, the husband is in no hurry to give up his harem,[2] or
to make himself the slave of a wife for whom he must assidu-

[2] The word harem applies only to the practices of young men
living in large cities, where those with manners and fortune are able
to form a harem better stocked than that of the great Sultan. There
are three classes of Odalisques—noble and virtuous women, women
of the petty bourgeoisie, and courtesans. This is why the young men
of large cities resist the ties of marriage so strongly, while in moral
and unexciting towns, like those in Switzerland, they fear it less.—
Fourier.

ously do his conjugal duty at the risk of leaving an easy access to other entreating suitors, or of having bestowed upon him children of doubtful paternity that he would be forced to accept according to the law *Is pater est quem justae nuptiae demonstrant, or the real father is he who is designated as such by marriage.* This law, bugbear to all men, authorizes a white woman to give birth to a mulatto child, even though the husband be white. And this is only one of the dangers to which marriage exposes men. No wonder they consider it as a tendered trap, as a perilous jump. Before stepping over the line they wear themselves out rusing and calculating. Nothing is more ridiculous than the instructions they give one another on how to mold a wife to the yoke of bondage and how to charm her with lessons of morality; nothing is as curious as these secret confabulations where they critically analyze the marriageable young ladies and the traps set out by fathers trying to get daughters off their hands.[3] After all these debates one hears them conclude that one must ally one's self with money; that if one must be cuckolded by the woman, one must at least not be cuckolded by the dowry. A man has to assure himself of an indemnity which compensates for the vexations of marriage. Thus do bachelors reason among themselves. Such are the philosophical dispositions they bring to the *sacred bond* of matrimony.

It is doubtlessly just as far from calculation to love as from household life to voluptuous pleasure. No doubt one lives well in wealthy households (of which there is only one out of eight) but the seven others vegetate and are seized with jealousy at the well-being enjoyed by the eighth. In the end, all, whether

[3] To speak frankly, fathers with marriageable daughters have a vile role to play in our civilization. I understand that paternal love may blind them to the infamy of their maneuvers and the cajolery that they use to allure suitors; but at least they should not close their eyes to the uneasiness and disgrace associated with such a role. How much must one who is overburdened with daughters desire that a new domestic order, without marriage, be invented so that fathers will be delivered of the problem of furnishing their daughters with husbands. How much they would owe to him who brings them this innovation.—Fourier.

rich or poor, are so fed up with themselves and with their monotonous life that we see them throw themselves at great cost
into the *undomestic pleasures* of haunting public places, theaters, balls, cafes, etc., keeping an open house if they are rich,
and alternately offering banquets to one another if they lack the
individual means to furnish themselves with the needed distractions.

These diversions, bought at such cost in the present system,
would be freely lavished on all in the seventh period, the arrangement of which I will presently describe. This society will
assure to all a constant variety of feasts and gatherings, and a
liberty the likes of which one finds not a hint in household
meals, where reigns a stilted atmosphere and a tyranny of prejudice much different from the ease found even at *picnics* and
pleasure outings today.

As for these household meals that are dulled by the uncom-
fortable assortment of ages and guests and by the fatigue of
preparation, we can observe that this mediocre amusement is
only possible for the rich. What is the fate of those numerous
spouses who, by lack of fortune, are deprived of what we call
pleasure, and are reduced to the internal war proverbially defined so well: *The mules fight among themselves when there
is no hay in the trough.* Oh how many families, in spite of
their opulence, fall even still into that discord which is almost
universal with those embittered by poverty!

There are exceptions, of course. There are not only individuals, but entire nations as well who adapt easily to the yoke of
matrimony. Such are the Germans whose patient and phleg-
matic character is better suited to conjugal servitude than the
flighty and restless nature of the French. These exceptions are
seized upon to plead the case in favor of marriage; only the
favorable instances are cited.

Such a knot is doubtless suited to a middle-aged man who
wants to isolate himself from society's corruption. I understand
that a wife may find some charm in the company of such a man,
and renounce society's tumult for him. But why does the masculine sex conceive of these wise proclivities for retirement only

after fifteen or twenty years of coquetry? Why, in retiring from the world, do men not take women matured, as they are, by experience? Will they always find in an adolescent girl virtues more precocious than theirs which were so late in coming? It is not ludicrous that the civilizees, who boast of surpassing women in reason, demand of a sixteen-year-old girl the reason that they did not acquire until the age of thirty or forty, after having wallowed in debauchery throughout their youth? If they only arrived at reason by taking the road of pleasure, should they be astonished that a woman takes the same route to arrive at the same place?

Domestic politics, founded on the fidelity of a young girl, enters not at all into God's design. If He gave young women an appetite for dissipation and pleasure it is obvious that he did not intend them either for marriage or for household life, which requires a taste for retirement. It follows then that men must be unhappy in matrimony since they want to marry young women to whom nature has not given penchants suitable to that condition.

Here step in philosophers who promise to *change the passions of women, to repress nature.* Ridiculous pretensions! One knows the success they have. In marriage as in all other contracts, misfortune falls to the man who is most deserving of a happy fate. He who merits a loyal wife finds the most libertine and false. The devotion of such a husband becomes the cause of his credulity; he will be better taken in by the pretense of modesty and the innocent airs that a liberal education bestows upon all young ladies to mask their nature. In spite of all the moralists' systems, happiness is not to be found in matrimony. A universal cry raises itself against the problems associated with this style of life. It is the very men who pity themselves who have made the laws and who should have made them to their advantage! What would women say if they had the right to complain? What must one think of an institution so wearying to the strong sex who established it, and even more wearying to the feeble sex from whom no complaint is permitted?

Some boast of the apparently harmonious marriages in which

a young victim supports with heroic devotion the persecution of a jealous husband who is retired from the world. Oh, is that not a state of war even worse than that in some German villages, where the husband keeps next to the hearth a stick called *the peace of marriage*, used as a last resort to settle all conjugal disagreement? The oppression, being less evident in the upper classes, is no less real. How can the two sexes not rise up against a system that subjects them to so many evils? Seeing this domestic war among all classes of citizens, how can one fail to recognize that the conjugal condition is not at all the destiny of man? Far from searching for some palliative to the disunion of husband and wife, we must look for a way to emancipate ourselves from a system that nurtures and ferments discord and unrest, without producing *a single good that would not be found in a state of total liberty*.

OC, Vol. I, pp. 111–17

THE OPPRESSION OF WOMEN

TENDENCY OF THE PHILOSOPHERS AND MORALISTS, PARTICULARLY AMONG THE FRENCH, TO UNDERVALUE AND DEGRADE THE FEMALE SEX

I know not on what grounds the French base their claim to the distinction of being the gallant nation; it seems to me as destitute of foundation as the epithets "Beautiful France" and "The Great Nation." But on this latter point we will not speak at present.

How happens it that the French, who are so versatile in their laws and constitutions, have adhered steadily to but a single one, that which excludes women from the throne? The *Salic Law* has maintained its ground under all dynasties. Nowhere is there more constancy and more unanimity than among the French to subordinate that sex which they pretend to honor so highly.

There is no nation among which women are so much deceived by lovers, so frequently cajoled by promises of marriage and excuses for delays, where they are more readily abandoned when *enciente,* or forgotten when love has ceased. With such characteristics the French call themselves gallant! They are in truth intriguing and selfish in love, very skillful in seduction, and very deceitful after success.

No people has, in the drama, more reproached women who have manifested a passion for study. Does this show a knowledge of nature? Are not women destined to exhibit in literature and the arts the same capacity they have exhibited on the throne, when, from the days of SEMIRAMIS to CATHERINE, there have been *seven great queens to one of inferior capacity, while among kings, seven have been incapable, to one that has been great?*

The same rule would hold good in literature and the arts; the female sex will carry off the palm in these departments, when, in the combined order, education shall have restored woman to the use of her faculties, smothered by a social system which engrosses her in the complicated functions of our isolated households.

I do not deny that, in the present state of society, it may be necessary to stifle in women the desire of distinction, their inclination to great deeds, their love of rank. Having, in civilization, as a general rule no higher function than that of housekeeper, it is well that their education should stultify their intellects, and make them fit for such menial occupations. In the same way, to fit the slave for his degraded condition, he is forbidden the studies which would render him sensible of his abject state. According to the precepts of Aristotle, who could not see the propriety of moral worth in a slave, he is to be denied the practice of the virtues. In like manner, there are many virtues which philosophy judges unsuitable to woman.

A husband will maintain that the demands of the household require the wife to be confined to the management of domestic affairs, while he gives his attention to business abroad. Such arguments are not applicable to the combined order, where household labors, being simplified by general combination, will require but one-eighth of the women now employed in them. There will be no necessity then of degrading the sex by a menial education; young girls may be inspired with a love of distinction which will be at once a path to fortune and to renown, because they will share in the magnificent rewards which the combined order will bestow upon success in science and the arts.

Moreover, if the rivalry of the sexes is well established, the feminine series will wish to possess the knowledge requisite to the prosecution of their functions, to join theory with practice, even in labors connected with the kitchen and laundry. In washing, for example, they would desire the head of the series to have a chemical knowledge of the nature of soaps and lyes, and their effects in cleansing; the series would consider themselves degraded, if they were constantly liable to mistakes for want of knowledge in these matters, and obliged to appeal to men whenever a difficulty arose.

The male sex among us invades nearly all the proper avocations of woman, depriving her even of the more profitable branches of needlework. This monstrous perversion will cease as soon as free scope, given to attraction, shall assign to each sex its natural sphere of action. Then all the prevalent prejudices in regard to the capacity of woman will vanish; and in the primary schools of the combined order, there will be a greater attendance of girls than boys.

If it were true, according to the doctrines of Mohammed and some modern philosophers, that woman is destined only to serve the pleasure of man, or to be a domestic drudge, the law of emulation between natural opposites or the law of emulative contrasts, which is the basis of the system of passional equilibrium, would be disregarded, both in social relations and in education! On what could emulation be based, if boys did not see themselves excelled by girls of their own age in different avocations—in the fine arts, for example? Otherwise it would be impossible to create in the male sex a sentiment of politeness and deference for woman. This respect for the sex should exist among one-half of the children, if for no other reason than to conceal from them the real motives of the courtesy which they see prevailing among adults.

Women should, from childhood up, secure respect by incontestible merit. But in what shall this merit consist? In the art of *skimming the pot?* In the combined order, that function will be performed by men rather than women. Much physical strength will be requisite to manage the great caldrons which will be used in the kitchens of an association, each holding at least a hundred pounds of beef. The most that young girls or women can do will be to manage the pots containing delicate dishes, the preparation of which requires great care; but men will be required to attend to the large earthen caldrons, hung in iron frames and moved by pulleys.

The ambition of girls, then, between the ages of nine and fifteen, will not be limited to mastering the art of *making the pot boil;* they will not, however, neglect this function, and will exercise it even with skill, but their greatest distinction will spring from the culture of the arts and sciences, which they will early learn to prosecute jointly with the light branches of agriculture and manufactures.

Without this contrast of merit between the sexes from childhood up, there would be no counterpoise to the natural rudeness of boys and their inclination to despise the other sex. Girls would be entirely discouraged, and boys left without the stimulus of emulation, if there were not provided for each sex in childhood avocations in which distinction could be attained, and claims to the respect of its natural rival set up.

This rivalry is the true destiny of the female sex. The picture given of the juvenile bands is a true mirror of its future eminence, and of the important part which it is to perform even in childhood, when nature shall have resumed her sway. I have not spoken yet of the position of the sex in adult years, but simply of its general relation to the other.

Far from suspecting that woman was destined to attain distinction even in childhood in industry, science, the arts and the social virtues, man has thought only of preparing her to submit to the marriage yoke in mercenary unions. I admit that the civilized order is obliged to adopt such an abject policy; it is advocated with more insidiousness in France than elsewhere, and upheld by sophisms which are promulgated to divert women from the paths of distinction.

In childhood, they are made slaves by moral teachings; in adult years they are impelled to coquetry, and a display of foolish pride by constant flattery of their transient charms; they are encouraged to employ cunning, and to make conquests of the other sex; their frivolity is stimulated by extravagant praise; as when Diderot said, that in writing to a lady, "the pen should be dipped in the rainbow's hues, and the sheet sanded with the dust of the butterfly's wing."

What is the result of such fulsome flattery? Both sexes are duped by it; for if the social destiny of woman be not discovered, that of man will remain an enigma. If an escape from the civilized order is forbidden one of the sexes, it will be equally so to the other. There are several issues from this social abyss, which could have been discovered by a study of the social destiny of woman.

In thus doing justice to the weaker sex, I am by no means aiming to gain her approval. There is nothing to be gained in praising a slave; for the slave respects only him who is his master; and this is but too generally the character of women in the civilized order, who are indifferent to their bondage, and submit passively to a system which consigns them to the isolation and drudgery of our petty households.

The Turks teach women that *they have no souls,* and are unworthy to enter paradise. The French would persuade them that *they have no intellects,* and are not made to engage in mental labors, and to tread the paths of art and science.

It is the same doctrine in both cases, expressed in different terms—in the East rudely expressed; in the West politely uttered, though concealed under the mask of gallantry to hide the selfishness of the stronger sex in its monopoly of power and distinction.

Woman is degraded and made to believe that nature destined her exclusively to menial domestic labors, which in the com-

bined order will be so abridged as to be performed without oppression to either sex.

Madams Sévigné and de Staël were not mere housekeepers,
skimmers of pots, any more than were Elizabeth and Catherine.
In such women, we catch a glimpse of the destiny of the weaker
sex, and of those powers of mind which it will exercise with
complete success, as soon as it shall be restored to its natural
position, which is not that of the SERVANT, but of the RIVAL
of man; not that of attending to petty or menial domestic labors,
but of confounding, as they will in association, the idle doctrines of the philosophers and moralists in defense of incoherent
industry, the isolated household and the degradation of woman.

To pay them off, the sex which they have considered as fit
only to be the domestic servant of man will demonstrate the
futility of all their theories, and show that, after thirty centuries
of theorizing, they have failed entirely in the study of man,
and promulgated doctrines which have tended only to pervert
and degrade woman and thwart the development of the child,
while at the same time they have convulsed the social world
with their visionary doctrines, which have produced no other
result than to enslave entirely one sex, and the great majority
of the other.

TSO, II, pp. 239–43

WOMEN IN THE COMBINED ORDER

SOCIAL FUNCTIONS OF THE JUVENILE BANDS:
COMPOUND ERROR IN REGARD TO THE CAPACITY OF
WOMAN

The juvenile bands must consist of girls, who constitute two-
thirds of this corps; in our speculations, then, we must have regard to the ruling passion in girls, which evidently is the love of
ORNAMENT AND DRESS.

But how can we draw from such a source of frivolity a
counterpoise to great virtues, like the devotion of the legions?

A moralist would say that the love of ornament and dress can only be a source of corruption. On the contrary we shall show that the passion for dress and finery, which is now foolishly occupied with trifles, will become, when rightly directed, a second fount of social concord and unity. . . .

This corporation is to be the conservator of what may be styled *social charm;* this is apparently a less brilliant function than that of guardians of *social honor,* assigned to the legions. We shall see, however, that the functions of the former are hardly less valuable than those of the latter; and when we can apply usefully that love of dress and ornament which characterizes young girls, we shall obtain as a result the four following singular advantages:

1. Industrial refinement.
2. The reign of good taste.
3. Compound instruction.
4. Compound friendship.

✕. UNITY OF MANNERS.

The combination of these several advantages will give rise to the reign of SOCIAL CHARM or elegance and refinement in manners, exciting enthusiasm in the association for itself and for its industry, and a kind regard for strangers that visit it. We can judge of these results after a description of the functions of the corporation.

I have said that the juvenile bands are entrusted with the general supervision of the vegetable kingdom. Whoever breaks a branch from a tree, gathers fruit or flowers when there is no need, negligently treads upon a plant, is cited before their senate, which tries such cases in accordance with a penal code framed for such delinquencies, as the council of the legions tries offences against animals.

As the arbiters of good taste and industrial refinement, and as guardians of the vegetable realm, they will take especial care of flowers, which are a source of charm and refinement. They will have the same care over the lawns and flower gardens that is exercised by the legions over the highways. Flowers will be their passion; they will take charge of all floral exhibitions, and the adorning of the altars and the public halls.

This passion may excite the censure of our utilitarians, who will declare flowers altogether useless. This is a gross error. Through the passion for flowers, nature aims to attract the female sex to agriculture; for the transition is slight from the flower to the vegetable garden, and to the greenhouses and orchards. But at first the culture of flowers will be for young girls an excellent means of instruction and of acquiring agricultural skill; and will gradually interest them in other branches of agriculture.

To attain this end, the juvenile bands will be led to consider the perfection of flowers a point of honor for their corporation; they will offer premiums for success in their cultivation, and will establish in each association a school of floral art.

The combined order, in its system of education, will encourage the cultivation of both kinds of flowers—the natural and the intellectual—convinced that in the system of nature, unity of plan pervades the whole; and that if no useful function can be discovered for the passion for flowers that charm the eye, rendering it an incentive to agriculture, there can be no useful function for the flowers of the intellect; that the love of the good cannot be developed by the love of the beautiful.

We shall, however, obtain this result from a band of young girls, animated with a *collective,* not an *individual,* passion of ornament and dress. Its inclination to collective display and elegance, encouraged at the outset in matters which may seem frivolous, such as dress and flowers, will soon extend to the fine arts, and at last to industry and the sciences. (*Compound instruction, and the development of a love for the good and the beautiful conjointly.*)

As one of the effects of the serial system is to unite all branches of industry, and so to connect them in their mutual relations that one shall necessarily lead to another, it is a matter of little importance that a part of the children develop a passion for labors commonly deemed frivolous; these trifling pursuits will prepare the way for those of a useful character.

In order to secure a full development of industrial talent, a part of the children of an association should be exercised in a branch of the arts which aims at elegance and grace. This will give a charm to industry and increase the attraction for it. The juvenile bands, then, will devote themselves to the embellishment of the palace and the domain of the association; and in addition as conservators of social charm, of good taste and unity of manners, they will exercise a function similar to that of the French Academy and the Crusca, namely, the correction of the use of bad language and of faulty pronunciation.

In the combined order, purity of language will be considered a unitary grace; and in this matter, every member of the juvenile bands will be authorized to act the part of the Athenian woman, who rallied Theophrastus for his bad pronunciation. The senate of the bands has not only the supervision of the language of children, but the right of criticizing adults themselves by written communications; it will make out a list of the errors in grammar or pronunciation to which any member of the association is addicted, and send him a copy of them, signed by the presiding officer of the body, with a recommendation to correct them.

But will they have attained sufficient knowledge of letters to perform so difficult a task? Doubtless this right of criticism would not be granted them, except to incite them to study. Every branch of industry needs its incentive; now, the *right of criticism* and the *honor of the corporation* are already a twofold incentive.

The distinction attached to these various functions will be needed to attract young boys of a studious turn to join juvenile bands and to counterbalance the influence of the rival corporation. This literary distinction of the bands, their supervision of good manners, will produce a further good result; they will give rise to *corporate pride,* and as a consequence to COMPOUND FRIENDSHIP, or that which extends from each member to the entire body. This sentiment is quite unknown in the civilized order, in which women generally criticize their own sex, are acquainted only with simple or individual friendship, and are penetrated with a selfish love of ostentation, prizing display only so far as their poorer neighbors are debarred from it.

The juvenile bands are enemies of this anti-social vanity; stimulated by the noble examples of virtue and charity exhibited by the legions, they strive to equal them so far as their functions will allow. They occupy themselves with elegance and ornament only in a collective capacity, and for the general credit of the association. A rich applicant, upon her admission, will present some ornament to her division, and if her means are sufficient, to the whole band. She would be condemned if she were suspected of being actuated by a contracted or mercenary spirit.

Like the legions, the bands have the privilege of initiating certain ceremonies and enterprises. Whenever works of pleasure and elegance are undertaken, such as the preparation of ornaments for a series, for a temple or its ritual, for halls of industry or the opera, the juvenile bands will take the lead, and open the work.

They will rarely appear at the industrial armies; but when they do, it will be in the capacity of attendants of the legions, who are allowed the privilege of opening and closing enterprises in which strength is required, such as the placing of the key-stone of an arch, after having already laid its corner-stone.

If the combined order, by granting certain honorable distinctions, has the skill to encourage the legions to engage in repulsive labors, it must by other distinctions attract the juvenile bands to works of skill and taste, particularly in literature, the arts, and delicate handicraft. As this corporation is in great part composed of females, it ought, according to the natural order of things, to have a fondness for all mental and material labors which do not require physical strength.

Besides, in the combined order study will be a much more easy pursuit than in the present order; this will be the result of unitary methods of instruction; in addition to the advantages derived from these methods will be the two which spring from the rivalries of the series, and the introduction of the science of universal analogy.

We already begin to discern the error which prevails in regard to woman's capacity; her genius has been very falsely estimated by our analysts, who have been unable to appreciate either the woman or the child.

As regards woman's capacity for study, they have fallen into a fourfold error. First, they have overlooked the principle of *compound adornment,* internal or external.

1. The *internal compound*—beauty of the body, separate from external vesture; this will be treated in the chapter devoted to integral gymnastics.

2. *Compound external*—the adorning of both body and mind, their simultaneous culture. We ought not only to encourage the passion for dress and ornament in women, but seek to make it contribute to the adorning of the mind by connecting it with the culture of the arts and sciences; and, on the ground of the necessity of establishing *compound unitary elegance,* should seek to make the adorning of the body and the mind keep pace with each other.

To these two oversights, two others are to be added.

3. They have been ignorant of the fact that this unitary elegance should be collective and not individual; and that it can produce beneficent results only as applied to masses, composed of persons who, possessing unequal fortunes, are still united by corporate sympathy.

4. Lastly, woman in this new career—with the three conditions above mentioned—would still be deprived of adequate incentives to action unless stimulated by the rivalry of the other sex.

If these four conditions, however, are observed, women will excel in those various arts and sciences from which the male sex would now exclude them. The true germ of this possible perfection in the development of woman's nature is to be found in the love of elegance and refinement, which is the incentive to all those works of collective embellishment and artistic refinement in which she will excel. The error committed in regard to the capacity of woman, then, is fourfold, based on a complete ignorance, analytical and synthetical, of her nature and social destiny.

Thus will be confounded that insulting and vandal philosophy, which, with all its pompous pretensions to be the disseminator of intelligence, would condemn to ignorance one half of the human species, by compelling woman to stultify herself in the petty and menial labors of the isolated household, where her natural faculties find no scope for expansion.

The combined order, on the contrary, pursuing an opposite policy, would make the female the COUNTERPOISE and not the SERVANT of the male sex; this equilibrium will be established even in childhood by means of the corporation of the juvenile bands. . . .

A cultivation of refined tastes is the function of the juvenile bands; they possess a faculty for the perception of delicate shades and varieties, which creates divisions, and gives rise to as many groups as there are varieties. This faculty is to be found in those children only who, having a passion for ornament and elegance in dress, are capable, as a consequence, of discerning artistic refinement in all those branches of industry in which they engage.

It is for the juvenile bands to inspire the whole body of children with that taste for graduated and contrasted shades or varieties, without which it would be impossible to transcend the lower degrees of skill in agriculture and the arts, or create higher incentives to industry. Now, if the association is to feel a pride and enthusiasm for itself and its works, it should provide itself with whatever will invest it with charms and attractions, such as flowers and elegant costumes, and consider the care of the one, and attention to the other, as opening the way from the beautiful to the good—from the culture of the arts to the study of the sciences. . . .

TSO, II, pp. 231–37

POLYGAMOUS BONDS

Let us proceed step by step toward the art of utilizing polygamous love, thought to be criminal. We will first examine its germ, consecutive infidelity, from which we will very quickly arrive at cumulative or plural love. Let us explain how harmony speculates upon this infidelity in order to arrive at the equilibrated testament, which is the most brilliant effect of familial harmony. Our philosophers, all of whom are fond of preaching against this branch of harmony, did not suspect that it was from this branch that would come harmony's luster and its most precious bond, the dissemination of heritages. Without this custom all visions of fraternity fail since fraternity cannot exist when the poor have nothing to hope from the rich, as is the case in our family system. We will see that infidelity and inconstancy, the goal of our jaded satyrs, is a gauge of the advent of fraternal union, so clamored for by philosophers. The secret views of everyone will be well served in teaching the art of utilizing infidelity. One sees nothing in civilizee love but the multitude's penchant for amorous bigamy and for the accumulation of two, three, or four intrigues. This merits a special chapter of analysis.

Our objective will be to understand the effects of libertinage and of impatience with the marital yoke in conjunction with the effect of the polygamous character. These effects of amorous infidelity have very precious properties unknown to civilization.

This is a very delicate question which will cause all prudes to crow over the fine principles they practice so little.

Let us begin by unmasking them. In regard to this subject every prude makes a rivalry of hypocrisy; however, nine-tenths of all civilizees are bigamists or polygamists in love.

In this fine world, which harps on morality, one meets everywhere people who exercise polygamy very basely, like young men who pride themselves on sharing a woman with her husband, or like women who extend this sharing to several lovers concurrently with the husband. Add to this a swarm of accessory and fleeting love affairs, or reminiscences, and it will be agreed that all this sanctimonious, prudish world which is surnamed high society, that this heap of libertines and intriguers who disguise themselves behind a verbiage of fidelity, is a bigamous, trigamous, and polygamous world in every degree. These hypocrites should thus not be astonished by a theory which is an apology of certain cases of polygamy, those of love alliances with friendship and familyism. I will not justify wholesale infidelity, but I will prove that it is useful and praiseworthy

in harmony when it is freely consented to. Those who hasten
to invalidate my thesis will surely be the most guilty in these
matters, because false prudes always rise up violently against
the vice from which they secretly profit.

There will be two principal modes of infidelity to distinguish,
consecutive and cumulative. Let us first treat infidelity in the
consecutive mode.

Inconstancy is almost universal in the case of all civilizees
who enjoy total freedom. Each civilizee, man or woman, is
secretly given to inconstancy. There are very few exceptions.
But in order to discern those who engage in simple infidelity,
which leads to forgetfulness of past loves, from those who practice composed infidelity, which carries on friendship despite the
end of love, some touchstone must be used. Properties useful
to inconstancy must be assigned and verified for each subject,
if he is gifted with the precious property of conserving friendship after love.

Let us first establish the vicious side of inconstancy. In attraction, all that which diminishes the number of bonds and
virtue is called vice, all which augments it [   ]. I refer to
the definition given [   ]. Thus, characters who are subject
to forgetting the ones they have loved, or who are subject to
conserving friendship for them after ceasing to love them, remain to be classified. The 130 polygynes, for the most part,
have the property of conserving friendship after love; their inconstancy turns entirely to the profit of virtue. A female polygyne who has had twelve lovers, and who conserves friendship
for the twelve while reserving love for the thirteenth, has by
means of this inconstancy formed twelve amicable bonds which
would not exist had she been constant. From among the 576
monogynes, divided into twelve classes, there are hardly three
who have friendship, ambition, or a composite dominant, or
who have the property of steadfastly conserving friendship after
love. Thus three-fourths of all monogynes are vicious (520 out
of 576) in regard to constancy.

Monogynes of familyism preserve affection for a wife or a
husband after love has ceased. This is a bond of family or house-

hold spirit rather than the effect of friendship, which is devotion of a very different kind. (Similarly there are monogynes of ambition who, after love has passed, conserve a bond of intrigue rather than of sentiment.) Thus monogyne spouses confuse this familial and household affection or this league of interest and cabalistic spirit with love or friendship, without having had either of them. These distinctions that I have established [   ] also include the league of ambition, which is often very strong between two inconstant spouses, and very different from love.

It may be objected that civilizee inconstancy has some very serious disadvantages, such as adultery, fornication, and other disorders not compensated by amicable bonds. But I speak here in a general sense in connection with known social periods, the seventh [   ], where adultery and permanent marriage do not exist. Here inconstancy becomes exempt of danger, and useful as well when it leaves behind bonds of friendship.

To give an example of this usefulness I will cite only the custom of legacy, which is very general in harmony, and bestowed upon all fond souvenirs of love, friendship, etc. If a wealthy woman has passionately and ardently loved fifty men in the course of her life, and in such a manner as to pass some time with each of them and to conserve friendship for them, she will not fail to leave them legacies in her will. If she fails to do this she will be accused during her lifetime of vice, and of ingratitude for those to whom she owes happy days. Legacies will not be extended to casual lovers. This lady will have had perhaps a thousand or two thousand men in caravan seraglios, orgies, adventures, and army bacchanals. Legacies are not left to this myriad of transient lovers, but only to those with whom she has carried on a passion of several months. She will be obliged, according to opinion, to bequeath to these lovers a sum or else run the risk of passing for a simple character, a civilizee soul unfitted to the social virtues, who has conserved no souvenir of the bonds which were one of the charms of her life.

Thus fraternity—the general good will so desired by our savants—will have one of its sources in virtuous inconstancy, the sort of inconstancy that leaves bonds of friendship after it.

This is truly a shameful aspect of civilizees; nothing is more odious than their almost universal custom of completely forgetting the very people they have idolized. One can say to them —either you were very blind, very stupidly inspired in that violent transport for a being unworthy of a friendly remembrance; or else you are today very ungrateful, very egoistic to conserve no affection for the being whom you must have [   ]; furthermore it is not unfounded to predict that you will similarly forget the person to whom you are attached today, and that in a year's time you will judge him worthy of nothing. This ingratitude remains one of the distasteful sides of civilization, where one encounters nothing but characters indifferent to all they have loved in the past. Civilizees concentrate all their affection upon one woman and a few children, and are encouraged in this vile egoism. They are titled tender fathers and tender republicans by a mob of moralists who esteem only one of the four bonds, that of parentism or the clublike factions disguised by fatherland. Monogynes are, for the most part, especially subject to this ignoble penchant of which I just spoke—they are forgetful of people they have loved and left. One half of the 576 monogynes will reply that a mistress [   ]⁴ would rightly suspect reminiscence [   ] proves civilization to be unskilled at two things—sincere friendship and celadony [sic]. If a friend were sincere he would not cuckold so much; if celadony were sincere one would not doubt so much; if truth and publicity were guaranteed one would not fear encountering old lovers so much.

The principal goal of harmony is to maintain the balance of the four affections and to blend them in every sense. Thus in an equilibrated testament, [   ] legacies should be classed according to bonds of the four affections. What rank will legacies of love occupy if men become austere republicans, favoring only their sanctimonious spouse and forgetting all the women they loved before her?

In harmony this egoism would cause even monogynes to

⁴ Illegible word in manuscript.—Ed.

blush, whose character is very inclined to forget all past bonds of love in favor of the present one. However this does not prevent the majority of polygynes from conserving a lively affection for past lovers. Still this is not yet composed fidelity, since it leaves only friendship after love has ceased. It is mixed fidelity which is as worthy of praise as simple fidelity, or consecutive forgetfulness, is worthy of scorn.

To conclude we will see whether the kind of fidelity of which I just spoke [   ] attains its goal of effecting alliances and composites of the four affectionate passions. The distribution of legacies to all loved ones creates a true alloy of love and of familyism—it assimilates lovers to the family, and extends the bond of family through inconstant love. Among us the family tends to be reduced [   ] by exclusive marriage; it prevents an alloy between love and familyism, and it confines the bonds of these two passions to a most circumscribed alliance, since the alliance of marriage restricts all bonds of inheritance to a single couple and to a single family line.

Does harmony exist in a bond which extends only to a very limited family? Does it exist in a bond that renders the family an enemy inclined to despoil all neighboring families? Such is the effect of the civilizee order.

From this chapter it can be concluded that good is always born of composition, as witnessed by inconstancy which in the simple order, as in civilization produces vices of all kinds. In a composed order which unites two passions—friendship for old lovers and love for present lovers—inconstancy becomes a germ of equilibrated testament. This is one of the most precious gauges of social harmony, and one of the principal springs of rallying between rich and poor. . . .

The question of fidelity and infidelity is similar to all questions around which debate gathers. The result is that one becomes attached only to the superficial, only to the witty repartee furnished by the debate. As many systems arise as there are individuals [   ], and he who, like certain vestals of whom I will speak, maintains that an infidelity is of no importance, that it is a small oversight, will be just as right as he who praises fidelity.

The first distinction to establish on this point is between simple fidelity and composed fidelity, which is unknown. Simple fidelity is what our philosophers demand. It is exclusive cohabitation with a single object; it has the very infamous property of successive forgetfulness. Men and women who remain totally faithful to each of their favorites are accustomed to forgetting all preceding lovers in favor of the dominant one. Oronte, a monogyne, was faithful for ten years to ten women with whom he lived successively; in the eleventh year he became fond of an eleventh woman and forgot the other ten, as if he had never known them. He became totally indifferent to their well-being, and soon he similarly forgot his eleventh mistress in favor of a twelfth that he took in the twelfth year. Monogynes are like this; they boast of a rigorous fidelity and truly observe it for as long as the amorous bond lasts, after which they fall into a perfect indifference toward those whom they have loved. This behavior, simple fidelity, is disdainful in that it leaves no trace of a bond. Only composed fidelity in a high degree is esteemed in harmony. This is the attribute of polygynes who create a pivotal love to which all other intrigues ally themselves. This kind of fidelity is often established in marriage through a spirit of ambition and parentism. A woman may have twenty consecutive lovers and yet conserve amorous tenderness for her husband, who binds together the whole. It is composed fidelity that becomes the pivot of other bonds of the same type, and is concurrently maintained with them. . . .

We have arrived at the most criticized type of infidelity, polygamy, in which several loves are carried on at the same time. This so-called vice has some brilliant functions in harmony that civilizees do not hasten to find fault with because, I repeat, the prudes who condemn polygamous love are in secret its most ardent disciples.

Amorous polygamy, graduated according to degrees, is the quality of essence and of alternation in the case of polygynes.

For example a trigyne will love three men simultaneously in her periods of alternation; the pentagyne will love five, the heptagyne seven at a time, and the omnigyne will love eight, with transition. Let us note that my estimates are based on the average; I do not mean that a heptagyne, each time she ends a liaison of exclusive love will become impassioned the following month for seven other lovers, but in periods of alternation she can love seven at a time, and accord to each a dose of love strong enough to charm him. Whereas when a trigyne loves three men in a period of alternation, she will not have love enough for a fourth aspirant, or if she accepts, she will cease to love one of the three others. Her cumulative degree is fixed at three, save by exception, as these estimations are merely averages which are not invariable. Thus a trigyne who enters into alternation of love twenty times will notice that she has sometimes two, sometimes four, but on the average three men at a time, which is also the customary proportion of honest civilizee women. A pentagyne, upon making the same count, will see that her average of alternation is five men at a time. If some lady is horrified by this number, she can be suspected of being a pentagyne herself and of secretly anticipating harmony's license. In harmony this plurality of loves has some very precious properties in the case of polygynes, such as the aforementioned equilibrated testament established by cumulative as well as by consecutive love, both of which are advantageous when they attain this goal.

Let us examine polygamous love in the various degrees, first in the case of monogynes, where it is reputed to be libertinism since it leaves no trace of friendship. However it is no less useful to the services of caravan seraglios in the army and to indulgenced[5] polygamy. A dancing girl would be vicious in the social mechanism if she were to love exclusively; she would then be unapproachable to all but transient lovers. Her destination is just the opposite. The more she flatters and satisfies aspirants the more she will excel in her duties. In harmony

[5] Fourier is alluding to the Roman Catholic practice of indulgences. —Ed.

virtue consists in forming the greatest possible number of bonds
of all kinds, which is to say that if loves of exclusive bond are
necessary, then loves of multiple bonds, like those of caravan
seraglios, are necessary as well. Social perfection is to effect for
each kind of love the number of functionaries suitable to the
balance. Whatever the number of dancing girls, it is certain that
they will only be esteemed in proportion to their ability to carry
on several loves at the same time. Even if there should remain
no trace of friendship, they will have excelled no less in their
kind of love, where sentimental souvenirs are unnecessary. They
deal with travellers who, if worse comes to worse, need only the
affection of a moment. Things will only go better if [   ] . . .

Let us go on to polygynes and first to the ninety-six digynes,
those who will be attached to corporate bodies of the priesthood; shamans, bacchants, dancers, etc. They will be as perfect
in their loves of religious function as in their fleeting loves.
They will be able to accumulate other sustained passions of several months' duration, inspiring an amicable souvenir. They
will have thus another bond with the tourbillon and will be of
greater weight in its general harmony.

Trigynes, tetragynes, etc., being able to carry on three and
four celadonic or polygamous loves simultaneously, will also
be valuable in the case of sacerdotal function. But we must
examine the practice of polygamy outside the priesthood. Polygamy furnishes us with three chances of speculative harmony
—wealth, poverty, and mixed.

First, the case of the wealthy. The omnigyne Artémise possesses a fortune of twelve million. According to the count of her
alternations, she will frequently carry on eight passions simultaneously. Consequently at the age of eighty she will have loved
in 400 alternations about 1200 men and 600 women from the
forty tourbillons subject to her passional administration. All this
is independent of sacerdotal loves and army loves which are
neither counted nor registered by the clerk of love, unless a passion is declared to him.

In making her will, Artémise leaves a sum of three million to
her lovers of alternation, from a total of twelve million (two

to her friends, three to her cabalists of the series, and four to her relatives). She divides them into three classes, the first = 750 to 2000 to 1,500,000, the second = 600 = 1600 to 960,-000 and the third = 450 = 1200 to 540,000 [sic]. These distinctions are all classified in the amorous archives of the court of love. Each regular liaison is mentioned in the records, and in the annual table of relationships, which are extremely accurate. Thus here are 1800 people who have modest legacies to inherit from the affluent Artémise. Today her colossal fortune would be the prey of a half-dozen wicked inheritors who would hasten her to her grave. In harmony she will subdivide her fortune, either in titles of love or in other cardinal titles to a host of legatees, for whom a small legacy (or a considerable inheritance) will not be a motive for desiring her death since each one of them annually receives similar legacies in the four titles, and since they all have a patrimony of industrial earnings, etc. Artémise will have 1800 friends simply in souvenir of her loves of alternation or inconstancy. Those among them who, by monogynie, conserve no friendship for her will get small sums by way of legacy, or by virtue of other motives arising from cabals of industrial function. Thus harmony knows how to take advantage of inconstancy to create legions of friends for everyone. Is this not the goal desired by the philosophers who want to render us all brothers? Is it not obvious that harmony knows how to attain this goal through the use of all the springs, inconstancy and others, that philosophers damn and call vices?

If we speculate upon the chance of poverty, we will see that the omnigyne Irus, without possessing a farthing of patrimony, will have at the age of eighty a swarm of legacies, perhaps a thousand more already collected than he still has to collect, due to the single factor of amorous polygamy, since all who die wealthy leave something to their loves of alternation (who are nonetheless related by secondary bonds because the notable favorites are classed as friends). This is how free love, reputed among us to be a vice, becomes the most philanthropic of all harmonian springs. Thus God, who well foresaw the extreme utility of love, made it the strongest of the four cardinal passions and multiplied the means of prolonging its duration beyond civilization's limits.

Harmonians, convinced of the philanthropic power of polygamous love, envision it in a way opposed to contemporary prejudice. In harmony seven men will honor one another for having been loved all at the same time by a certain heptagyne. They will admire her vast sensibility and the varied development of her tenderness which sufficed to charm all seven of them simultaneously. A very beautiful effect of amorous alternation is to stimulate corporative friendship between harmonians who have cumulatively figured in an alternation. It must be remarked that this friendship is stayed by a swarm of bonds and cabals described in the treatise on the series, bonds which are replaced by seeds of enmity in civilization.

We have seen that the alternations of each polygyne generally exist in harmony in relation to their degree with the year; which is to say that a digyne will commonly have six months of exclusive love and then six months of multiple love with two passions, the trigyne will have a third of the year, four months, of exclusive love and a third of multiple with three loves, and thus the omnigyne will have an eighth of the year in exclusive love and one-eighth in multiple of eight loves. This is an estimate of the average.

The polygynes in this [   ] fill their character destination of double scale which should give effects proportionately contrasted in constancy and inconstancy, like all other [   ] of passion.

When a tourbillon is well balanced, when its general keyboard of characters is regularly assorted with all kinds of keys, it will frequently happen that the polygynes have in their cumulative loves an assortment analogous to their dominants. The tetragyne Henry IV will love in alternation or in *papillon* four women, each having as dominant one of Henry's dominants, then he will love pivotally a polygyne of his degree. These proportions seem unimportant in the civilizee mechanism; they are precious in harmony in relation to interest, etc. . . . because a tourbillon that is well equilibrated in love affairs will be

equally so in industrial attraction, and its products will be
proportionately superior to a tourbillon of the same situation
whose general keyboard of character and of sympathy is poorly
balanced. All the branches of harmony are bound together, and
what was stated in the antiphon of the ninth section regarding
the bonds of amorous harmony with industrial and productive
harmony could well be repeated here.

Thus are monogynes utilized and collocated in transcendent
love. In the measure that harmony extends bonds in a superior
degree, it rallies that which was not capable of being rallied in
an inferior degree.

The more one is steeped in these details, the more one is
tempted to believe that they are pure fantasy, since civilization
in no sense offers a similar development. But civilization is a
mechanism of general subversion which suppresses and traves-
ties everything. Kings, for example [   ] in every sense by
etiquette, have almost no means of abandoning themselves to
multiple and alternating loves. They would be obliged to
[   ] a *parc aux cerfs,* like Louis XV, or disguised seraglios
like certain educational establishments very accessible to kings.
The travesty takes on other forms in the case of private individuals.

From this sketch let us conclude against the philosophic system which restricts love. The examples of Artémise and Irus,
omnigynes having immensely varied liaisons, permit us to estimate in decreasing progression the sum of legacies that the
mixed class receives, of whom I have not spoken. A tetragyne
who has markedly fewer liaisons than Irus will have fewer
legacies in the title of love; perhaps he will have more in function of friendship or constant love. But let us limit ourselves to
our subject, to polygamous love envisioned in the order that I
have just described.

Here are men organized by this single spring into great families having as support, as legatees, all that surrounds them. Irus
has 1800 legacies to collect in the title of love alone, some of
which may come from women far away whom he has loved in
his travels. Is not this mode of inheritance, which is subdivided

into four titles and distributed from each of the four to a large number of lovers, friends, leaguers, and parents, the true bond of family? Is not the man who supports the poor with a parcel of his fortune their true parent? Of what use is a blood bond if it fails to assure the poor the pecuniary aid of the rich? To make a large family of mankind, to invent one or another kind of love bond matters little, provided that the goal is attained—to interest the rich in support of the poor and to interest the poor in loving the rich who support them. Such is the way in which harmony develops the four cardinal affections, and desires their infinite development in opposition to the philosophic system of restriction limited to couples, to the tender household, which leaves only a minimum development and transforms each family into a group of tigers and political serpents set upon despoiling and triumphing over all their neighbors. Civilization has made the human heart the receptacle of all vice. What is needed to correct this is not a heap of volumes and precepts, but a mechanism conceived in opposition to this civilization which establishes man in a state of war with all his fellows and makes each family the secret enemy of every other family. Since the contemporary system of minimum association restricted by the isolation of households has led mankind to an excess of perversity, it is necessary to put to the test the opposite system of immense association (of which the treatise on the series, sections 3 and 4, determine the highest possible degree), if one wants to elevate mankind to reason, so often used as embellishment.

Association only grows by extending bonds; to arrive at its highest degree each bond must be raised from the simple to the composed, to the omnimode, and to all mixed or ambiguous modes. But the civilizee order is set up in such a way that the bonds become detrimental to the mass as soon as they are extended. Large commercial association only engenders monopolists, hoarders, and stockjobbers who reduce the people to famine; large assemblies of pleasure only engender adultery, fornication, debauchery, and other proscribed pleasures; large political meetings only work to undermine the government, and to ferment revolt and conflagration. It follows that the oracles

of incoherence, the philosophers and the theologians, condemn
all bonds that tend toward the highest degree of expression, and
toward the omnimode. They are right, since these bonds produce
evil in civilization, and because association is suited only to the
order of the passional series. But they are wrong in the abstract
because bonds are commendable in and of themselves. Instead
of rigidly proscribing them as harmful to civilization, one must
seek another society where these bonds can become practicable
and beneficial. Now that this order is discovered we can discard
all the theories of incoherence that condemn the bonds that
civilization does not know how to utilize; harmony will know
how to employ these bonds for the happiness of mankind.

NMA, pp. 272–85

THE NEW FAMILY

Children, like savages, give us warnings in social politics:
their repugnance for our work is a judgment of reprobation
pronounced by nature.

Nature serves to notify us, by way of savages and children,
that our industrial method is contrary to her design. When
children want to work on Sundays, and savages want to labor
and plant, we will be able to believe that humanity has taken
nature's path, that it has at last discovered its destiny.

In order to lead humanity in this direction it is necessary
that it be made to see, through an experiment of combined industry, that family households or fragmented industry are the
source of evil morals and poverty.

Future generations, and our own shortly, will have trouble
understanding that a century possessed of so many treatises and
sects of economism did not envision the necessity of uniting into
combined households at least the lower classes and the needy
families who are unable to keep separate, tiny households.

Upon seeing the advantages, the conveniences, and the
enormous profits which will be born of this union, when it
includes a sufficient number of families (*minimum* 120), the

rich will promptly imitate it. From this will be engendered the seventh social period which will organize the combined family into three classes of fortune. The discovery of the means to unite the three classes in combined exercise will directly follow.

If well-off families want to live in isolated households there is no disadvantage other than the expense, which they can afford. But since the people are not able to pay the cost of isolated cooking and heating, they must be brought to the associative family *willingly or in spite of themselves*. They must be made to accept the combined education of children which is the most costly branch of the civilizee system, since the care of children occupies ten times more women than in the combined order, and the mortality rate of children is three times as great.

When municipalities or charitable institutions build fires in winter for the poor, 500 to 600 people are assembled and heated cheaply, since two or three large stoves heat one vast hall, instead of one hundred stoves to heat 100 isolated families.

Experiments of combination in cooking and the care of small children must be made with small households. Large economic unions must be tried as in the case of heating for large numbers of people. But these must be graduated and unequal unions because equality is antipathetic to harmony; Owen's reunions failed because of equality. If only this could have been tried with 120 families, classed in three degrees and with three slightly different prices of subscription, the natural procedure or series of groups ranked by nuances of function and character would have been discovered. This would establish the accord of the masses upon individual discord and the scale of inequality.

As long as we are ignorant of the means to utilize discord we are outside the path of nature which, having created as many discords as accords, must have considered the means of utilizing both. This is in spite of philosophers who desire that we all be *brothers*, that we all be of one opinion like the brothers Cain and Abel, Eteocles and Polynices, Don Pedro and Don Miguel. . . . Cain cannot help but be Abel's brother; whereas two friends separate if they no longer suit one another, as do two lovers or two associates. The three groups friendship, love, and corporative ambition are free bonds; the bond of family is not. Thus God would be an enemy of freedom if he had chosen as the base and pivot of social mechanism the only group which is not free.

His choice is just the opposite. Here is the system:

Out of the four groups He gives preference to the two *major* groups, corporative ambition and friendship, because they do not depend upon the material, as do the two *minor* groups, love and family. The major groups are more identical to God who is the soul of the universe, the prime mover of matter.

He admits in support of these two groups the influence of certain branches such as the group of love, in so far as it is *free*, which it will be during the eras when marriage will comprise twelve degrees, rather than one single degree as it does in the confused method of the civilizees. This order will be postponed for about one century. But God in no case admits that the family group shall direct the harmonian mechanism.

On the contrary, the family group will be absorbed and will lose all influence in favor of work, the sharing of profit, and *industrial* advancement.

The family group will conserve its influence in hereditary advancement, which will be much more assured than in the civilizee era, for the branches of administration will be hereditarily constituted, like legacies and sovereignties of all degrees from the first to the thirteenth. . . .

Children's affection for fathers will already be three times what it is today because fathers, instead of moralizing to and constraining the child, will only have to admire him. This triple affection of children will be only one of the three sources of filial love that fathers will enjoy. Thus in family bonds fathers will be nine times happier than they are at present, thanks to the exclusion of the family group from social politics, of which it is presently the pivot.

The twenty-eight characters allotted below to the family group would furnish matter for twenty-eight chapters.

It will be necessary to slide over such a vast subject. Let us limit ourselves to a general conclusion: philosophy is very deceptive; it pretends to analysis while only writing apologies for civilization. Philosophy is very much an enemy of truth. In light of the preceding picture, and those that I have painted elsewhere, it can be seen how fertile such a subject can be if it is sketched with a truthful pen.

If philosophers thought by analogy, as they claim to do, they would have considered that the family, materially envisioned, has the property of *degeneration by internal alliance*. A family that will not marry outside itself, and that, like Adam's family, marries brothers with sisters, falls in a few generations into physical degeneration.

It should be inferred that nature, which desires material growth, desires by analogy also spiritual growth. Thus she gives children characters and tastes different from those of their father. It follows that the family group is heterogeneous within itself: a doctor's son will not like the profession of medicine; a wealthy merchant's son will not like business; a housewife's daughter will be coquettish.

In daily life the members of a family seek only to flee from one another. The child wants to play with the neighborhood children; the young man wants to go to a spectacle or a coffeehouse against the wishes of a frugal father; the young lady would rather go to a ball than to a sermon. The tender mother would like to neglect the pots and pans to pander in neighborhood gossip, and to make acquaintances dangerous to conjugal honor. Finally, the father wants to maintain relationships at his club, at coffeehouses, and at cabalistic meetings, for which he neglects his sad household.

The familial union presents as well a mixture of inconvenient ages and characters that inhibit conversation. Morality engenders a frigid atmosphere, as in all places where it reigns.

Thus the family is a group which needs to escape from itself, and to branch out in all directions, in social relations as in the material relation of reproduction.

It follows that in order to utilize the family and to satisfy its natural impulses, an order must be invented that operates a spiritual intermingling of characters, passions, instincts, and tastes, in industry as in pleasure. Our sluggards, called philosophers, have never taken the trouble to research the function nature intended for this raw material named *families*. In order to dispense with invention, they imagined the family to be the pivot of the social mechanism, of which it is but a crude element. They wanted to co-ordinate all relations to the design of the family, which is the enemy of the social state. Each family seeks to deceive the mass; to usurp by astuteness, larceny, and violence. The family refuses the collective solidarity that would benefit the poor branches of society such as children, the infirm, and the unemployed.

The family is thus an antisocial spring in both an individual and a collective sense. The invention of a new order was needed to transform this caterpillar into a butterfly.

OC, VIII, pp. 197–99, 202–4

V. LOVE

A SOCIOLOGY OF LOVE

What are you thinking of to choose such a subject? Write on love? One must have the pen of Tibullus or Parthenius—it requires so much finesse, such a light touch!

Really! According to Diderot it requires a pen dipped in a rainbow and the dust of butterfly wings. By paying us with such talk sophists give us the change for their ineptitude in calculations of amorous or minor politics; they occupy us exclusively with the ambitious or major politics they have so cleverly treated, especially in this generation.

Without having recourse to either rainbows or butterflies I am going to present love from a point of view more worthy of interesting honest people. I am going to show them that in the theory of love one error alone is enough to overturn the whole structure of politics and civilizee morals.

The regime of love is organized upon *general constraint* and consequently upon *general falsity;* it is a coercive regime because there is falsity everywhere. Prohibition and contraband are inseparable in love, as in merchandise. If love is opposed by prohibitive laws you can be sure that it will retort with general contraband.

Consequently all family relations are corrupt. Fathers are deceived by wives and daughters who hide their love and are obstinately opposed to fathers' impulses of fidelity, marriage, etc. Moreover fathers are deceived about the origin of their own children. This is the most odious of all social perfidies, although the subject of many jokes. (Kean, Beaumarchais, Joconde.)

Meanwhile our equilibrists want to found public and private happiness on the respectable order of the family. We will thus examine how the falsity of love throws disorder into families, and consequently into the whole social system. This will be a *graduated thesis*, treating first the parts and then moving progressively to the whole.

This seems necessary in response to premature criticism. . . . Everyone will rise up against the idea of giving freedom of choice to young ladies, despite my observation that this regime will be established only after two generations, and that it will be conducted so as to give happiness to fathers as well as to children.

It is fitting to calm these impatient souls with a negative reply —with a picture of the disorders engendered by their methods, which produce effects contrary to the good they promise. This is the practice of philosophy; is it not followed in the regime of love, as in all branches of the social mechanism?

Yet if sophists have the zeal for truth that they boast of, should they not applaud the idea of making truth dominant in love? Truth has been so well banished from love that the means of introducing it have never been considered. The difficulty seemed insurmountable.

This obstacle, like so many others, collapses in face of the passional series. But let us concentrate on the object of this interlude, which is purely negative, having no other goal than to record contemporary evil and to dampen the fire of the sophists who cry out "that all is lost if their coercive and fomenting methods of masking falseness under the guise of truth are departed from."

Love, in appearance a most frivolous subject, will be linked to the gravest problem, *the reign of truth*. First let us give a fixed compass reading on the function of truth. . . .

We will go on in the next book to the calculations most frightening to human politics: *passional equilibrium*. How great our frustration will be, in a study such as this, if we do not have a theoretical and practical compass reading on the function of truth, gauge of all material and passional equilibrium!

As for the present, where is truth to be found in the two principal passional branches, the relations of love and ambition? These are pits of falsity. We have hardly worried about love, because we thought it was outside the domain of social politics and good only to occupy Colin and Colette.

Far from it—this passion will present to us problems of equilibrium even more difficult than those of ambition because in passional mechanism, as in music, the minor order has fewer accords than the major.

What will become, however, of the calculations of attraction or spontaneous harmony if they do not extend to love as well as to ambition, and if we do not manage to establish the full dominance of truth in love? This will be the most complicated of all equilibriums, with the most far-reaching ramifications and springs. Minds must be disposed far in advance: thus the object of this interpreliminary is to analyze our social absurdities in the minor mode, and to analyze the errors of the civilizee regime in relations of love and family.

The question should be envisioned in a political, moral and religious sense according to a pledge taken to simultaneously satisfy these three authorities.

Moreover the three interests will become more and more complicated in the course of discussion. I remind you that under the name of *social truth* I designate practicable and practiced truth, reality rather than illusion.

1. POLITICS. Its object is to found domestic happiness upon respectable morals and family union, and consequently upon the practice of truth. Ruse and perfidy can only engender discord.

As a general principle truth cannot be introduced into family relations if it does not prevail in love relations. Let us analyze the state of truth in both of them.

Politics establishes quadruplicity of action in the system of education, the primordial branch of familyism.

The whole system of politics in love is similarly falsified and organized by a quadruplicity of action and conflict which I will analyze.

QUADRILLE OF EROTIC CONFLICT
K. Composed Seraglios

1. Venal love;   3. Morals of low society;
2. Secret love;   4. Morals of high society;

X. Constrained or Legal Love.

The detailed examination of these vices will prove the sound-
ness of the principle that "domestic or familial happiness is inseparable from truth in the regime of love. If politics lacks
equilibrium in love relations, equilibrium will also be lacking
in family relations; and if falsity prevails in love then it will
prevail as a consequence in the domestic or familial mechanism."
Let us proceed to an examination of falsity and conflict in the
regime of civilizee love.

K. COMPOSED SERAGLIOS.

True seraglios exist in all civilizee countries where slavery
prevails. Colonialists make seraglios of their black woman; the
staid Dutch in Batavia have seraglios stocked with white,
mulatto, and black women. This is a meshing of barbarian customs characteristic of transition; I note it with the sign K.

Seraglios exist, although in small number, in countries
exempt from slavery. One existed at Versailles under the name
Parc aux Cerfs. How many houses, disguised under a mask of
decency and a pompous title, have been fine seraglios secretly
open to high and powerful masters! Furthermore, does not a
rich civilizee have full license to form for himself a small seraglio, either at home or elsewhere? to set to work intelligent
matrons who know how to procure for him women and girls
of noble lineage, the numerous family d'Argencour?[1]

Up to now the abuse has been simple, merely an imitation
of barbarian customs which proscribe religion and morals. But
the civilizee order, as I have pointed out more than once, has the
property of elevating to the composed mode all the vices that
barbarism exercises in the simple mode. The latter has only

[1] Pun in French upon the words "argent" = money and "court" =
conjugation of the verb "to run."—Translator's note.

permanent and *compulsive* seraglios; civilization, as we have just seen, establishes similar ones and includes *vague* or *free* seraglios as well.

What is a vague seraglio? It is the following of all young men much favored by nature and even slightly favored by fortune.

How is a vague seraglio organized? For this information we can turn to the Knight Joconde, who appears on stage to tell the story of his style of life in a *vague seraglio.*

> Without being proud of my fidelity,
> I flew from love to love.
> I've always loved only beauties;
> But for scarcely more than a day.
> This was not inconstancy;
> Rather it was prudence;
> Because as for women, truly,
> I know their flightiness,
> And I leave them in advance,
> Only in order not to be left.

Thus Joconde had 365 women a year! Let us reduce this figure and subscribe to an estimate of 50. This is approximately the life style of rich young men, at least for the numerous class whose characters are inclined to fickleness. In the treatise on characters it will be seen that this class composes a three-fourths majority. The proof is that the boastful Joconde is loudly applauded by women as well as men.

"Applauded! By what class?" it will be asked. "By a rabble of profligates who frequent the theaters?" But if others do not imitate them it is often because they are not able to. Fear of syphilitic maladies keep some faithful; interest, esprit de corps, and title of character constrain others. But suppose that the reins were dropped and humans were abandoned to good nature; you would see the majority imitate Solomon and Joconde. What is more moral than a Dutchman in his own country? Look at the same men in Batavia.

Analysis concludes that civilizees elevate the vice of plurigamy to the composed mode, which is simple in the case of

barbarians; the latter have *permanent seraglios,* whereas civilizees have both *permanent* and *vague seraglios.* All young city
dwellers slightly favored by nature and fortune know how to
form a *vague seraglio* stocked with women of all ranks, and
without having to pay for their keep as do the barbarians. Far
from it! the majority of civilizees fleece and rob the women.

I spoke of the vice of transition; let us examine more briefly
the vices of the quadrille of conflict.

First, *venal love.* There are many species; venality in love
is not limited to harlots. How many men and women of noble
lineage are inclined to this kind of corruption! Sanchez[2] is of
the opinion that a woman has the right to wear a revealing neck-
line when she appeals a lawsuit; in this case are not the female
petitioner and the judge who is taken in two champions of venal
love? Many other classes, even the most fashionable, could be
joined with them; but let us be discreet in speaking of respectable society.

As for the people, their venality in love is no mystery; the
prices are as well known as the current rates at the stock exchange. Must one be astonished when he sees a price set for
virtues of the highest caliber, such as those of a nation's rep-
resentatives? Did not Walpole say that he had in his portfolio
the tariff of all the honesty in England's Parliament?

Under the reign of such morals how will politics, morality,
and religion attain their goals of domestic happiness, which are
founded upon the conjugal bliss of the spouses, the continence
of girls, and the reign of august truth in domestic relations?

Second, *secret love.* This is another voluminous confusion.
I abandon the figures to statisticians; for the city of Paris alone
they would fill ten volumes as thick as the royal almanac. This
whole merry-go-round, however, is in violation of moral, civil,
and religious law—what insubordination in this world of love;
what rebellion against gentle, pure morality! In the face of so
many notorious or secret infractions, how can we fail to recognize either that the regime of love is organized in opposition to
the conventions of truth and morality; or, that if such a regime

---

[2] Perhaps the reference is to Thomas Sanchez, a 16th century
Spanish casviste.—Ed.

is inseparable from civilization, then this society is the antipode
of morality and truth?

Third, *morals of low society,* especially of the petit bourgeois category—shopgirls, working girls, etc. Before marrying
they are an entirely free class of women, especially in large
cities. They have lovers to flaunt under fathers' and mothers'
noses; they have a new lover for each occasion; and finally,
they enjoy in profusion what is refused to young ladies of a
higher class. Their youth is spent in flitting from one man to
another. True Jocondines, they are but more intelligent at their
work and more skillful at hoodwinking the innocent who weds
them when they are on their decline.

This class is in actual fact as *emancipated* as if full liberty
in love existed. And yet this class, openly disengaged from the
constraint of civilizee religious and moral laws, makes up half of
the feminine population of big cities, where sane doctrines of
mild and pure morality are lavished on the people.

As regards low society, I abstain from citing soubrettes and
chambermaids who appear to have no acquaintance with the
laws of continence; at least they behave as if they had never
heard of them. Although they, like the young ladies of the petit
bourgeoisie, regularly attend sermons where they are taught
these precepts. What must be thought, after all this, of the
measures taken by politics, religion and morality to curb love?
Must one not suspect a trio of errors in the three repressive
systems?

Fourth, *the morals of high society,* or the class of well-bred
people [*comme il faut*] who dispense with moral laws, while
at the same time defending them as a good means to keep the
lower classes in line. In the case of respectable people the husband has his known mistresses, and the wife her known lovers.
This concurs with the harmony of the household; it is known
as *savoir vivre.*

A slight disadvantage to these morals, which are called "respectable," is that the paternity of the children is never certain.
But the law is *is pater est,* etc., under which no equivocation is
allowed, in spite of certain resemblances which may throw suspicion on the origin of the dear children.

Doctors come to the support of the law by declaring that these resemblances can result from a look cast by the pregnant woman upon some man whose physiognomy attracted her attention. Had she looked at a black man it would be enough for her to give birth to a mulatto! Now if the matter depends only on looks it would be very ungracious for a husband to entertain doubts against the testimony of the law and medicine, one being as infallible as the other.

On the other hand well-indoctrinated neighbors and friends assure the father that the child looks very much like him. People who don't believe it keep silent; all concur to favor and legitimate fraud in such matters.

Anyway, is it not in very bad taste to be jealous of one's wife? If one wants to merit the title of good husband he must have active faith and believe that nothing can happen between respectable people. This is a moral precept of the bourgeoisie.

But do husbands in high society look so closely? Most of them have speculated on a dowry or a useful alliance. Perhaps they are not deceived in these matters. More often they have the accessory and very convenient gambit of attracting to their households many women and young ladies, ostensibly as friends of their wives. These they court even with the consent of their spouses, who close their eyes according to the law: "You scratch my back, I'll scratch yours."

In the case of this antimoral concert of husband and wife, conspiring to make marriage a mask for scheming, the house becomes an arena of high intrigue where public opinion and reputations are made and unmade. Such a clique has great prestige; it exercises *composed matronage*, one of the finest excrements of civilization, one of the trophies of august truth. A house such as this has full access to power—it obtains favors and sinecures; and it *makes colonels,* as admitted even by Bonaparte, who reproached such women for boasting of their intriguery. If they did this under Napoleon, under what regime will it not be done?

A simple matron causes herself to be scolded and fleeced by the police; a composed matron, operating under the protection of marriage and husband, heads for high fortune and distributes sinecures. It is as true for vice as for virtue that nature attaches happiness only to composed movement.

So goes the civilized world; there are only the dupes and those who have the last laugh. Make marriage and morality a mask for orgy and everything will be given you—a hackneyed criticism perhaps, but necessary in replying to the partisans of constraint. They must be overcome by a picture of the results of their system.

Here, in five articles, is an exposition of the role that august truth plays in the erotic world.

This is the quadrille of conflict well established in *love*, and also in *familyism*. These politics, whose governors lay claim to unity of action and swear only by unity and truth, produce strange effects indeed. The falsity and quadruplicity of action could not be more obvious or better established in the minor order; can they fail to invade as well the major relations, *ambition and love*?

X—Constrained or Legal Love.

The pivot in the erotic world remains to be discussed; it is the constrained and legally virtuous class. There exist some young people so well supervised by fathers and mothers that they are obliged to be continent, or to be faithful. Their number, much smaller than it would appear, serves to accuse a law that rallies so few to its standard and consists only of those soldiers that it fetters. If the class of voluntarily faithful wives is distinguished from the class of wives who are faithful by force, could it be guaranteed that after ten years of marriage there would remain

> One out of a million spontaneously faithful;
> One out of a hundred faithful of necessity.
>
> (La Bruyère)

When legislation has arrived at such results it can be summoned to pass judgment upon itself. Are not laws a work of madness when there is not one out of a hundred who observe them? The laws have created four classes from the 99/100—

each operates in opposition to the will of the law, in opposition to truth and unity; each adds some shocking vice to an infraction such as venality, fraud of paternity, etc., etc.

Upon seeing such peculiarities, such conflict of falsity, how can the philosophy called *politics* have lagged behind for 300 years? How can it have failed to ask if there is not an *aberration of the social genius* in this legislation that so oppresses love? Is this indeed the spring that will conduct nations on the path of truth?

2. MORALITY. Let us examine whether, by speculating on the repressive system, morality will have succeeded better than politics in establishing the reign of truth in minor relations. I have analyzed them politically in regard to love; we will now look at the minor relations in regard to familyism.

Since love is considered by morality to be an accessory, and since morality places the happiness of man only in family pleasures, in household union, and in pastoral virtues, we will have to treat the familial branch of minor relations separately, if we are to be attuned to it.

Let us distinguish *conjugal pleasures* and *paternal pleasures*.

For the tables below keep in mind that I speak only of the very largest class which has, as a consequence, only a mediocre fortune. The rich class, being a very small exception, will not be considered in a general analysis where the exception, as always, confirms the rule.

SCALE OF DISGRACES IN THE CONJUGAL STATE

K. Widowerhood	Ʞ Composed Orphanhood
1. unhappiness risked	7. discord in education
2. disparity of taste	8. placements and dowries
3. complicating incidents	9. separation of children
4. expense	10. deceitful alliance
5. vigilance	11. faulty information
6. monotony	12. adultery called cuckoldom
Y. Sterility	⅄ False Paternity

1. *Unhappiness risked* and anticipated anxiety. Is there a game of chance more frightful than that of an exclusive, indissoluble bond, in which life's happiness and unhappiness depends on a throw of dice? Men and women have been known to worry several years in advance and with good reason. How inept social politics are to subordinate life's fortune to the most incertain of all bets!

2. *Disparity of taste and character* often emerges directly following the ceremony, if only about cooking, which is of one variety in humble households; then about adornment; then relations. The good wife wants to entertain and visit certain habitual friends and relatives that she says are very respectable, true friends of commerce and of the Charter; the husband has no faith in their merits. In short, hardly two weeks have passed before incompatible tastes and habits are discovered on both sides. Household happiness is immediately disappointing, and from the moment that the illusion is dispelled, happiness progressively diminishes.

3. *Complicating incidents.* It is rare that six months pass without some event that changes the aspect of things. I saw a young husband whose father-in-law went bankrupt and paid the dowry with a statement of insolvency. The worst was that the son-in-law, having given a receipt in full in exchange for unpaid debts, found himself compromised in such a way that he was obliged to pay the sum of 80,000 francs for a dowry he never received.

This is an incident of major mode, ambition; others are of minor mode, love.

A husband, for example, may recognize after one month that his wife is a Messalina,[3] and that if he does not continue as during the first month he runs great risk of having to have the court intervene.

One hundred pages could be filled with incidents that soon dispel the charm of marriage and show both spouses the trap into which they have fallen. Sometimes a husband is disap-

[3] Unfaithful.—Ed.

pointed from the first night, not finding what he hoped to find. The disappointments and snares are no fewer for wives.

4. *The expense.* In general everything accords to engage young couples in expenditure. Many a husband is heard to complain after three months, and to speak of economy to the wife who, in response, accuses him of avarice. Household life is so expensive that the budget that was agreed upon is always exceeded; it then must be cut back. Love disappears as soon as marriage causes such debate. Illusion vanishes and the chains remain.

5. *Vigilance.* There is an obligation to keep watch over the details of a household in which it is not prudent to blindly trust the wife. If she disposed of everything as she wished the table would suffer in favor of the wardrobe. How many other dangers oblige husbands to a vigilance which they could dispense with in the condition of liberty!

6. *Monotony.* The monotony must be great in our isolated households, since husbands, in spite of the distraction of their work, run in hordes to public places, coffeehouses, clubs, theaters, etc., to divert themselves from the proverbial satiety of always eating from the same dish. This monotony is even worse for wives who want to be faithful to duty.

7. *Discord in education.* There is a source of misunderstanding when the father, wiser than his wife, does not consent to spoiling the children. A father becomes tired of their squabbling, feels sorry for himself, and deserts them. The wife consoles herself with a neighbor, and discord is born of these same children that morality proposes as a pledge of ineffable accord.

8. *Placements and dowries.* It is at the time of these irksome tasks that men become finally disillusioned with the pleasure of marriage. However, his daughters will remain on his hands if he does not arrange a dowry for them; what can he do? He has only just enough to get by on. Then he must place his sons; meet the expense of education. What tortures in the conjugal state, depicted like a bed of roses!

9. *Separation of children.* If one only has daughters they follow their husbands to various regions or to another house-

hold in the same town. Ordinarily marriage takes from the parents their favorite daughter, and they sadly remain alone. The son finds a good situation in some region where he settles. How many parents are deprived of the company of their children, or are reduced to keeping only those whom they enjoyed the least, or to visiting them from afar in their separate households, where their fathers' company becomes parasitic!

10. *Deceitful alliance.* Annoyance is caused by the families with whom one is allied by marriage. Their subsequent conduct only rarely fulfills the hopes founded on kinship, and often they engage in numerous duperies. Their misconduct forces discord and rupture that replaces the tender familial pleasure promised by morality.

11. *Faulty information.* This pertains to events during or prior to the wedding, and about the wife or her parents. How many husbands, believing they have married an Agnes,[4] cry out, "If I had known such a thing I would not have entered this family!" How many fathers, having concluded the marriage, exclaim, "I would not have given him my daughter!" Information is so inexact that three-fourths are heard to make similar complaints.

12. *Adultery.* This is called cuckoldom in the theaters of France. This must be an unfortunate accident since the husband exhausts himself to avoid it in spite of the certainty that he will suffer the same fate to which he subjected so many others before marrying. The analysis of this twelfth disgrace would require a single article as long as this interlude.

Y. STERILITY. It threatens to undo all plans for happiness, and would alone suffice to appall whoever takes a wife in the hope of progeny. The poor always have legions of children; *the worst befalls the poor.* It rains children in the case of those who have nothing to feed them, whereas sterility seems especially to strike the rich. Sterility disconcerts spouses and their parents; it delivers their inheritance to other relatives, whose known or disguised avidity and ingratitude are the despair of the rightful heirs; it inspires in the husband an aversion to his

---

[4] Reference to a Molière heroine who is a sweet innocent.—Trans.

sterile wife and to the conjugal knot which has made impossible all their hopes. Sterility is a true social trap, sovereignly impolitic in this respect, and even more in the next.

Λ. FALSE PATERNITY. This is the most odious perfidy engendered by the conjugal system. Yet in France it is the subject of public witticism, even in the theater, where jokes about it are made in verse and in prose—jokes very worthy of a social order where all is false, and where falsity is the only path to success. Thus law and opinion unite to prohibit a husband from complaining in this regard, or to nullify any charges he may make. Justice answers that it is not proven, and she sends him packing like Guillaume reclaiming his sheep stolen by Agnelet. Opinion tells him *what one does not know does not hurt; when one knows it is unimportant.* Here he is, charged with others' children and ridiculed for having noticed. Composed injustice, the essence of civilization, never begets evil in the simple mode.

K. WIDOWERHOOD. It reduces the father of a family to a life of forced labor, a disgrace much worse than the small annoyances of bachelorhood! A father, unless he has a large fortune, is transformed into a galley-slave if he remains a widower with several children whom he wants to raise with good manners and industry. If the father dies before their majority he is dogged by bitter anxiety until the moment of death—his children may be delivered into mercenary hands; ruin may await his young family.

Ϟ. COMPOSED ORPHANHOOD. The principal pleasure for fathers and mothers is the guarantee of happiness for their children; the conjugal state in no way guarantees the well-being of orphans. The precautions of trustees and guardians are in no way sufficient to keep an orphan from injury and spoliation.

There is more. The child is often a *negative orphan* in the very frequent case of incompetent parents who dissipate the inheritance which should fall to the child. He is as unhappy, perhaps more so, than if he were a *positive orphan* through the premature death of his parents. It thus follows that the conjugal state exposes children to two orphanhoods, without guarantee against the harm which may result. None of these vices can exist in the associative era which does not make use of the conjugal bond.

Corollary. If it is true that this marital union is a pledge of happiness, how does it happen that a young widow with a small fortune is reputed to be very happy, happier than she would be with her husband alive?

Both sexes proclaim the happiness of young widows, especially when they know how to conserve their freedom and how not to fall from Charybdis to Scylla, from the yoke of a husband to the yoke of a sentimental braggart; when they reserve independence in love and the right to change lovers.

Such is the class of civilizee women whose happiness is so highly extolled. Happiness exists neither for women nor for men in the conjugal bond. In fact a young woman is reputed to be happy only when she is a widow; or when she has a husband affable enough to dispense with conjugal rights, to not suspect her of illicit liaisons, to raise her to the rank of Bachelor [*licenciée*] of Marriage, or to place her under the guardianship of a fictitious tutor. These are the two kinds of young women cited as happy; but in both cases, *widow* or *licenciée*, the woman's happiness consists in escaping from the conjugal yoke. This bond, then, when the statutes are strictly observed, constitutes the unhappiness rather than the happiness of women.

If one were to gather men's votes one would find seven-eighths of them lamenting the tribulations of marriage, especially in the case of the poor, who know only the distress of matrimony. But even in consulting the rich who complain neither of misconduct, nor of damage regarding the dowry, nor of the wife's bad humor, the great majority are heard to cry, "what foolishness, what drudgery marriage is. Ah! if it were all to do over, I would not be caught!"

This perpetual bond was thus invented for the unhappiness of men and women; the rare exceptions confirm the general principle. This must be ceaselessly repeated to all quibblers who cite the exceptions as if they were the rule.

To resume this analysis, I will ask what husband is able to flatter himself in escaping these sixteen disgraces, of which often a single one is enough to make his life miserable? Out of 100 individuals married for ten years, are there not 99 who complain, not of a single disgrace, but of two or three? How happiness serves as a lure to the bond of matrimony which is always disappointing unless there is wealth! What poverty of genius there is in these politics and in this morality that, in opposition to the vexations that the seraglio imposes only on women, can only create a conjugal bond that imposes vexations on both women and men at the same time! It is all too true that civilization reproduces in the composed mode all the vices that exist in barbarism in the simple mode!

As indemnity for these conjugal miseries, whose description could be doubled and tripled, morality promises paternal joy to the spouses. What guarantee does it offer? Imagine a growing family, and see how many disappointments plague a civilizee father.

A synoptic table will allow us to judge the leaven of discord that civilization creates between children and fathers in the regions most praised for their morality and sane doctrine, like modern Europe, ancient Greece, and China, so highly spoken of by Father Raynal.

This is one of those truths that must be silenced if one does not bring the remedy to the evil; but since the remedy is no longer unknown, fathers should read with pleasure the picture of their disappointments and their wrongs, either to convince themselves of the unreason which reigns in the calculations and duties of reciprocal affection between children and fathers, or to recognize how much is needed a science other than philosophy, and a society other than civilization, in order to arrive at passional equilibrium in family relations.

OC, IV, pp. 51–54, 60–77

LOVE IN CIVILIZATION

Allow me to consider amorous relations in modern or perfectibilized civilization.

Among the essential discords of our social system is the battle of the young against the old which reigns perpetually, sometimes openly and sometimes covertly. This war seems to be an effect of nature, an inevitable schism—a prejudice that will soon be dispelled. In treating conflicts of major order we have seen that science, called in to reconcile extremes, fails because it has neither principles nor rules on the function of the passional minimum, nor the guarantee of any spring in regard to the twelve passions. These would be the natural remedies, which are inadmissible in civilization due to the crudeness and the poverty of the people and the absence of industrial attraction.

This is the first vice defeating politics, which has not even dared to present itself on the battlefield. Does politics fare better in the treatment of minor vices? in the amorous war that the young secretly fight against old age, and that the old fight openly against youth?

Let us look at some facts which will enable us to conclude that our customs in this matter are the absence of any politics or plan, unless our legislators intended to establish the greatest possible constraint and falsity. If this is the case they could not have chosen better than the institution of exclusive and permanent marriage.

Of all our relations there is none more false than love; dissimulation exists so universally in love that we can no longer read either the modern or the classic works that deal frankly with love, like those of Plutarch, Virgil, and others who were models of decency in their time. Ambiguous or unisexual love was accepted in that era. If the great men of Greece lived today they would all be burned alive; Solon, Lycurgus, Agesilaus, Epaminondas, Sappho, Julius Cæsar, and Severus would all be led to the scaffold for pederasty or homosexuality. These same ancients scorned the corruption and lies so honored in civilization; bankruptcy and stockjobbing are today as innocent as ambiguous love was in ancient times. There is ground for litigation between the ancients and the moderns, so opposed in these matters! The ancients extolled the chaste morals of the Roman ladies who celebrated the phallus in religious processions. Which of the two ages has advanced or regressed along nature's path? It is not yet time to treat such a very new question. Let us limit ourselves to observing that in love, as in commerce, all civilization's progress is in social falseness. Tangible proof of the increasing falsity can be found by establishing parallels from one century to another. Molière's comedies are disagreeable today because they speak openly of cuckolds and cuckoldom. Academies want to strike from the French vocabulary the word designating a husband whose wife is unfaithful. Is this proof that there are fewer cuckolds today than in Molière's era or in those preceding his? The number of adulterers has not diminished, and it is certain that amorous license has increased as a result of the three following causes.

First, *the growth of the mercantile and fiscal systems,* concentrating more and more wealth in the large cities, causes the increase of venality and corruption. These spread to the villages which become increasingly accustomed to city morals due to the progress of commerce and other developments. Today even in hamlets there are cafes which a century ago were found only in the capital. Is it to be believed that the customs of amorous license have made less progress in the hamlets than the customs of gourmandism? They have made even more; secret orgies are more vilely organized in hamlets than in large cities.

Second, *the loosening of various reins,* among others diminishing religious prestige and the weakening of venereal virus which, being better known and better treated, does not inspire the same horror. The curb of religion was destroyed by the revolution; it will take a century to accustom the peasants to believe in hell. Women believe still less when it comes to love, which they call God's secret. This is now an idea so well established among young ladies that sacred armies could not lead them to declare their loves in confession.

Third, there are *revolutionary morals.* A counter-revolution can change authorities and practices, but it cannot change private morals. It is unable to keep military invasions from carrying the libidinous spirit everywhere, or to keep former soldiers from converting the most isolated countrysides to debauchery. In a

hamlet of forty cottages where I went to live and to work on
this book, I saw in the pretended refuge of country innocence
secret orgies as well organized as in a large city. Twenty-year-
old girls were more practiced and more artful than Laius and
Phryne could have been at four years; peasants were accustomed
to seeing their daughters deflowered at the age of ten. Fathers
and mothers, well informed of all these tricks, put out their
hands as coldly as Tahitian mothers lend a hand in the prostitution of their daughters. All this licentiousness is well camou-
flaged and patched over with the prudishness of communion and
sacrilege.

This is what can be seen, as I saw it, in a hamlet. At that
time I left a large city where obviously cuckoldom had not gone
out of style, since I was able to make up a list of seventy-two
very distinct varieties; this inventory corresponded to as many
living models who frequent the public path.

In this era, when philosophers are heard to boast of social
perfection and the progress of reason, the belief that the perfection of reason rests upon the progress of falsity is not unfounded since other branches of the civilizee system (commerce,
chicanery, etc.) have, like love, made tremendous progress in
this direction. Our savants, however, claim to seek august
truth; they must therefore seek something other than civilization since they only advance on the path of falsehood.

Let us untangle these contradictions in a few words. The
class of civilizees who legislate and direct morals are not able to
invent anything; consequently they adopt all the practices that
chance introduces as if they were the wishes of nature and the
final destiny of man. Exclusive marriage and arbitrary commerce
are the dominant customs which have been glorified, and are
still being glorified, only because legislators know how to invent
nothing else.

For societies prior to harmony, however, there are seven
methods for the social exchange of products. Full liberty in
love and total truth in commerce will reign only in harmony
or the eighth period. Thus there are seven other methods which
could be the object of research for legislators. If they were

knowledgeable about social mechanisms they would compose a table including the seven procedures of conjugal union and the seven procedures of social exchange prior to total truth; then, supported by a reasoned analysis of the fourteen customs, they would opt for two. But knowing nothing outside the civilizee mechanism, and looking only backward in social movement, they all prefer their civilizee customs to barbarian or patriarchal customs, which are still worse.

In Love:

Third—patriarchal. Mixed monogamy with simple concubinage;

Fourth—barbarism. Forced polygamy or seraglios;

Fifth—civilization. Exclusive and permanent monogamy.

In Commerce:

Third—patriarchal;

Fourth—barbarism, maximation and requisition;

Fifth—civilization.

Comparing these three periods, and finding civilizee practices in some way preferable, they pronounce boldly that it is the perfection of perfectibility perfectibilized. Instead of looking backward in movement, if they were to look forward, according to the following order—

Fifth—civilization,

Sixth—guaranteeism,

Seventh—serieosophy,

they would find in periods six and seven (which I will treat in the minor octave) mechanisms of conjugal union and of truthful commerce very different from and very preferable to ours, although not yet the full liberty and truth reserved to the eighth period. How have champions of liberty and truth been able to adopt excessive constraint in love and excessive falsity in commerce? Because there is no method more coercive than the legal system of civilizee love, *if it were rigorously observed* by both sexes, married or single. There is no method more favorable to deceit than the legal system of civilizee commerce and free competition, the mother of all social crimes. How have legislators, these learned friends of liberty and truth, become tied to these two processes, which are the most inimical? How can this peculiarity be explained if not by their characteristically knotted genius, their lack of knowledge with regard to social conventions? It is a property inherent to all classes of savants who speculate on the past and look backward in movement.

Marriage, like all civilizee customs, has led to the opposite of its intended objective. It has produced nothing but secret and general debauchery, and the protection of the laws by those who violate them most audaciously. Justice is mocked by saying that she can catch only little thieves, never big ones. Justice protects houses of pleasure as well, where women give freely without speaking of marriage. They have the protection of everyone—of fathers and mothers who are pleased that their sons find free women without risk of marriage; of young men, some of whom have taken a piece of the forbidden pastry; and lastly, of other ladies and young women who enjoy the savor of the feast and find vicarious pleasure in frequenting the houses of these gallant women painted with sanctimoniousness.

Philosophers should take into account these observations, these experimental truths, and speculate upon the function of that which they cannot prevent. In a region like France or Italy, for example, what is the relation of licit to illicit unions; which is the greater in number? It is doubtless illicit unions. Forbidden amorous pleasure can surely be estimated, without exaggeration, to be seven times greater than conjugal pleasure sanctioned by a municipality. Since there is no legislative resource to stop this ever increasing infraction, why not utilize it by extending the framework of licit love to negotiate a compromise between heaven and the law? A double advantage would be gained by preventing secret violation of the law and by snatching a good number of victims from hell. An order of things which tolerated a triple or quadruple development of love, which legally elevated love to the degree that it has risen illegally, would, as a result, commute into social and useful divertissement that pleasure whose prescription now becomes the leaven of disorder. If philosophers had speculated about love in this way they would long since have discovered the path of guaranteeism or the sixth social period, very happy not only in love, but in all social relations. Then from guaranteeism society would have risen to the seventh period, and soon to harmony, since one progress leads to another. Sophists, who boast of studying nature but who do not want to consider her universal impulses, could only arrive at empiricism in amorous relations, as in all others. Before showing them the salutary operations to which love is susceptible, it is fitting to point out the principle that they missed—*Speculate on the function of that which cannot be prevented.*

If a horde of one hundred miserable men, like the Luddites, ravage the countryside because they lack bread and work, is it not obvious that there will be great benefits in quickly returning them to work by some conciliatory path? The cost of common defense, of military and judicial pursuit, of the waste caused by bands that pillage much and lose as much as they consume, would be saved; furthermore the production of the hundred brigands returned to the workshops would be gained, instead of the great plunder that is stimulated by refusing them the work and the subsistence they can not do without. The same operation presents itself in matters of love. This passion has been too restrained; the proof is that no man wants to follow the law of continence outside marriage. The infraction of men carries with it that of women. Civilizee society, in all that concerns love, is universal anarchy and secret insurrection. But here the remedy is much simpler than with political rebels; it is limited to a decree, to any modification of the amorous regime. In truth this innovation had to be created, and we saw above that modern minds are not apt at invention. They know how to speculate only in retrograde, by looking backward in movement. Consequently philosophers, envisioning love only in comparison with barbarian and patriarchal societies, have missed the easiest path of social progress, the reform of the amorous system.

AP, pp. 198–205

LOVE AND COMMUNITY

The equilibrium of the affective passions cannot be established so long as affections and corporative sympathies are made to exist between classes today antipathetic, such as rich and poor, or young and old. The affection which should exist between them will be created by accords which will align and unite natural or extremely divergent antipathies.

The accords of alignment should be of at least eight kinds, two for each of the affective passions. Since equilibrium cannot be established by simple function, but rather by composed function, at least two rallying points must operate on each passion, and preferably four in bi-composed modulation. But we will limit ourselves to two.

Each of the four passions is the product of two elementary springs, one spiritual (s) and the other material (m). None of the four is of a simple nature; the following can be distinguished:

TABLE OF AFFECTIVE SPRINGS.

In friendship,	S spring	{ affinity of character
	M "	affinity of industry
In ambition,	S spring	{ of glory
	M "	of interest
In love,	M spring	{ of lubricity
	S "	of celadony
In familyism,	M spring	{ of consanguinity
	S "	of adoption

An S spring entitled *celadony* appears in this table; it is love based upon a long period of expectation for which it would be quite difficult to give a theory of equilibrium satisfactory to civilizee readers. The two celadonies, simple and composed, are

not practicable in civilization where a man is exposed to ridicule
and dupery if he puts off for a single day physical possession of
the one he loves, or does not at least attempt such success.

Only a few glimmers of obligatory celadony are to be seen
in cases of constraint as when lovers are restrained by chap-
erones or other obstacles. But spontaneous celadony, a bond
more spiritual than material, is generally inapplicable to the
cunning morals of civilized people, even though a pretense is
made to persuade fathers and husbands that no secret favors are
obtained, or to mask scenes of seduction. This display of sentimental love, causing laughter in secret, is opposed to the social
function of celadony which is a love anterior to physical pleasure
titled *dominance of the spiritual to the material spring.*

Simple and composed celadony can only develop from customs that do not yet exist, of which only one has been described,
the Vestalat. It will therefore be the only spiritual rallying point
cited in love. We will be troubled similarly by that which concerns the springs of familyism. Without these obstacles I would
have analyzed in each of the cardinal passions four functions
of alignment or paths of equilibrium which are easy to discover.

In a new science the fragmenting of proofs must be avoided;
all that is superfluous is more tiresome than instructive. It will
suffice therefore to know that I can, if desired, quadruple the
proof of the property of alignment inherent in the associative
order. I can demonstrate that in this order each of the cardinal
passions presents four guarantees of aligning extremes, and of
passionate concert between what are today the most irreconcilable classes.

OC, Vol. V, pp. 378–80

THE ORGY

Civilizees may think that the harmonian orgy is an assembly
of pure sensuality, as is the foul civilizee orgy; but the two have
nothing in common. An orgy may be fortuitous, as in the assemblies of the army and the caravan seraglios, but in the regu-

lar sessions of the court of love, orgies are prepared by the minister and the female pontiff who arrange delightful reunions and cumulative sympathies that heighten one another. It will suffice to cite a single orgy in order to demonstrate the range and the delicacy of the functions entrusted to the genies, fairies, and other officers of the ministry of the pontiff.

Because these scenes are incompatible with our morals I am obliged to glide over their description. However it will be necessary to raise just a corner of the curtain to make it understood that the functions of the court of love's ministry are of great interest to the pleasures of youth, and that the rallying of love indicated . . . between youth and the aged is founded upon the double bond of custom and childhood cabals and upon the daily services rendered to lovers.

The most brilliant use of the pivots of polygyne love consist of the *composed marriage of their scales*. It is one of the court of love's most refined operations, and as it is a source of very brilliant illusions I will describe it [   ]. . . .

It occasionally happens that a polygyne will have a regular sympathetic scale, that is to say, a series of women who match his dominants. The pentagyne Cléon has as dominant passions the four affectives and the *papillonne*. His regular scale should be composed of five women, one in the title of *papillonne* and four others in the title of each of his four affectives. When Cléon, in an alternating period, loves five women assorted in this way, he loves in regular scale. But this happens rarely since his alternating loves will vary from one session to another.

As a base for marriage of matched sympathetic scale it is necessary that a pentagyne woman similarly encounter five monogyne men, or others titled with each one of her five dominant passions. And if these two scales are united by joining the two pivots of the pentagynes of scale it will happen that within several days they will suddenly be enamored of one another and both pentagynes will be enamored of one another's pivot. I assume that they will be acquainted with one another since this union could not take place between travellers, but would rather occur in the habitual relations of the court of love, where much thought is given to forming these marriages of sympathetic scale. They result in very brilliant orgies that furnish charming illusions and precious and durable souvenirs.[5]

This sort of marriage is rare since polygynes love a series of people precisely corresponding to each of their dominants. But when this happens in the case of two polygynes of the opposite sex, their two scales are found to be in composed sympathy through the intervention of the two pivots. They fall into collective love through this single [   ] and their orgy can be repeated with full success, and their love sustained for quite a while, perhaps two weeks, resulting in delectable suppers and parties.

Thus monogynes, even though they are an amorous populace not highly considered by the court of love, become interesting by the coincidence of certain possibilities, such as in marriages of sympathetic scale.

The effect being rare, it is rewarded in harmony, as among us is rewarded the gunner who put the shell in the barrel and each time by accident.[6] But it is important to encourage tentatives that are able to bring about this effect. Every marriage of sympathetic scale obtains indulgences from the provincial pontiff in proportion to its degree. These are accorded upon verification by the detectives of love who visit the tourbillons under their administration to verify these marriages and to carry on other transactions within their competence.

One could describe many other scales of orgy if these details were not, as I have observed, incompatible with our antiamorous prejudices. I have similarly avoided giving explanations that would be appropriate but offensive to chaste ears. The little that I have said will suffice to infer some properties of the harmonic orgy.

First, this is not an assembly of fortuitous and confused libertinage; it is rather a lasting society skillfully prepared by the

[5] The editor of the French edition states that this passage has been crossed out in the manuscript. Trans.

[6] This is no doubt an allusion to a French proverb or adage.— Trans.

ministry of fairies to form amorous scales in a manner suitable to composed marriage.

Second, it creates among the initiates a super-tonic founded upon the opposition of two scales of contrasted character; it reinforces everyone's sympathies through a common collective passion, creating a new bond for them all.

Third, lasting memories are founded upon honorable and symmetrical bonds that are difficult to coalesce, and more precious to the contracting parties for this reason, as a difficult victory is precious to all those who personally contribute to it. However, I cannot enlarge upon this description of the properties of harmonic orgy for one of two reasons—either because it would require inadmissible details, or because I have not yet spoken of the various amorous transitions that I will treat in the last chapter.

These will be lesbianism and pederasty.

Up to this point I have only shown the framework of the edifice, only the material aspect of polygamous love. I admit that this is to present it in repugnant colors, but could I follow any other course? Theory requires that the material be described before the spiritual. I had no choice but to conform to the law of nature. Can an architect arrange the carpets and mirrors in a drawing room before the walls and the framework are finished? Doubtlessly not. I am experiencing the same difficulty. I am obliged, in describing the loves of harmony, to first construct the carcass of the edifice, the material, which is admittedly distasteful in isolation, as is a skeleton stripped of muscles and epidermis. . . .

The mechanical aspect, the theory, of polygamous love requires that the material be described before the spiritual.

We are going to fill in this sketch and analyze sentimental charm. This polygamous love could be paralleled with the orgies of respectable civilizee society.

Various readers will accuse me here of clumsiness, indeed even of indecency, and will say that I should not offend respectable society by calling its orgies crude, since it flatters itself by claiming refinement in love, and since courtesans, even

the demi-venal Ninons and the Aspasias, were artful in exciting
a lasting charm over their lovers. Civilizees must have all the
more reason to be enthusiastic about women who are exempt
from venality, as amiable as they are unselfish, as were the
Sévignés and the Maintenons. And not to render homage to the
amiability of the men of the gallant world would be, they say,
to deny the obvious.

To admit that these celebrated women were exceptions is not
the same as to win the case for civilizee love. All exceptions
confirm the rule, and if a few lovers have merited distinction
regarding honor it is but a stamp of disgrace upon the great
number who misunderstand the laws of honor in love, whose
rights I will reestablish.

I have been long in coming to the heart of this matter, and
from the beginning I have not ceased promising without
[   ]; all the details up to this point seem to give the victory to cynicism in harmonian love. I have brought several
noble springs into play but they have appeared weak and have
served only to give a material complexion to the whole system of love in harmony.

Already convinced that noble affection (in love) cannot coincide with exclusive or conjugal and egoistic love [sic].

No one has considered defining a pleasure attached to all
reunions, that of sacrificing a portion of one's joy to the convention of the mass. Let us cite some examples before applying
it to love. A dozen people are seated around a table; each one
of them covets one of the dishes served and yet no one will
seize the platter for himself before he is served. Far from it;
each one enjoys deferring his pleasure and awaiting his turn
to assure order and harmony.

If you were seated alone at a well-laden table you would
forget this kind of pleasure, this delay of general convention
and you would directly begin to attack the dishes that appealed
to you. But, seated among company, you would be very offended
if one were to suspect you of wanting to anticipate upon the
order of service and to grab a certain piece before it were carved
and passed to the company.

Let sixteen people be placed in a quadrille, and not one of them will want to violate the timing or order of the movements of the dance. If the dance were their only pleasure everyone would hasten to take off from the first sound of the violin. But on the contrary their pleasure is in working together, in retarding the movements according to general convention. Let each dancer be placed alone in a room where he will hear the orchestra; he will be able to dance upon the instant, without delay and without stopping for another's turn. Yet he will be much less satisfied than in the quadrille of a country dance that obliges him to subordinate each of his movements to general convention.

The case of a concert musician is similar; he is obliged to pause, to rush or to retard his playing, to fully sacrifice his will to the noble orders he slavishly obeys. He has much more pleasure than if he were alone in his room playing variations and arpeggios without being subjected to any method. It is thus certain that in all material exercise of passion *developed harmonically* or by concerted body that there is more pleasure in subordinating all movement to the interests of the mass than in exercising it freely and in isolation. And this kind of pleasure, very different from joy itself, is a pleasure of *unityism* [   ] which has the property of doubling the intensity of a pleasure all the while contrarying it and subjecting it in all its flight. But this opposition is balanced by a feeling of unity and of [   ] which diffuses a powerful charm upon the subservience and transforms it into true voluptuousness, because it flatters the self-esteem of the individual while attributing to him the honor of the beautiful order that reigns collectively.

If one supposes as well that each individual has a very lively good will for each of the members with whom he is in a quadrille of music, dance, gastronomy, etc. he will enjoy that much more having contributed to diverting and drawing out a dozen friends. This second effect does not take place in civilization where collective friendship is unknown and where quadrilles are but the vehicle of self-love, which is already sufficient charm. But in harmony the vehicles of collective and individual friend-

ship are joined, which increases still more the charm of the
small sacrifices each one makes to the profit of the multitude. It
follows that quadrilles or passional orchestras in harmony are
much more voluptuous than they could ever be in civilization,
and that one lends oneself to them with much more ardor and
with fervent dedication to the conventions.

Such is the spirit that harmonians bring to the formation of
quadrilles or orchestras of love. It is a kind of distraction
incomprehensible to civilizees whose hates and jealousies do not
lend themselves at all to this sort of illusion.

There is, nevertheless, a slight hint of this collective spirit in
the orgies of respectable society where the women are secretly
in demi-community, in periodic relay with all the initiated.
These coteries have a germ of collective friendship which sur-
mounts jealousy, or at least keeps it in balance. They will understand that in the amorous reunions of harmony there will reign
no mistrust, no rivalry of interests, but rather a total friendship.
There will be great pleasure in setting aside all jealousy in order
to exercise harmonic polygamy or to subordinate its varieties to
the conventions of a quadrille that will become famous for its
accord and the unity of its manoeuvres.

The property that we should pay special attention to in the
polygamous quadrilles, or orchestras of love, is the subordination of gallantry to the noble passions, to the springs of honor,
emulation, friendship and unity that have no import whatever
in gallant civilizee society, where titles of celebrity are purely
arbitrary. A certain man who is idolized by women is often as
insipid as their little dog; often he is nothing but an egoist, a
double-dealer stuffed with every vice. But he only succeeds better in capturing all feminine hearts because in civilization honor
carries no weight in a woman's mind; their totally disordered inclinations are only guided by trivial and cynical motives. Often
it takes mere jealousy to make a boor the hero of a dozen little
mistresses. Let one of them appropriate him, and immediately
all the others want to try him, admire him, and favor him, forgetting that they all scoffed at him a month ago.

Another reason that civilizee women become accustomed to

baseness at an early age is the spirit of conjugal servitude with
which they are indoctrinated. They are raised to revere in advance all the actions of a husband. Moreover the practice of
marriage reinforces the [   ] by [   ] them to certain pleasures that they have long desired. As soon as a woman marries a
Robespierre she thinks herself obliged to admire him at every
moment and in every way. The more she cuckolds him, the
more she hastens to repair her gallant pranks in the eyes of the
world by a servile [   ] for her sweet husband's cruelties. A
woman must follow the straight and narrow path by maintaining
that her Robespierre is an angel of virtue because she finds him
so in the marriage bed.

The baseness of gallant civilizees can only be corrected by
the spring of honor that is put into play by means of the
quadrilles. Those women who are too weak to embark on the
career of the vestalate will find in the [   ] other [   ] that
will support them in the league of [   ]. . . .

I have already cited the classification of nobility and of commoners. The quadrilles present an even stronger spring; they
place each individual in the position of distinguishing himself
by liberal penchants in gallant harmony, or of being classed
among the ranks of commoners and egoists.

Reputation in harmony is not founded upon cynicism or upon
the caprice of some little women who lack judgment, as in
civilization. Men and women can only attain renown in as
much as they have proven themselves. This does not depend
upon [   ] as in civilization, where one hears a troop of
women say of a man, he is charming, he is unique. And what
has he done? He went to bed with all of you and then he treated
you very impertinently; the most lowly wagon driver would do
as much.

To obtain the title worthy of love, to deserve the rank of focus
of a quadrille in harmony, one must enjoy a renown established by a succession of exploits very different from cynicism.
One must have proved by degrees that he excels in the art
of charming entire companies, to have proved oneself in this
double [   ] with companies of love and of friendship simul-

taneously, which he has not enjoyed upon the [   ]. . . .

Harmony puts all pretenders to a host of tests too long to enumerate, which are the object of court of love sessions. After the preparatory trials one must be tried in quadrille, where one must excel in the art of assembling a company of loved ones and favorites and in the art of setting them off so as to cause them to be sought out by another company bound in friendship.

Thus the half of youth that neglects the vestal career and gives itself early to gallantry finds [   ] that continuously bring it to the conventions of honor and friendship. They risk disdain if they do not give themselves over to excelling in the composition of their scales of love; they risk being classed among the commoners and judged incapable of becoming the head of a quadrille. The least blemish on their record would render them unsuited to this rank; no one would want to form a quadrille under a discredited leader.

A quadrille's success principally depends upon the reputation of its two foci. We see among us that value is attached to the conquest of a woman in proportion to the merit of the man who possesses her. If she is loved by a vulgar man she is disdained; if she is courted by a man in vogue all the gallant world pursues and courts her. Thus in a small quadrille such as I depicted, the four women of high and low scale will lose their hearts suddenly to the four men of high and low scale when the latter have a very renown woman as focus. All are eager to obtain those who are loved by the Coryphaeus of gallantry; they alone are suited to be the foci of a quadrille because they alone have the property of setting off those they love and of attracting to them [   ]. If Cloris is [   ] the four favorites of Télamon will hasten to [   ] Cloris' four favorites.

One will thus be assured of promptly inflaming the one for the two other [   ] of the quadrille if the two leaders are [   ] distinguished in a gallant career. (*sic.*)

A suitable match of the favorites with the focus' dominant passions, either of identity or contrast, will be a second gauge of success. Let us theorize upon identity. The four men who love Cloris will love her detailed image, her character reproduced in the four other women loved by Télamon, who proposed them in quadrille; they will similarly love the four women who are in perfect contrast to Cloris since love is established by contrast as well as by identity.

The third gauge of success will be in the personal merit of the people proposed in scale. If Cloris is a libertine who has attached herself to four men in common love, it would be in vain that she propose them in quadrille. Far from causing any sensation, they will be scorned, and their focus along with them. Télamon and his four favorites, whom I assume to be of the amorous nobility, will think themselves compromised by this disparate union.

Thus to become the focus of a quadrille one must enjoy a reputation well established upon the foundations that I just cited; personal merit, the favorites' assortment of characters of the scale, and their consideration.

Here are the three [   ] to which a young person who begins in the gallant world should attach himself. It is here that we will see honor become the banner of precocious maidens in gallantry, as of those who resist the charm of the honors of the vestalate.

Cloris, after hesitating in regard to the vestal career, has taken a lover at the age of sixteen. Not a word will be said to her about her first inclination, which is reputed to be praiseworthy and exempt from [   ], whatever the mediocrity might be of the individual whom she has chosen. However if she has taken a common lover this is an unfortunate augury. When this first bond begins to falter her friends will make her feel the necessity of being well matched in future loves, and of not acquiring the reputation of a cynic devoted to the lowest commoners and to the material. She will be made to feel that far from succeeding in becoming the focus of a quadrille, she would degrade the quadrilles she might want to participate in; her very pretention of figuring in them would become an obstacle to their formation. These [   ] will stimulate Cloris; she will seek respectable company, namely the nobility of pivotal love or love of high scale, then love of low scale. She will attach herself to respectable commoners, to the monogynes respected among their class. Thus honor will have a fixed influence upon her choices which will be founded upon a goal; upon the ambition of raising herself to the rank of focus of a quadrille, a title which is the sign of amiability, the gauge of respect and whose [   ] is worn as a decoration. All men and women who have worn a cross in the court of love advance in steps proportionate to the number of foci they have formed.

Among us what goal does youth have in love? What [   ] of rallying to honor? None whatsoever. All is vague in the dignity of being loved. There is no touchstone, no test which decides; reputations are all the effect of chance, of an unreflective vogue which often gives victory to the stupidest people. In the end it is cynicism or cleverness that decides popularity; reputations in the gallant world depend entirely upon these two titles. They will have no influence in harmony because every woman is assured an overabundance of the physical, and because wiles, far from being meritorious, as they are today, will be attributes of the two idiotic classes of low commoners. These are the only ones to whom ruse will be permitted; they will be scorned simply because they practice these wiles, which today are the gauge of reputation.

Half of youth, called the class of young lads and young ladies, who abandon themselves to love at an early age, must seem quite weak in *point d'honneur* in love affairs. It remains to clear them of this accusation and to prove that this corporate body, without equaling the devotion and the magnanimity of the vestalate, is no less faithful to the principle of harmony which requires that honor surpass all other passions, even love. Love can obtain the greatest influence in the particular, but in the general it is completely subordinated to honor, so unknown in civilizee love.

The quarrel will be judged impertinent but in order to be worthy of the subject I will begin by throwing down the gauntlet even if this allows both sexes to use all means of defense.

It has been desired that honor be placed in the domain of unsocial or exclusive love; experience, however, speaks out against this. In civilization gallant society produces men who are tyrants and dupes behind masks of courtesy and finesse, and abject and perfidious women behind masks of modesty and sincerity.

Such results prove well enough that the civilizee system in affairs of love is far from the path of honor.

This subject will parallel the obscure loves of civilization. Everyone is quite awkward when it comes to citing brilliant matches that leave charming and durable souvenirs. The most astonishing exploits become reduced to a few square or hexagonal affairs, to a few mean orgies of respectable society, where a half dozen Agneses or Pamelas abandon themselves in turn to a certain man who has no merit other than being their initiate, their confederate in orgy. Nothing is designed to exalt the soul through a succession of well-graduated and contrasted intrigues; all the charm is reduced to secret perfidity, to the pleasure of taking a man away from the one who possesses him by title. Civilization, with its display of sentiment, is far from believing it possible to arrive openly and in total friendship to plurality, which today is merely the effect of reciprocal treason.

The omnigyne quadrille is the most extended that is practicable; it includes in the simple order thirty-two persons and two foci. If it is composed, the number is double, each person being replaced by a couple.

The distribution is the same as that of the thirty-two planets. The two foci first elect the four cardinal sub-foci of the quadrille; these are the four who are loved in title of favoritism and unityism. Then each one elects, from fourteen loved ones, seven that are pivotal in high scale and seven in low scale. Next are elected four ambiguous in low scale; the surplus form the twelve major and the twelve minor keys, of which seven are pivotal in each octave.

Since all the functions of these thirty-two characters are of love, their description would require a *tableau* of the kind given [   ].

But because this would take us too far, it will suffice to de-

scribe some of them. There is, for example, a vestal of manoeuvre; a woman who loves in simple celadony. One will judge that
her role is unfortunate since she is the only woman who will not
enjoy the sixteen men. But for her it is a great contrast, a special
charm that cannot be comparatively appreciated in civilization.
To compensate for this privation she will have a swarm of advantages.

The manoeuvres of this quadrille and its methodically varied
unions will be similar [   ] to the aromal copulations of
heavenly bodies, which I am obliged to illustrate. I refer you to
that chapter which will serve as a description of the present
quadrille.

Everyone will unite in turn with the thirty-one others, but
not in the confused manner of civilizee orgies. There will be
a method for setting into relief the people chosen each day as
pivot of the manoeuvre, and they will not be possessed until
everyone has felt a true passion for them through these [   ]
founded on carefully arranged conventions of contrast or
identity.

These unions will be quite similar to a sympathy where a motif is fugued between all the instruments; each character in turn
will become the motif. This will engender a passion in each of
the sixteen men for one of the women of the minor octave who,
enjoying one of them each day, will find in this union the charm
of a vehement passion sixteen times repeated in as many successive days. If the first pleasure with a single object of love
already leaves us precious souvenirs from the first day, imagine
the pleasure to be had in a quadrille, where everyone will be
able to procure sixteen times the pleasure, and to add to it a
host of other [   ] which will derive from manoeuvres which
I cannot here disclose.

After these shocking tenets of love, here are some even more
shocking, which thus have an even greater need to be supported
by the principles that theory always demands. Let us recount
the most notable principles that have been enunciated and
established in the course of this work, as much on the function of love as on the function of the other passions.

The omnigamous mode, with which we are dealing, is to the four other modes—already described under the name of simple, composed, polygamous and amphiomnigous—what the foci are to all modes, and what fire is to the four elements. We have seen that the focus reunites extreme properties, and is always double in an infinite sense, that is to say it is devoid of properties contradictory in the infinitely large and the infinitely small. A mode having the rank of focus in love should similarly have these double properties; it should cumulate the two most contradictory functions by analogy with the following table:

Classes   Orders   Types   Species
Confusion . . . . .Variety

The focus is composed of the two extreme modes, confusion and variety; the first or direct mode includes the infinitely large bonds of love and the second or inverse mode includes the infinitely small bonds.

The infinitely large bond of love is that of the orgy, which establishes a general confusion among the initiates; the infinitely small bond is that of amorous manias or habitual manias and fantasies that everyone acquires in love, as in all passions. Harmony will class all these fantasies and will associate in sects all those given to each mania. To render the definition more immediate, let us consider a comparison using the sense of taste.

Let a dish be prepared in whatever manner, even the best and most renown; there will always be guests who find something to criticize, who will desire a certain modification in the degree of cooking, salting, kneading, dressing, etc. If one wanted to count these various fantasies, they would number in the dozen, in the hundreds for each dish. No matter how skillful the cook, a dish will give rise to a hundred criticisms, a hundred desires for improvement.

On the other hand if you were to serve the same dish to crude peasants, who are always hungry and poorly nourished, they would all find it excellent and would express no desire to modify the preparation. Which table is closest to perfection; the twelve peasants, each of whom finds the dish excellent without proferring any criticism, or a society of twelve sybarites, each one of whom desires a modification? Assuredly the last company is as refined, as perfected in gastronomy as the first is crude and gross; it is the same in love. Not twenty peasants have with their wives a secret mania; they take their pleasure brutally and simply, without refining their pleasure by manias or customs. Twenty sybarites will each have their special mania in pleasure.

To form infinitely small or omnigamous bonds in love, sectarians from the whole globe must be compared and must be leagued together to support this or that fantasy. Even in gastronomy the bonds of infinitely small manias will be composed by corporate bodies who will support nuances of preparation and will unite over all the globe to assure an honorable rank to their fantasy.

This kind of bond, adapted to minute and infinitely small manias, is inverse omnigamy. It becomes direct when it is applied to the method of universal union like in the bacchanal of love and the public banquet of gastronomy. We will treat two opposed unions which form the bond of focus, always double in the passional, as in the material. We must define the infinitely small bonds from which the infinitely large necessarily result.

It is so necessary to understand the passions' infinitesimal manoeuvres that it is fitting to give some lengthy details, which will seem very ridiculous until the moment when conclusions are drawn and applied. I am going to bring to the scene personages as absurd as Molière's hypochondriac when he asks his doctor, "How does one put grains of salt in an egg?" We will see the globe all in a fluster about whether a sauce should be more or less seasoned with salt or vinegar. The utility of this so-called trivia will be seen when we arrive at conclusions. In the meantime let us observe that if health is the first good, then hygiene or the guaranteed regime of health is the first of the sciences. In order to stabilize and adapt it to each of the 810 temperaments, all uncertainty must be eradicated in regard to these so-called trivialities. The globe must decide the most minute questions of hygiene according to each temperament. To advance toward this point, as toward all others, is the goal of harmony—to confederate throughout the globe the partisans of each branch of passion, each of which will be distinguished into two and three leagues comprised of those who want seven or eight or nine grains of salt in an egg; and to found upon their rivalries unitarian [   ] according to the mechanism of the passional series. It matters little if a bond is born of a cabal; it is important that a bond be useful, and that it lead to associating industrials over all the earth.

Philosophers and theologians admit this principle; they desire that all men be brothers in Jesus Christ or in equality. This is to desire a direct omnimode bond or infinitely large bond of friendship. They would like all family branches to be united; they would like the richest to lend support to the poorest. This is to want a direct omnimode or infinitely large bond in familyism. Lastly philosophers and theologians allow and encourage very extensive bonds of the three cardinal passions, which they do not know how to establish. Why is love, the fourth, the only passion to which they want to admit the fewest possible bonds? A strange contradiction. If bonds are advantageous in social harmony they must be approved in a general system allowing the principle that "that which benefits some while hurting none is necessarily good."

They reply that all bonds in love clash with the laws of exclusive marriage, which is the foundation of their social regime. To benefit this institution they misunderstand the necessity of amorous bonds while producing nothing in favor of marriage, whose laws are violated in every sense. They fail to obtain the effect that would otherwise develop through bonds of love; they fail to consider that to thwart the development of one of the cardinal passions is to thwart them all. Thus is born the universal falsity that reigns in our societies.

Love is the cardinal passion whose development must be reestablished in all degrees. Since the three others are tolerated and even induced, we will not occupy ourselves with them. It will suffice in the following section (major pivotals) to expose their course in harmony. This will offend no one; on the contrary it will gain general favor. But a wagon is not able to run on three wheels if the fourth is broken . . . therefore all our theory hinges on the restoration of love, the single passion proscribed by civilizees. We will show love's mechanism in its highest degree, omnigamy.

(It must first be proven that civilizees have a penchant for orgy or direct omnigamy; that this penchant manifests itself among the most polite classes; and that they tend by all possible means to give to their orgies a sentimental veneer that civilization is unable to allow.)

We will recognize in this regard civilizees' troublesome talent for changing gold into copper. There is nothing more repugnant, more foul, than their amorous or omnigamous orgies where all is pure materialism, thus leaving no door open to sentiment. Consequently all chaste readers will be predisposed against a theory of amorous orgy. Let them rest assured that harmony never speculates on lewdness; simple movement is allowed only in relays of the composed. Thus in orgies, as in all effects of passion, it is necessary to establish a sentimental bond between all the co-operators. Before describing the springs, some signs of them must be indicated among our customs.

We will begin with the material in accordance with the rule requiring that all movement proceed from the material to the spiritual, and from the simple to the composed. We are going to treat omnigamy in the material sense, even if it incites the rigorists; it will be easy to clear ourselves of their accusations when we consider spiritual omnigamy or sentimental orgy.

Even in dealing with the material, harmony does not allow the infamous [   ] of civilization. If the material is dominant in an orgy, harmony would desire that it be embellished by some illusion or other which derives from noble passion. First we are going to contrast orgies of the lowest species in harmony to those of the highest species in civilization. It will be seen that the lowest harmonic degrees are infinitely superior to the highest degrees of civilization.

Let us keep in mind that I am describing only the lowest or

least noble degree that exists in all the mechanism of harmony.

We will first seek a germ of [   ] in the most cynical re-unions. I will cite two of them, one in confusion, the other in [   ] . . .

First, confusion. I know of nothing more remarkable than an association of Muscovites (I speak from hearsay) called the Club of the Sensual. The associates are first admitted by a concierge who knows them; they then undress in a chamber and enter nude into the meeting room, which is dark; here everyone feels about, forages, and manoeuvres by chance not knowing with whom they are dealing.

This [   ], which at first glance seems foul, is perhaps the most prudish that has ever existed in civilization. It is the only one in which civilizees have known how to disguise their vile customs and their too heinous sentiments; too mistrustful to accept light, they need the support of darkness to forget their ignominy.

Despite these aversions [   ] they sense their need for nature, for *orgy* or omnimode love. The Muscovites had a very fine idea; they knew how, by means of darkness, to conciliate the natural penchant for orgy with the obstacles imposed by civilizee suspicion and jealousy. The invention of a session in the dark rallies to nature those whom civilization would hinder and those who feel the need to be hidden.

I began with this example because it [   ] a tacit avowal of natural impulse. It is certain that nature urges us to orgies of love as to orgies of feasting; that which is culpable in excess will be commendable in an order that knows how to effect a balance. We have heard the sensitive Anacreon, who prefers men to women, extol the orgies of young pederasts and intrepid drunkards among the soothsayers. If the champions of antiquity admire excess, so condemned today, it is because they quite agree that orgy is one of man's natural needs. What should be regulated is the exercise of this pleasure which is, like so many others, incompatible with civilization.

It is nature's wish, nonetheless, to excite us to pleasures of all

degrees—to the simple, the composed, the polygamous, the omnigamous, and the ambiguous.

The amorous or omnigamous orgy is so natural that it is dominant on the island of Tahiti, which is surely well on the path of
benevolent nature. The savages' orgies exist in the composed,
which is to say, that they combine both men and women. It
exists in the simple in the case of all barbarians who exercise in
love the simple orgy adapted to the sensual pleasure of a single
sex. Every barbarian pasha has orgies with his women, and the
majority have pederastic or ambiguous orgies as well. Certain
barbarians have orgies of ambiguous contrast. Giradon.[7]

Civilizees, on the other hand, surrender themselves to orgy
every time they are able, as witnessed by the custom of the lords
of Moscow who are served in underground apartments by nude
Georgian women. The respectable women of our capitals are
quite fond of this sort of amusement, frequent even among the
innocents of the countryside. All coteries of hexagonal and octagonal groups strongly incline to orgy; I have been astonished
more than once upon seeing the [   ] that the apparently most
prudish women do in secret assemblies. I have occasionally attended these assemblies and have always been surprised at the
ease with which women suddenly forget all these [   ] of
morality that are so regularly observed in public.

Let us carefully distinguish the orgy from prostitution and
debauchery, because orgy is a transcendent love, [   ] . . .

Prostitution is but a very subordinate love; it thus prevails
among the people of the poor class who will give over their wives
and daughters for a small sum. The orgy, on the contrary, is a
penchant of the free and opulent class who tend through excess
of well-being to general friendship or unityism. Thus the orgy
occurs naturally following banquets, especially in rich and licen-
tious society as was the regent's court of Louis XIV.

Thus orgy is the noble development of free love. Sometimes
it doubtless takes on [   ] colors at certain vulgar reunions,
carried to [   ] by the fumes of wine or venality; but when

[7] Obscure allusion. Fourier may be referring here to the sculptor
François Giradon (1628–1715). [Note by S. D.-O.]

it is spontaneous and disengaged from sordid calculations, as in the secret bambocciades[8] of respectable women, it becomes a very noble and philanthropic passion, as I have already shown in depicting square, hectagonal and octagonal unions, etc.

When the need for a kind of pleasure is so well established by the uniformity of secret impulse, one cannot refuse to recognize it as a spring of nature. It only remains to regulate its course with the wishes of harmony, to always ally sentimental charm with material pleasure. That is why [   ] . . .

Nevertheless I can barely hint at the subject. The reader will well understand that I am forced to restrict to three or four pages what would otherwise be the subject of an ample and brilliant account, were it not rendered inadmissible by our mores.

NMA, pp. 309–29

[8] Perhaps from the Greek verb *bambaino,* meaning to chatter or stammer.—Ed.

VI. EDUCATION

THE TYRANNY OF PARENTS

What! The family, the gentle moral household that raises tender children to love commerce and the honorable Charter, this loving bond is the germ of falsity and immorality? Yes, and the following details will prove that civilizee family life perverts every character, that it throws three-fourths of the population into crime, and that it thrusts the other fourth into a labyrinth of obligatory or speculative or palliative vice.

To speak frankly, the family bond in the *civilizee regime* causes fathers to desire the death of their children and children to desire the death of their fathers. It is much worse in the case of distant relatives. Could there be anything more infamous? A few rich families are the exception that confirms the rule, which applies mainly to the poor who make up seven-eighths of the population. This rule, however, applies as well to many families of the middle and wealthy classes, where brothers love one another like Cain and Abel.

Let us first hear the facts about a subject so contrary to preconceived notions. We will look at the manners which prevail for the majority; for those who are starving and make up two-thirds of the population, and for the needy who, joined with the working people, compose seven-eighths of the social body.

Moralists take little account of this class. They envision it as the Athenians envisioned the slaves. They count on prisons and the gallows to develop the muscles of the people. They write only for notables. Like the poet Delille, they see the human species only in the castles of marquis or in the drawing rooms of bankers.

If I have succeeded in studying attraction, I owe it in part to the precautions I have taken to study the people, to prefer localities where their conversation, nature's interpreter, is heard. On a boat where there is a choice, I disdain the salon of high society where nothing is learned, where nothing but hypocritical conversation is heard. In the lower-class salons I hear many astonishing and artless remarks which plainly reveal the morals of the people and refute all the philosophers' theories on the progress of morality and liberalism.

If our century, which establishes the price of morality, had researched the causes of evil morals, it would have recognized that the principal cause is the subdivision of the people into small, poor households (whose number is being reduced in Austria). I am going to give an example of the depravity which is introduced by this fragmentation, not only among the working people, but even among the demi-bourgeois class, only slightly superior to the lowest class. Here is a conversation that I overheard in Paris, the center of morality and mire.

Four men sat down at a table near my own. They were artisans, a little above the poorest class. One of them was saying,

"I'm asking that girl in marriage because she'll have money; the family is comfortably set. You can be sure I don't want to be a sucker again. Take a wife who hasn't a penny, then the children come; it's the devil to take care of them, it's hell."

"Then you had a lot of them?" said one of them.

"I had six—feed all that and the wife!!!"

"What? Six? Oh! good heavens! a worker who hardly earns a thing, to feed six children!"

"Yes, six; but they all died, fortunately for me. And the mother's dead too."

Notice the words *fortunately for me!* This exclamation surprised me little because I know the frightful position of a worker without fortune reduced to feeding six children and a mother who is unable to work. She is obliged to comfort an urchin who cries, wipe up another, spank this one, whip that one. These wretched children ask for bread as if it were to be had. They are given the whip when they are hungry.

The interest of this conversation lies in the unanimity of the three companions in regard to the father's exclamation, "fortunately for me they are all dead, and the mother too." All three expressed agreement that it was indeed very fortunate for him.

This then is the paternal and conjugal sentiment of the people that philosophers depict so movingly on the stage. They do not see that the poverty of lowly households transforms fathers into brutes worse than ferocious animals. Even a lioness grieves if she loses her young; she is furious if they are taken from her. Then as soon as you wish, gentlemen of progress, elevate moral man to the moral height of wild beasts! You will do well to set down the principle that the social body should dispense all fathers from providing nourishment, care, and education for their children. Wild animals are exempt from similar worries. Before you elevate men to sovereignty, before you give them the proud name of free men, assure them first the same help nature gives to animals in their paternal relations. Nature is responsible for clothing and educating the offspring of animals, and as they are nourished by the mother, the animal father truly enjoys a freedom denied to seven-eighths of civilizee fathers, who are no more than chained prisoners as soon as they have children. If children are a joy for the well-to-do, they are a torment for seven-eighths of all civilizees, who cannot afford to maintain and educate them.

Marriage and dependent children are a trap for the people! Morality carefully hides this distressing truth from us because it knows no remedy for the evil. But I, who bring a remedy, must not dissimulate these woes from fathers, and I must not dissimulate from society its radical vice of pushing seven-eighths of all families into evil practices through poverty.

There is no antidote other than quadrupling production, limiting the population, and granting a minimum standard of living to the people. These three conditions can only be fulfilled by combined and attractive industry. Production alone, even if it were quadrupled or increased tenfold, would not guarantee a sufficient minimum to the people, who would multiply unchecked and abandon themselves to idleness outside the regime of attractive industry.

Thus, all the conditions upon which the establishment of good morals depend are bound together; all must be fulfilled simultaneously. Philosophers see this well, and it is what disorients them.

To shirk this huge problem philosophers resurrect the demagogic visions of antiquity. The most recent of their sect, Owen and Saint Simon, reproduce the agrarian law in a poorly disguised form; they want to take from the rich and give to the poor. This is the opposite of combined industry, which doubles the revenue of the rich, while increasing the revenue of the poor sevenfold.

We have seen above that seven-eighths of all civilizee fathers are forced by poverty to desire the death of their children, and often that of the mother. If they have not desired their death, at least they console themselves willingly when their death does come.

With rare exceptions, the same depravity prevails among the wealthier class. This corruption is so notorious, so common, that opinion sanctions it by saying at the father's death, "now the son is going to rejoice." Did he not rejoice, then, when his father lived? In villages where nature manifests itself more crudely, a father who possesses some land and who puts off dying too long is openly nicknamed *père vit trop*, father who lives too long.

You who speak of good morals and of familial harmony, invent a regime where poor fathers find it in their interest to conserve their children, and where poor sons find it in their interest to prolong the life of their parents, and even of legators.

Compare these vile impulses, born of the civilizee order, to those engendered by the associative regime—a poor father does not wish his children's death and does not rejoice in it; he gives himself fully to paternal affection because his children cost him nothing. Raised at the expense of the Phalanstery until the age of three, children are then ready to earn their keep. The mother earns more than she consumes because she has no children to care for. But if she is inclined toward this kind of work she can enlist as a children's maid, or as a kindergarten teacher, whose duty is to guide young children from the age of one to five.

In this situation a father is materially elevated to the height of animals. He is without anxiety regarding the upkeep of his wife and children and his children's education. Released from this servitude he can call himself proud of the noble name *materially free man*.

SPIRITUAL freedom—or the spring of paternal notions and the chance of a brilliant future for his children, his wife and himself—remains to be acquired. Animals have no such desire, but since nature inspires it in men, she must also see to its satisfaction. If not, men are spiritually much lower than animals. Our bards of progress, with their sublime flight toward rapid development, are not aware that the fate of civilizee fathers is, in every detail, inferior to the fate of the lowest animal.

If the father that I quoted had kept his six children, they would have gone in rags until the age of fifteen, and they would have lacked the education that he could not afford. After the age of fifteen the sons would have become cannon fodder and the daughters prostitutes.

In harmony these children will be very well brought up at no expense. At fifteen they will already have acquired a fortune and recognition, which abounds for harmonian children. They will have eminent ranks of all kinds, and sovereignties of all degrees, from prince and princess of a Phalanstery, of a district, of a province, up to the thirteenth degree, which furnishes the First Prince and First Princess of the whole globe.

They will have military titles in the Phalanstery and in the industrial armies, like the minor khans who command the little hordes of the children's cavalry. They will also have numerous grades in industry like colonel, captain and lieutenant of the industrial series, and bannerets and other offices which are extended to girls as well as to boys. A harmonian child of twelve or thirteen has printed on his letterheads all his great titles of

dignity, which are as copious and as long as the prototitles of
the Great Sultan, the King of Spain, the Duke of Wellington,
and a Piedmontese Marquis.

In this order fathers delightfully rejoice in the charms of
paternity. Even if their children are born poor, at the age of
fifteen they will have a fortune in savings, various legacies by
virtue of industrial inheritance, numerous titles, and a magnificent future. This is especially so for girls who enter the corps
of vestals whereby they often arrive at sovereign alliances, at
the throne of an empire, at a Cæsarate, an Augustate, or an
Omniarchate.

But in civilization paternity and the tender moral household
without bread are hell for three-fourths of all fathers who must
endure this suffering morning and evening. In harmony family
reunions are meals of joy and reciprocal praise, although they
take place barely two times a week because the mother and the
father have too many intrigues to follow, too many cabalistic
coteries to attend during meals and at work.

In our society philosophers praise women who are totally occupied with children and urchins, with pans and casseroles.
These are virtues of last resort, diversions springing from boredom. This fragmented household drudgery will be quickly forgotten when women have thirty industrial groups to go to, with
a chance for profit and advancement, and when women see their
children better cared for in the nursery halls than are a king's
children today. Because today, even in the case of princes, it is
not possible to educate a child's senses at an early age.

Civilizee children have crippled senses. The son of a wealthy
man often has a tin ear and a fractured voice; his auditory senses
have been crippled by a bad education. Moreover, the sharp-
ness as well as the accuracy of his hearing are faulty. He does
not know how to hear the sound of troops marching at a distance
of one league by placing his ear to the ground as do the Cos-
sacks and the savages.

I could point out similar infirmities of the four other senses
of our perfectible civilizees. Faulty taste, for example, which is
among the most important of the five senses, indicative of a

fault of the sensory compass. It is perhaps more defective in the case of city dwellers than in the case of country people.

For the instruction of civilizee fathers, I insist on a very essential point, specifically: if the senses are not educated from the age of one to three years, the instinctive education from the ages of three to five years is missed as a consequence. Next the industrial education from three to seven years fails; then the intellectual education, whose various degrees should occupy the years from five to fifteen fails as well. On the one hand a ladder of success, on the other, a rebound of stumbling blocks.

Being ignorant of the gradation required by nature, our philosophers only occupy themselves with intellectual education. They also fail to prepare for it by not first cultivating the two sensitive and instinctive branches which are obligatory steps to progress.

This natural course is so ignored that the last sect of sophists to appear, the Saint-Simonians, re-echoed morality and only wanted to implement the *morality of morals* and the *morals of morality*. They did not even grant quarter to two-year-old children. Neglecting to educate the senses and the instincts, they wanted children to be moral, and moralized to them in the bassinette. They imitated the melomanic who orders that one sing and dance at birth.

Nature, on the contrary, desires that the sensory and instinctual faculties be cultivated first.

The soul is comparable to a prince or a great lord, who comes to inhabit his castle only when his subordinates have made the preparations necessary to the master's reception. In the same sense, the preparatory faculties upon which the soul will operate should be developed in a child before the age of five. As it is at the age of five that the soul begins its development, its manifestation of character, and its choice of roles, the corporeal envelope must be fashioned, the senses must be refined, and the instincts must be aroused. The gifts of material nature that the soul will put into play must be developed before this age.

In this chapter I aim to dispel the prejudices of fathers whom morality has persuaded to become the natural instructors of children. Nature refutes this false principle in many ways.

First, the father is subject to death; this risk does not exist in harmonian education since the child is educated by a hundred corporate bodies whose support can never fail him. These corporate bodies do not die, as they are renewed by apprenticeship.

Second, the father, either through ineptitude in the art of educating, or through powerlessness to arouse and to satisfy the natural penchants of the child, is almost always a clumsy teacher.

Third, the civilizee father is often so poorly educated that he gives only vicious stimuli to the child. I could cite a string of ludicrous examples on this subject factually demonstrating that a child is more often corrupted than cultivated when his education is entrusted to fathers, most of whom are incompetent.

Fourth, the civilizee and barbarian eras do not furnish children with the means to develop their faculties. It often happens that the father and the preceptor judge the child to be vicious because he manifests penchants that, harmful in the civilizee order, would be of the highest utility to the mechanism of harmony.

I will only cite one of these penchants which are repressed and condemned by our customs. The penchant for filth, for un-clean functions, is a proclivity that nature gives to two-thirds of all male children between the ages of five and thirteen.

Their mania for dirt is the most precious spring of social harmony. It is this that establishes a society of citizens, not of subjects, by maintaining consideration for the inferior classes who exercise the repugnant and dirty functions today.

As soon as any work is scorned and discredited, the little horde will make it theirs, will excercise it with religious devotion, in cooperation with the regular workers. Hence no work can be disdained, and the lowest classes of people will enjoy consideration and a good dividend for performing repugnant duties.

The little horde, upon which this mechanism rests, is often composed of potentate's children, since it attracts two-thirds of all boys and one-third of all girls. The little band, which satisfies the opposite penchant for adornment, contains two-thirds of all girls and one-third of all boys. These two corporate bodies furnish to children of all characters various means of distinguishing themselves through advancement and enrichment, of becoming impassioned of particular branches of study, of arriving by a hundred different routes at a general knowledge of the arts and sciences, and of achieving excellence in some branches.

In such an order, fathers will have only to applaud their children. They will see them elevate themselves willingly to knowledge, to useful work, and to brilliant and lucrative situations. Everyone will see that it is not the father who is the natural teacher of the child; it is nature. She alone will suffice to educate him when he is surrounded by a hundred series which will develop his instincts and will find some very useful ones, even in children considered to be most unmanageable in the contemporary order.

It will be recognized that a civilized father enjoys little or none of the charms of the paternal bond. Being obliged to remonstrate and constrain the child, to repress, suppress, and restrain his passions and instincts, the father is necessarily little loved by the child who, on the contrary, attaches himself to the one parent or servant who spoils him.

OC, VIII, pp. 188–97

THE NEW EDUCATION

There is no problem on which men have reasoned more diversely and vaguely than on public instruction and its methods. In this department of social polity, nature has confounded all their theories.

To escape from the chaos of present systems, let us lay down some positive principles for our guidance; let us determine the end to be attained, and then the course to be pursued to attain it.

In every operation of association the end is unity; to secure it, education must be COMPOUND and INTEGRAL.

COMPOUND—developing at the same time the physical and the spiritual, or the body and the soul, neither of which is accomplished by our present systems of education. We shall prove in the course of the present treatise that our civilized methods neglect the body and pervert the soul.

INTEGRAL—extending to and embracing all parts of the body, and all the faculties of the soul, perfecting both to the highest degree. It will be seen that our civilized systems thwart the natural developments of the body and neglect the soul or corrupt it by selfishness and duplicity.

In these introductory remarks, we will omit the consideration of physical education, and speak of education only in its moral and political aspect, that is, in its unitary sense, for there can be no true social nor moral polity that diverges from unity, which is the polity of God.

The first object of harmonic education will be to develop in earliest childhood those vocations for which there is a natural aptitude, a natural instinct, and to guide each individual to those functions to which nature destined him. Our civilized methods pay, with rare exceptions, no attention to this first principle of a true education, but seek to mould the young mind to suit the prejudices of parents or the interests of classes.

No question is less understood than that of *natural vocations*, or the instinct for industrial and other functions. This problem will be cleared up by the system of harmonic education. It will develop in the child, not a talent for a single vocation, but for some thirty, graduated and predominant in different degrees.

The first aim of nature being to direct man to material wealth, to riches and luxury—the first focus of attraction—education should aid nature in her designs and attract him to productive labor. But she can only do this by removing an evil that disgraces civilization, and which does not exist in the savage state; it is the coarseness and rudeness of the lower classes, and the discordance between them and the upper classes in language and manners. This coarseness may be necessary in the present social state, in which the masses, oppressed by poverty and toil, would feel too keenly their privations if they were polished and cultivated; but in association, in which wealth will be universal and the whole people will possess the guarantee of abundance, it will not be necessary to render them coarse and ignorant in order to inure them to privations that will cease to exist, and enable them to undergo labors which will not be repulsive and oppressive, as the serial organization will render them attractive.

Industry, having become attractive by a proper organization, will render necessary the education and refinement of the laboring classes; for if associated industry is to attract the rich as well as the poor, the coarseness and rudeness of the latter would be alone sufficient to counterbalance the attractions which the new industrial system would offer to the former. The polished classes would never consent to labor in concert with rude boors, and mingle with them in their works. Thus, for the purpose of securing the welfare of the people, and to induce the rich to engage in productive industry, the masses must in the combined order be no longer rude and unrefined; on the contrary, they must rival the rich in politeness, so that the pleasure of agreeable social relations may be combined with that of industry in the pursuits of agriculture and manufactures.

General politeness and unity of language and of manners can result only from a system of collective education, which shall give to the poor the culture and polish of the rich.

If the combined order had, like civilization, different degrees of education, some for the rich and some for the poor, it would arrive at the same result which we have, namely, the incompatibility of classes and duplicity of manners, the latter being coarse and rude among the poor, and refined among the rich. Such a state of things would be a source of general discord; it is therefore the first thing to be avoided in the social polity of the combined order, which will guard against it by a system of education which will be ONE for the entire association, and for the entire globe, and which will everywhere establish unity of manners and general politeness.

Let us not confound *unity* with *equality*. Unity of habits, manners and language does not imply equality of fortunes, characters, etc., or uniformity of any kind. It will not be pretended, for example, that in order to avoid equality and monotonous uniformity—both entirely opposed to the social nature of man, which requires graduated inequalities and diversities of every kind—the poorer classes should be smaller in stature, or physically different from the richer. *Physical unity* requires the bodies of all classes of men to be of the same stature; this constitutes *simple unity*, limited to the material or physical nature of man.

Compound unity, which embraces both the *material and the passional*, and which can be established only in the combined or harmonic order, demands that human beings should be identical as respects the development of the faculties of the soul, and the functions of the body, and that they should be homogeneous in habits and manners, though unequal in fortune and in many other respects.

From the moment labor is rendered attractive, it will be necessary that the industrial classes be intelligent and refined. It would destroy the pleasure of the industrial unions of the series if they retained the coarse manners of civilization. To give charm and emulation to those unions, unity of manners and general politeness must reign. The harmonians will feel as much sympathy for each other as the civilizees feel indifference or antipathy; an association will consider itself as one family, well united; now, an opulent family can not allow one of its members to be deprived of the education which the others have received.

To educate the entire body of the children of an association in politeness and establish unity in their manners, the most efficient instrumentality will be the OPERA—the school of material harmonies—attendance upon which will be for them a semi-religious exercise; for the opera in the combined order is emblematic of Divine harmony, of the unity which God causes to reign in the system of the universe. It is the combination of all material unities; as a consequence, the children in association will take part in it in order to exercise themselves in material harmony, which prepares the way for passional or spiritual harmony.

The opera will be as necessary to an association as its flocks and agricultural implements; and this not alone for the purpose of furnishing its members with an entertainment of an elevating and refining character, but to educate the young, and form and fashion them to material harmonies. Every association will have, when the combined order is fully established over the earth, an opera equal to those of our largest capitals.

The opera—this assemblage of the material harmonies—will satisfy the demands both of attraction and reason; the first, as it will draw the young passionately to it, and will instruct them in its harmonies; second, as parents will see in it the basis of a true physical and industrial education, and a symbolic initiation into the principles of social harmony.

GENERAL PLAN OF THE PHASES AND EXERCISES OF EDUCATION IN THE COMBINED ORDER

I divide education into two vibrations, and four phases, which include the young choirs in the following order:

(Children less than three years of age not reckoned in the scale.)

INFERIOR VIBRATION—TWO PHASES.

1ST PHASE—Choirs of *Infantiles* comprising the children from three to four and a half years of age.

2D PHASE—
{ Choirs of *Cherubs*: children from four and a half to six and a half.
{ Choirs of *Seraphs*: children from six and a half to nine.

SUPERIOR VIBRATION—TWO PHASES.

3D PHASE—
{ Choirs of *Lyceans*: children from nine to twelve.
{ Choirs of *Gymnasians*: youths from twelve to fifteen and a half.

4TH PHASE—
{ Choirs of *Juveniles*: young persons from fifteen and a half to twenty.

Each of these four phases is subject to a special system, as regards both instruction and the amount of liberty allowed it. Although children in the combined order enjoy perfect freedom in everything not injurious to them, there are limits to be set to their freedom; it would be folly to allow a child of three years to handle the little hatchets and other edge tools scattered about the workshops. He is admitted to such privileges only by degrees, that is, as he enters the older choirs; when admitted to that of the cherubs, he gains the right to handle certain utensils, such as little saws; but the use of hatchets will not be allowed him till he enters the choir of the seraphs.

In the first two phases of infancy, a preponderance will be given to material over spiritual education, without, however, neglecting the latter.

In the last two phases, spiritual education will preponderate over the material.

This contrast corresponds to the faculties of the different ages. In the choirs of the first two phases, including children from three to nine, it is of more importance to develop the body than the mind; and in the two choirs of lyceans and gymnasians, from the age of nine to fifteen and a half, more attention will be bestowed upon the cultivation of the mind.

It does not follow, however, that the combined order will entirely neglect to cultivate the mind and heart of the young at any age. Children in this order will be more developed spiritually at four years of age than the children of the civilized order are at ten. The cultivation of the physical nature does not forbid that of the mind; but as there is danger in exercising the mind too early, corporeal training should preponderate in infancy. . . .

I have likewise avoided everything arbitrary in regard to the development in the child of any particular class of sentiments or opinions. A moralist would propose that the child should be reared with a love for truth, and a contempt for riches; a political economist would recommend that it should be inspired with a love of commerce, and, as a consequence, of fraud and falsehood, which are inseparable from it. I shall not run the risk of involving myself in such contradictions; to determine the true ends to be attained, I shall have a sure guide, which is attraction, studied analytically and synthetically.

Whither does it lead us?

First, to *Material Wealth*. Second, to *Groups*. Third, to *Series*. ✕. To UNITY.

The methods of education should be planned with a reference to these primary attractions.

Our civilized systems would first of all train the child to virtue; but according to the primary focus of attraction, we must first of all train him to the attainment of compound wealth, that is,

To dexterity and health, which are the source of internal wealth.

To productive industry, which is the source of external wealth.

But what relation is there between health and the training of our schools?

In them the child is shut up, often chilled with cold, to plod over obstruse subjects in which it feels no interest. The mind is dulled, while the growth of the body is injured. Our systems of education are then contrary to nature, for they are opposed to the primordial impulses of attraction, which tends to compound wealth, that is, to health or internal riches, and to industry, the source of external riches.

Such are the two aims which the education of the combined order has in view. It attracts the child, even at four years of age, to engage in many branches of industry, to develop the different parts of the body methodically, to make him dexterous in various functions and by such a variety of exercises to obtain the two guarantees of wealth, which are *integral health* and *industrial skill*. At four and a half years of age, the child should have attained these results.

We will now examine the means by which they are to be secured.

TSO, II, pp. 123–27, 129–30

COMMUNAL EDUCATION

THE THREE ORDERS OF INFANCY

In the phase of early infancy we include all children under the age of four and a half years. If a child should reach the age of five without fulfilling the conditions necessary for admission to the class of cherubs, it would be considered an idiot, or at least as of inferior capacity. It would be ranked among the accessory or complimentary choirs, which are made up of children that display the least activity of mind and body.

Infancy is divided into three classes, as follows.

> 1. Nurslings of ages between 0 and 18 months.
> 2. Weanlings of ages between 18 and 36 months.
> K 3. Infantiles of ages between 36 and 54 months.

This last age begins to take part in industry and to frequent the gardens and workshops. In them may also be found a few children of ages varying between thirty and thirty-three months, but they are not considered as regular pupils; I will therefore give to the orders 1 and 2, the name of sub-choir, while the infantiles constitute a regular choir. They form the transition, marked K, to active industrial life.

Each of these orders of infancy are to be sub-divided into three categories, having three separate nurseries, halls and systems of instruction. For example, the infantiles may be classed by differences of age as follows.

1. Sub-order of ages between 36 and 41 months = 5 months.
2. Sub-order of ages between 41 and 47 months = 6 months.
3. Sub-order of ages between 47 and 54 months = 7 months.

If the architect and the founders of the experimental association should neglect to take all these gradations into account, and graduate the dimensions of their apartments accordingly, the

seristeries[1] would be ill-arranged and unsuitable for their purposes; attraction consequently could not be developed, and it
would be necessary to resort to that method of government employed by the Algerines and the philosophers, namely, *constraint*. A fair trial of association can only be made by a careful
estimate of all the material and passional gradations which nature establishes. Let us then study them as manifested in childhood, at which period they are more subject to analysis than
in adult age.

In addition to this classification of ages, we shall have to indicate a classification of faculties, of which we shall speak in the
next chapter. Let us first establish a proper sub-division of the
three orders of infantiles, weanlings and nurslings, that we may
foresee and prevent the errors liable to be committed in the
construction of their seristeries. Association would be a failure
if errors are committed either in the material or passional education of the young.

On the contrary, the associative mechanism will operate without hindrance, and difficulties will be easily overcome, if we
organize properly everything relating to the industrial relations
of childhood. For these relations will have the most important
influence on industrial attraction; and in this respect the influence of the sexes will be in inverse ratio to the physical strength
of each; that is,

The male sex, which is physically the strongest, exerts the
least influence in industrial attraction. In this respect, children
occupy the first rank, women the second, and men the third.

I assign the third rank of influence to men because attraction
should, in direct contrast to compulsion, proceed from the
weaker to the stronger. That state of things which shall give
rise to industrial attraction will allure children more strongly
than fathers and mothers, and women with more power than
men; so that in the combined order, it will be the children who
will give the chief impulse to labor, and after them, the women
will allure the men to the exercise of industry.

It is evident from these considerations how important it will

[1] Series of groups.—Ed.

be, in the first association, to bestow the greatest possible attention to organizing the industry of the children, the proper arrangement of their seristeries, and a proper choice as regards
numbers and ages.

If the requirements of attraction and of progressive graduation are duly observed, we shall see in the very first association
a child four years old, left to himself, more prudent and more
expert at his vocation than the generality of adults at the age of
thirty or forty in the civilized order. In the combined order a
child of four years, were he the son of a millionaire, would know
how to make his living in several callings, to exercise every
organ in due measure, and secure perfect health and vigor,
with the full development of the physical and mental powers;
and this, moreover, with the subordination of every act and
deed to the requirements of the collective interest.

How far are our present systems of education from securing
such a result! A youth of fifteen, reared under them, would not
have acquired that relative perfection of faculties to be found
in a child of four years, reared in the combined order.

I lay special stress on these features of association in order to
interest the reader in the method which I am about to unfold,
and which, as regards education, will realize all those advantages, on some of which men have speculated, but which they
have not been able to attain, and have formed nothing better
than legions of *little vandals,* which are ever on the alert for an
opportunity to destroy instead of produce, and which, when
adults, will become *full grown vandals,* spoliating, pillaging,
sacking and massacring to promote some commercial interests,
or to secure the triumph of some political abstractions.

Such are the fruits of a social order in which education tends
only to stifle attraction, and thwart nature and the development
of individual character. I am going to show how the opposite
result may be achieved, how attraction may be consulted and
taken as a guide. If this power has been wisely distributed by
God to all his creatures, it must draw the child to productive
industry, which is the source of wealth and the first demand of
attraction, the first focus to which it tends. But in the solution

of this problem, and in explaining the art of attracting a child without compulsion to industry, we must rely on means very different from those adopted by our moral and political sciences, which, when they do not form characters like a Nero or a Tiberius, form fashionable idlers. Among the means which I shall explain in the following chapters, I will indicate the principal one, namely, natural and progressive emulation between children, which is unknown in civilization; it is the result of the industrial and other material arrangements of association, and can not therefore exist in the present order.

The principal incentive to this emulation will be the influence of the older children on those a little younger; a child admires only what is within its capacity to attain; an infantile of the age of three or four will admire the choir next above it (the cherubs from four and a half to six and a half), and will look upon the children composing it, wearing their little uniforms and taking part in the manœuvres of the grand parade, as important personages. This spectacle will be for the young child what the trophies of Miltiades were for Themistocles, whose sleep they disturbed.

In the hope of reaching the rank of cherubs, a child will perform a hundred industrial exploits, which it would avoid, if ordered by the father or the teacher. Advice will have no weight with it; the unnatural discipline and artificial teachings of our schools tend only to bewilder the child, and disgust it with study; it needs an enthusiasm which our methods can not excite in it, and which nothing can call out but a vision of the trophies of the choirs of older children.

For the want of such incentives, other motives are presented to the child, such as duty to parents, respect for superiors, and other moral precepts. The child in civilization lacks the only incentive that can allure it to useful labor, and that is the spectacle of the choirs or orders a little superior to it in age, which are already skilled in industry. They are the only models which delight the child.

While education in the present order can hardly be undertaken before the age of five years, in the combined order the child at the age of four and a half years will already have passed the first stage of his education; he will possess physical dexterity, take part in several useful avocations, earn more than he spends, form his body to health and vigor, and his mind to social unity and the practice of truth. How far superior are such results to those which our vain theories propose!

MATERIAL MEANS OF ATTRACTING EARLY CHILDHOOD TO INDUSTRY

It would seem more methodical to treat first of the two youngest orders of infancy, the nurslings and weanlings; but a variety of considerations induce me to commence with those between three and four and a half, the oldest of the orders who are entering upon their industrial education.

We are to determine how the sentiment of industrial honor and emulation is to be awakened in them; a sentiment which is so foreign to the children of civilization, who have a sense of honor only for subversive ends. They emulate each other only in doing mischief; and he is highest, and most respected by the rest, who does the most. Association, on the contrary, inspires the child at an early age with inclinations quite the opposite of this, with a desire for distinction in several kinds of industry.

It is between the ages of two and a half and three years, that the question of natural vocations and talents begins to be solved; in every child, at the age of three years, twenty or thirty vocations, I repeat, manifest themselves, while in the civilized state it is with difficulty that a single one is discovered and called out in a youth of twenty.

The combined order possesses various means of developing in the child the inclination to these industrial vocations; I will point out seventeen.

MATERIAL MEANS FOR DEVELOPING NATURAL APTITUDES FOR VOCATIONS.

1. The elegance of little workshops, with tools adapted to the different ages of children.

2. The charm of graduated ornaments, of little uniforms, and badges of distinction.

3. The privilege of handling little tools and of appearing at the industrial parades; they exercise a great influence
on children.

4. The advantage of choosing in each branch of industry
the detail which the child feels capable of performing.

5. The gaiety natural to groups of children when they
work as an amusement.

6. The pride of having performed some trifle which appears of high importance in the eyes of the child.

7. Mimicry or the imitative propensity which is so
strong in children, and acquires a tenfold energy when the
child is stimulated by the achievements of those a little
older than itself.

SPIRITUAL MEANS OF DEVELOPING VOCATIONS.

8. The absence of parental flattery, inadmissible in the
education of the combined order, where the child is judged
and admonished by his equals.

9. The *aspiring impulse,* or inclination of children to
follow the example of companions a little older than themselves.

10. The pleasure arising from short and gay sessions,
with rivalry and frequent variations.

11. The emulation existing between contiguous choirs
and sub-choirs, and between the groups of a choir, increased
by the example of those who have already obtained admission to a higher order.

12. The admiration and enthusiasm for the prodigies
performed by older orders, according to the law of defense
for the more advanced.

13. The full liberty of choice as to the kind of occupation, and its duration.

14. Independence from arbitrary control, or dispensa-
tion from following any leader who is not selected from
choice.

15. The kindly intervention of the patriarchs or the old in instruction, who are the favorites of childhood; children receive instruction profitably only so far as they solicit it.

16. Material harmony, or labors executed in concert, unknown in the workshops of the civilized order, but observed in those of the combined order; they will be the delight of children.

17. Collective impulse, or the charm of following colleagues, when animated by songs, gay dresses and ceremonies.

PIVOT.—The influence of the serial organization, with its accords and rivalries, and its short periods of occupation—the only system which can charm children and inspire in them the docility requisite to master industrial studies.

A fine plume is often alone sufficient in the civilized order to captivate a peasant, to induce him to enlist and sign away his liberty. What then will be the effect of such ornaments in attracting a child to amusing occupations, to pleasing cooperation with his fellows?

We spoke of *privileges*; we will say a few words in explanation. Since the idea of privilege may seem inconsistent with that entire liberty which children will enjoy in the combined order, we will therefore define the sense in which we use it.

To say that children will be entirely free is not to assert that dangerous liberties will be granted to them. It would be folly to allow a child of seven years of age to handle fire-arms, or one of five to handle a hatchet. The liberty granted to children will consist in choosing any function and any pleasure which is without danger to them, and does not interfere with the usages of another choir or body of children. If a young child were to take a fancy to tear up the flowers cultivated by an older group, it would be a trespass, and its liberty must be restricted.

The various orders of children, therefore, should have special privileges, graduated according to their ages. The sixth order of the young, who are just entering on the age of puberty, may be allowed certain studies which can not be allowed to those who are below this age. The fifth order, the gymnasians, of ages between twelve and fifteen and a half years, will enjoy the privilege of hunting with fire-arms, a favor which could not be prudently granted to the lyceans, whose ages vary from nine to twelve years. These latter are allowed the use of ponies, and to appear in companies on parade. But this privilege could not be safely granted to the order aged from six and a half to nine years. This class is too weak to manage a horse, but it is allowed the use of little hatchets and other utensils, which are forbidden to the class below, whose ages vary between four and a half and six and a half years. These latter are allowed the use of knives, chisels, planes and saws; to drive little wagons drawn by dogs, and engage in a multitude of functions which excite the admiration of the next younger age, but are forbidden to them, though allowed functions and utensils somewhat similar. Thus the advanced infantiles are allowed the use of small saws to cut little sticks and matches, so as to discipline and accustom them early to the use of tools.

Desire for admission to these privileges is a great incentive for children who are always eager to rise from order to order and from grade to grade, and to engage in things beyond their years, when not restrained by severe examinations and test-performances; the choice of branches in which to be examined is left to the pupil, as it is indifferent as to the industrial group he enters; he is only to give proof of his capacity in a certain number of groups, which, by the very fact of their accepting him, certify as to the utility of his becoming a member of them.

These trials of capacity are practically tested, and no favoritism can influence the decisions, since a skillful performance of these functions, which are made a test, will be requisite. The groups and series, working from emulation much more than from interest, admit to their ranks no applicant who does not possess the necessary capacity to cooperate with them efficiently, and sustain with honor the ambitious aspirations of the group in its contest with those of neighboring associations.

The choirs of children, even the youngest, which are the infantiles, are in open rivalry with similar choirs of the neighboring Phalanxes. Groups of the same age from several associations, are frequently brought together to contend in the manœuvres of the parade, in processions, in operatic performances, and in the little workshops.

Owing to this incentive, even the youngest choirs are filled with pride and emulation, and would not admit to their number an awkward and incapable member; such an one would be remanded month after month from one examination to another, so long as he would be likely to hazard, by his want of skill, the reputation of his choir or group. Children are very severe judges in such matters; and the rebuff is very keenly felt by those that have already passed the age of admission to a higher class. After six months' delay and repeated trials of capacity, they are, if still incapable, dropped from the regular line of advance, and entered among the "irregulars" or order of semi-character.

Our special theme in this chapter is the education of the first order of childhood, the choir of infantiles; but as there is a strict connection between all departments of the harmonian education, to get an adequate view of the subject, it will be requisite to consider the mechanisms of the older orders, of which that of the infantiles is an imitation.

Each of the choirs of children will find occupations adapted to its strength and capacity; the Deity has provided them for every age. Take for example, cartage; the groups of cherubs which cultivate and gather the smaller vegetables, will carry them to the kitchens in little carts drawn by dogs; the groups of seraphs will drive carts of a little larger size drawn by asses, and capable of carrying heavier objects; the groups of lyceans will drive carts drawn by ponies; the groups of gymnasians, those drawn by horses of the middle size; and the juveniles will drive large carts and large horses. Care will be taken to establish this graduated order in all employments and in all the workshops, in order to exercise each child according to its capacity. There will be a similar scale of industrial occupations for the female groups.

As children are very prompt to follow the impulses of nature, and not being preoccupied by any considerations of pecuniary interest, they will be the first to organize in the experimental association their five orders. The first, that of infantiles, aged from three to four and a half, which we are now to consider, will be most difficult to form, because it can act only as an echo of the other five. These groups will afford a singular instance of children furnishing their parents with models of social harmony; for these children, within the first month, will organize the rivalries of the series, which the parents will have hardly formed at the end of three months.

The industry of the infantile choir will be the initiation to the system of harmonian education, since it is at the age of from three to four and a half years that the development of aptitudes for the various industrial avocations must take place.

To call out these aptitudes in the child, full liberty is allowed him to run about the workshops as soon as he can walk and go alone, at the age of two or two and a half years, or even before, under the oversight, however, of persons appointed to watch and guide the children.

When there is no attendant at hand, the child, when a group disperses, may be accompanied by a member who goes with it to another industrial group in which the child wishes to take part. Every one, in case of need, will fill the place of guide to the child.

We may then, at the age of two or two and a half years, or as soon as the child is able to run alone, leave it to its attractions; for these will always impel it to those quarters of the edifice, the gardens and workshops, where there are parties of children annexed to groups of an older age, provided with little instruments of labor, and where a patriarch or some elderly person present at the sitting will take pleasure in instructing them.

We will here give two classifications of the first infant order, one according to age and the other according to industrial skill. Classing them by ages, we divide them into

> Older;
> Middle; and
> Younger Infantiles.

But talent or skill does not always correspond to the advance in age, and the infantiles, considered from this point of view, are to be divided, like all other industrial bodies, into three grades of proficients in each branch of labor; namely, into

> Novices;
> Graduates;
> Licentiates.

So that one of the older infantiles may be a licentiate in the match-making group; a graduate in the group of shellers; and a novice in the group of mignonettes, with ornaments indicative of his position in these different grades.

There will be a certain ceremony and display in the distribution of these grades, which will take place periodically each month and each week. After the grand parade, a signal will give note of an examination for promotions. Then the whole troop, with its band, will advance towards the canopies, under which sit the two choirs of patriarchs, holding the ornaments to be distributed. The little drums beat the signal, and the heralds of the infantile groups proclaim:

By order of the most honorable choir of infantiles of gnidos—Hyles, aged thirty-five months, is promoted to the order of infantiles, allowed to wear the decorations of its younger groups, and to share in the privileges of this noble body, his skill permitting us to anticipate the time of his admission to our order by a month.

Then the leader of the choir of infantiles conducts Hyles before one of the patriarchs, who bestows upon him the decorations of his new dignity. Other children are brought before the patriarchs as soon as the heralds have announced their merit, and the band greets each successful candidate with a brief salvo.

After promotion according to age comes that according to talent. The herald proclaims:

By order, etc., Zelia, of the younger groups of infantiles, is promoted to such or such a grade. Here her title is announced, as also the list of her merits; then it is added, Zelia is promoted to the rank of *graduate in the group of mignonettes*. A young officer of the group conducts her to the patriarch, from whom she receives the *insignia* or decorations belonging to her new function; and thus with other infantiles who rise in grade after passing an examination of talent and capacity before a jury of their equals.

This second classification, according to talent, applies as well to groups of persons thirty years of age as to those composed of children three years old; it exerts a powerful influence upon children of the younger classes, especially when they are stimulated by the expectation of decorations and industrial distinctions. In consequence of these twofold honors, the distinction of the three grades excites much more emulation in the child than it can call forth in an adult, and therefore it is of importance to allude to it among the first details of the education of the young.

We shall devote to the subject of emulation among children two special chapters, and show that if this sentiment is successfully aroused in the youngest of the youthful orders, it will necessarily spring up among all the others. Here, as in horticulture, the greatest care must be bestowed on the first developments of the shoot; the tree may be left to itself as soon as it has taken sufficient root.

Let us then study the art of attracting to industry the two choirs of infantiles and weanlings; an art in view of which the entire system of early education in regard to the three youngest orders should be planned. The whole system of primary instruction would be vitiated throughout if we should fail to discover the art of alluring early childhood to productive labor; for otherwise children would contract habits of idleness, as is the case in the civilized order. Let us analyze with care the method which is to secure the children of association against this defect, and to form in them from infancy a love of useful industry.

SPIRITUAL INCENTIVES TO INDUSTRY ADAPTED TO INFANCY

In the opening of the last chapter, I gave a table of nine spiritual incentives to industry. I will enter into some details in regard to two only; first, I will speak of the seventh, *mimicry* or the *imitative propensity,* which is the transition to all spiritual incentives.

This propensity is common to all children; they wish to imitate what they see done by those older than themselves. It is upon this propensity, which I have termed the *aspiring impulse,* or the desire to follow those next advanced in age, that nearly the entire system of attractive education of the infantile order is to rest.

This propensity is now developed in children as soon as they witness manœuvres that display harmony of action; such as

> Military parades;
> Processions on festival occasions;
> Groups of dancers in the ballet.

Let a hundred young children, selected at random, witness these various performances, and they will be eager to imitate them. For want of guns, each one will get a stick; for a flag, they will fasten a handkerchief to a pole. But if they are supplied with little guns and little flags, we shall see them transported with delight and listening with respectful docility to instructions in regard to their evolutions, which an older child might be pleased to give them. Their attention would be further increased if they could also have a proper uniform and equipage, and if they were allowed little soldier's caps for the drill, and uniforms for procession.

The children will always find in the seristeries for education such toys adapted to the wants of different ages. At first they will get only wooden guns; then, older, they will have little ones of iron; then, in the third degree, those of a larger size. This progressive method will be one of the great incentives to emulation among them.

The young children will at times be assembled for practice in manœuvring. There will be, in the gardens as well as in the edifice, certain points fitted up for their use; and there all the toys and playthings which civilization creates, but without advantage to education, will be turned to account. The young child will there find little wagons and wooden horses; but he must know how to harness his wooden horse before he will be allowed a little wagon, drawn by a dog to work in the vegetable gardens. Progression will be observed in these matters as in everything else, and the child will handle nothing which does not aid in his industrial education.

The supply of costumes and toys, necessary to infant education, should be of three grades at least, and better of five, so that the children may be always taught in divisions and classes, and become early habituated to harmony and dexterity. In the civilized order, the child draws a little wagon awkwardly about all day alone, which will be broken by evening. In the seristeries of the infant order, the use of such playthings will only be allowed when the child has proved itself capable of employing them.

The furnishing of such means of education, which would be an enormous and useless expense for a single family, is for the harmonians the sowing of a precious seed; they find in them the inestimable benefit of alluring the child to industry, and of inspiring it at thirty months of age with a passion for a variety of labors, in which it will become in a brief period sufficiently expert to stand at least three examinations, and secure admission to the class of infantiles; the latter at three years old are already skillful workers, paying at least their support. No advantage can be derived from these stores of infant playthings but by uniting a large number of weanlings, and dividing them into three classes according to age and talent; only the third of these classes, whose average age is thirty-five months, and the second, whose age is thirty months, are admitted to industrial exercises.

How can such a system of collective education be tried in civilization, in which the proper number of children, and the proper graduation of ages cannot be combined, and in which no regular graduation of apartments, costumes and toys is to be found.

It is only with large numbers, distributed into companies, divisions and subdivisions, that emulation can be aroused, and the incentive of graduated privileges, such as decorations and the use of little instruments of industry, be brought to bear.

Their influence is such that from the time the child has

finished its third month in the seristery of the infantiles, its education will proceed spontaneously to its completion, simply through its desire to advance from stage to stage. Rivalries and pride in the success of its groups, will induce it to become acquainted with various details of industry; and preceptors will have nothing more to do than to meet the demand for instruction. The simple desire to advance from the class of applicants to that of novices, and thence to that of graduates, will suffice to inspire the child with the highest ambition in its works and studies. It will require less trouble to enkindle its emulation than to moderate its impatience, or to soothe its chagrin at some error which it will be eager to remedy.

One great advantage of the combined education of association is to neutralize the influence of parents, who flatter the child, defer to its fancies, or seek to communicate to it their tastes—a very frequent cause in civilization of misdirection and perversion. "You wish, then," it will be said, "to take the child away from its natural teacher, who is the father?" I have no wish in the matter; I am no imitator of the sophists, who lay down their foolish caprices for laws of education; who would, for example, plunge a child in winter into cold water in imitation of some usages of antiquity. I seek simply to determine the aims of attraction. Now attraction seeks to guide the child by the *ascending impulse,* or the *deference of inferiors to superiors*—a law the opposite to that which prevails in the family group. The real teachers of the child are the choirs of children, older than itself by six months or a year, who excite its admiration and emulation by their privileges, their uniforms and their exploits.

In the groups which the child frequents, it will be sufficiently criticized by its equals or those a little older. The rebuffs which an awkward child receives on seeking admission to a higher order will inspire it with an emulation and with an energy that would never be called out by the flatteries or excuses of a father or mother. A different rule presides among children; they neither pay compliments nor show mercy. The youngster that has some little skill has no pity for bunglers; on the other hand, the child that has been taunted will neither dare cry nor show

spite before children older than itself, who would laugh at its
vexation and send it away.

After the criticism which the child has received during the
day from its equals, it will matter little that the parents before
retiring to rest amuse themselves with humoring and flattering it,
praising its charms, and telling it that its fellows have been too
harsh. Such talk will produce but little effect. The impression
will have been made. The child, humbled by the taunts of
seven or eight groups which it has frequented during the day,
will not be influenced by the assurances of the parents that the
companions, who have criticized it, are unfeeling and unjust;
the parental praises will pass unheeded. The child, returning the
next day to the infantile groups, will remember only the checks
and rebuffs of the day before; and in the end it will correct the
father of his propensity TO FLATTER AND SPOIL by its redoubled
efforts, proving thereby its consciousness of inferiority.

This art of fascinating and subduing the child by *attractive
authority* is at present entirely unknown. It is well worth the
attention of those who are interested in the study of the methods
of nature; the principal means employed is the *ascending corporate charm, or the charm of associated groups, organized in
ascending grades.*

NOTE

PASSIONAL SUBORDINATION OF CHILDREN.

I here collect and bring together the theoretic proofs bearing
on this thorny problem, and the indications which point to a
solution.

The art of rendering young children of three years docile
through the attractions of pleasure, and what is more, eager to
engage only in useful industry—that would truly be a double
prodigy, one of the magic effects of the combined order.

Let us make the miracle fourfold greater, by inspiring these
same children with enthusiastic attachment to their superiors,
and giving them the faculty of bringing a flattering father back
to reason by showing themselves wiser than he.

"But such children would be celestial beings in a human form!" Yes, truly so, if compared with the young of the civilized order, which are but a demoniac breed, carrying perversity to its climax, and exhibiting the four following marked defects—

Aversion to all useful industry;

Antipathy and disrespect for superiors;

Mischievous combinations to destroy and waste;

Disposition to overreach and blind parents.

Such is the child of civilization, such is the result of our philosophic methods of education.

In education, as in every department of the associative system, let us bear in mind that *if we are wrong at the outset, we shall go further and further astray as we proceed.* Now in education, what is the point of departure? It is the transition period of human life, the early phase of infancy comprising the three classes, nurslings, weanlings, and infantiles. If we discover the art of applying the principle of passional subordination to this first phase, we shall be able afterwards to apply it to the three other phases. The method will be the same for all.

Let us enter, then, with care upon this research for a charm that will lead to industry, and that can be applied to the child as soon as it can go alone. What may be regarded as certain in this matter is that the charm in question can be found only in methods *transcending those of the civilized order, and opposed to them,* since the methods of this order arrive at the opposite result, and inspire the child only with inclinations for mischief and destruction.

Man is the only creature which by natural instinct destroys the work of its kind. A child, as such, is not depraved by the passions of gain or hatred, and yet it makes use of its liberty only to destroy and waste. This single fact is sufficient to prove that there is an inverted action in the passional mechanism, and that in rising from the savage, or brute condition, to the civilized state, the human race has advanced like the crab, in a direction the opposite of its destiny.

Let us go back to the source of the evil, and determine the radical defect of our methods. It is this—they are incapable of creating and applying the principle of natural authority, or the talisman of attraction, which fascinates the child, inspires it with passional docility, and allures it by *pleasure* to industry.

This natural authority assuredly is not that of fathers and mothers; the child makes two slaves of them, which it rules like a tyrant by its cries. The nurse gains its affection only so far as she yields to all its whims. So it is with the grandparents, another couple of slaves, who are its flatterers, and exercise no controlling authority, directing it to industry.

The insubordination of the child presents the same problem as that of the zebra, an animal which seems more rebellious than all others but which is, under *proper conditions,* the most docile of the equine species. In the combined order it will be much tamer than the ass. It will become so docile as to be used for the petty cavalry service of the groups of lyceans (from nine to twelve years of age). But to render it thus docile, it must be fascinated by some talisman of attraction which our usages can create, neither for the animal nor the child. If you can bring that compound charm, which gives rise at once to enthusiasm and affection, to bear upon both, you will see the lion lie down at the feet of Androcles, and the child as docile to the lessons of industry, as was Hercules holding the distaff of Omphale.

Who are more blustering than those bullies that can hardly hold a conversation without boasting in a menacing way of their exploits? Yet these braggadocios are the mildest and most cautious of men in the presence of skillful fencers. Then all their boastings cease; their tone is moderate; they no longer imagine they can terrify the whole world; they recognize all the bystanders as equals and peers.

In such cases we see that characters the most ungovernable apparently become the most tractable when they find their natural counterpoise, an influence which fascinates them and imposes upon them the sway of attraction. I have already remarked that this magic and quite unknown power which is to charm the disobedient child, is nought but its own predilection, its enthusiasm for the choirs and sub-choirs composed of children a little older than itself—from six months to one or two years.

They are the object of its admiration, the class with which it aspires to associate, and whose caprices, examples and impulses it subserviently and eagerly follows. They are its adopted masters; and here we find the natural or attractive educator, in search of whom the brains of philosophers have been vainly racked.

Civilization, instead of affording the child this incentive of emulation, surrounds it with influences that deprave it, as every neighborhood harbors a crowd of impudent and vulgar boys, to whose society it is irresistibly attracted. They incite it only to mischief and to play games dangerous to life and limb; they encourage it in disobedience, in vulgarity of language and manners, and in practicing deception upon parents and teachers. Is it not natural, then, that civilization, which is the source of all manner of evils, should pervert and transform into a social scourge that very instrument which, in association, could direct children from infancy in the paths of usefulness?

In our higher seminaries we see this pernicious influence exerted by the more advanced upon lower classes. The freshman respects those of the class next above his own, and reveres those of a still higher grade. He accepts their decisions as oracles and thinks it an honor to share in their mischievous plots, while he makes sport of the precepts and commands of the heads of the institution, and takes pleasure in disregarding them.

Children will pursue a course directly the reverse in the combined order, in which the choirs and sub-choirs of both sexes, composed of as many as forty children, and the graduated scale of honors and distinctions, will afford incentives to every kind and variety of industry, and for every age.

As things now are, if children turn out mischievous or vicious, the fault lies with the civilized order, which is organized on a system entirely hostile to natural education. God has formed natural characters to suit the organization of the combined order; hence it is that children which are beings in most intimate sympathy with nature, and least imbued with sophistical prejudices, are the first to revolt against an *anti*-natural order, and make use of their liberty only to do mischief.

The end of education, therefore, should be to create for children an industrial charm sufficient to subdue and fascinate them. The instrumentality of fascination is so essential in the system of nature, that it provides even for subversive charms, like that which the serpent employs to stupefy the bird before devouring it.

The treacherous system of civilization is thickly strewn with such subversive charms which allure men at every period of life into all manner of snares—the old man is beset with inheritance hunters, and the young with the seductions of other intriguers. The civilized order affords to every age enticements to evil; whence it follows that the combined order (according to the law of counter-movement) will lavishly provide for every age attractions to good; especially will it richly provide industrial charms for infancy, which, at that age, open the only path to wisdom. The discovery of this instrumentality was the only problem to be solved as regards education; and this at last finds its solution in the *charm produced by choirs of the different ages, organized in ascending grades,* or in the theory of the passional series, contrasted, rivalized, and interlinked.

COROLLARIES IN REGARD TO THE EDUCATION OF EARLY INFANCY

We have not yet touched upon the primary processes of the associative system of education as applied to children under fifteen months; and critics will already be disposed to find fault with the methods of training children recommended for the two succeeding ages.

I must warn impartial readers, then, that the system of associative education cannot be judged by an exposition of parts of the theory; it is a vast organization, in which each result attained springs from the action of the whole, and the reciprocal cooperation of all the parts. No correct judgment can be rendered upon it before the exposition of the four phases shall have been read.

We are investigating a system of education adapted to the

wants and requirements of all mankind—the savage, patriarchal, barbarian and civilized races. I shall treat of the subject in briefer compass than theorists generally employ to develop methods applicable to but a small portion of the civilizees. The theory of Rousseau, for example, is adapted only to families with an income of ten thousand a year—to less than a thousandth part of the human race. These families, however, can make no practical use of his reveries, which were not followed even by himself.

One objection which will be raised is that I attribute to children of three years of age an intelligence and dexterity, or powers of mind and body, which could hardly be expected in a child of six years. It will be refuted, a few pages on, in a chapter on the *compound precocity* of children in the combined order.

Many other objections, and on no better grounds, will also be urged; for example, that the petty labors of such young children are of no value. A great expense is to be incurred, it will be said, in fitting up little workshops and procuring little tools, implements and uniforms adapted to the different ages; but what profit is to result from it? These children will have split out and put up a few bundles of matches and fagots; but what an insignificant achievement! Two adults in an hour would do more of this kind of work than twenty children.

This reasoning is entirely fallacious; these petty labors of children produce in the gross an enormous return, which proceeds from four sources.

1. *A positive material gain*—for children, performing tasks which in civilization are executed by grown persons, do it much better, and with more rapidity. Six children of the younger choirs, seated at an octagonal table constructed for the purpose, will shell a basket of peas in less time than six of our servants, and the sorting of them will be much better done. The kitchens, the workshops, the gardens, the orchards, and the stables will abound in these petty labors which the younger choirs will perform with celerity, and thus at four years of age a child will often be able in such matters to do a day's work of an adult.

2. *A positive spiritual gain*—children will be the charm of an

association by their dexterity, their emulation, their early participation in industry, in the opera, and in ceremonies, and their general regard for good manners, which always accompany industrious habits. This industrial harmony among the children will be a powerful incentive to harmony among the parents; and thus the children will achieve in social polity what multitudes of philosophers and legislators have in vain essayed.

3. *A negative internal advantage*—if industrial habits are formed at the age of three or four years, that precious time will be saved which a youth in the civilized order devotes to his apprenticeship between the ages of fifteen and twenty years, and often without success, for the workmen of the present order are for the most part bunglers; the child in the combined order, becoming dexterous at a very early age, will be, when nine years old, as expert in his work as are performers in legerdemain. A similar dexterity will appear in all the labors of the children of the combined order of that age, and in a still greater degree in those of adults.

4. *A negative external advantage*—by avoiding the waste which children in the present order occasion. I will mention but a single case. When three years old, I was one day left alone in the garden of an ecclesiastic who was attending vespers; it was in a season of the year when the fruit is just formed, and pears, apples and peaches are about the size of hazel-nuts. Arranged in beautiful rows, the garden was full of these trees. I spent half an hour in gathering the young fruit, of which I destroyed a very large quantity. The ground was strewn with them. I brought a large number of them in my apron to the two domestics, my own and one that waited on the priest. At the sight of my fruit gathering they swore roundly, and overwhelmed me with reproaches.

But the two servants were to blame; they had been enjoying themselves over a bottle of wine from the priest's cellar and had left me alone in the garden. Complaining bitterly, they picked up the destroyed fruit and threw it over the wall.

Such are children, untrained to industry and to ideas of order; their instincts tend to destructiveness, even when their intentions are harmless, for I had committed this waste from no malice, but simply for amusement.

This instinct for mischief is a characteristic of all children brought up in our incoherent order. Just yesterday I saw a child busy breaking all the grafts which had just been set in some hundred small trees of a garden; his next exploit was to try to pull up the stocks; I arrived in time to stop him and call a servant. The children of the combined order should be seen at work to form an adequate idea of the incapacity of children in civilization. Averse to every kind of useful industry, they never weary when there is any mischief to be done; they spare neither time nor trouble; it would be no small economy to prevent the waste which children occasion, and avoid the expense of employing persons to restrain their mischievous propensities.

In these petty labors of the youngest choirs, I have pointed out a fourfold advantage to spring from them. I must add a fifth, the pivotal one, which is HEALTH AND A VIGOROUS GROWTH, the result of their industrial occupations, constantly varied, and never excessive. The regular development of the body depends upon this variety of exercises applied to all its parts; it is by such means that the children of the combined order at four years of age will be rendered equal in vigor to those of six years of age in civilization, and in intelligence to those of ten.

As to the labors of the young and the tools and implements they will use, let us recall the rule of progressive adaptation. For example, in ordering the hoes and spades for an association, its founders would doubtless forget that in providing these implements for adults, they would require to be of three sizes, slightly varied, to adapt them to the three grades of adult strength, and that the same rule should be followed in providing implements for childhood, which in every department imitates the industry of mature age. The children, then, will have little hoes and spades of three grades, adapted to the different orders.

A similar gradation should prevail in all the implements of industry; it should be in every sense progressive on a *compound* plan. For illustration, let us take some branch of infantile labor, such as the shelling of peas, beans, etc.

It should be performed by two concurrent processes, and there would be used for this purpose a table of eight sides, with the surface slightly inclined and concave toward the lower edges.

At the upper sides are seated three children, say four years of age, and before them a supply of peas in the pod; as fast as the shelling goes on, the inclination of the table causes the peas to roll down to the lower sides, where sit three children of the next lower choir, whose business it is to sort them. The table is so constructed and placed as to render this process easy.

Suppose three sorts are to be selected for three varieties of culinary preparation. The youngest (thirty months old we will suppose) picks out the large ones, which are easy to lay hold of; the second child, a little older (say thirty-two months) selects those of a middle size; and the eldest child (say thirty-four months) selects the smallest, which are the most difficult to choose. If one of these children performs its work badly, it will be sent away in disgrace; it will not be allowed to take part in the work, and will go complaining to a patriarch to be instructed. Those who execute their task well will be allowed to make a trial on other vegetables, and in the following month can be admitted as novices to the group for sorting vegetables. After admission into three such groups, they will be prepared to enter the order next above.

In this distribution of the six workers, there are two concurrent processes carried on by *competitors of threes*; the order is compound and the method regular, though the two series are restricted to the lowest possible number—three in the group above, and three in the group below. Here is a principle which should be consulted in preparing the tools and implements of the experimental association. I shall renew this advice when I have shown its utility by other examples.

Upon these points more than others I shall be obliged to have recourse to frequent repetitions, and explain in various ways the means of exciting industrial emulation among children.

There prevail so many prejudices in regard to the natural inclinations or impulses of children, and science is so incapable of discerning them, that we need more than one definition to render them intelligible.

I have made use of the following locutions at different times:

Ascending corporate charm;

Imitative corporate progression;

Imitative passional subordination.

These various expressions leave a choice to the reader. Some will prefer one of these expressions, while others another; it is well to repeat under various forms a principle upon which will depend the success of the experiment in association. The organizing of the groups and choirs of children should draw after it that of the parents, and should be completed some three or four months earlier than that of the latter; and therefore this step will be the first to be taken in the work of organization.

The association of the children will be very promptly achieved if the founders and directors of the experimental association are careful not to commit errors in the employment of motives and impulses, and to make a proper use of the principle of emulation, mutual criticism, and authority, which are very improperly employed in the education of children in the present order.

Our methods bearing on these points are entirely defective, because they can neither discover the *impulses* on which to operate, nor organize the children in such choirs or corporations that these impulses can be called forth. They employ, for example, the impulse of friendship when that of ambition should be resorted to; and if they choose the right impulse, they never use it in its proper degree.

To say, for instance, that the child should be drawn to industry by the *ascending corporate charm* is not to assert that the charm can be exercised directly on a child three years old by the choirs of children eight or nine years old. The progressive scale would be violated; the charm would not proceed from the proximate or VICINAL choir. It is only from the choir next above whose members are between four and six that the child of three feels the *emulative impulse,* and the impression of *corporate charm.*

The child's ambitious views never aspire very high; the younger it is, the more limited its aspirations. At three years of age, it will not envy the position of children eight or ten years old; the functions and distinctions of such children would be no stimulus to it. It can be influenced only by the exploits of the next higher choir of children, four or five years of age; they are its gods, and chosen leaders.

The charm, then, which is to influence the child must proceed from the VICINAL choir; the incentive which will attract it to, and delight it with industry, must issue from the choirs *next above in age.* This is a secret which our subtle analysts of human nature have been unable to penetrate.

In strict truth, we should say that the incentive to emulation as adapted to children should be,

An ascending corporate charm—and in its mode of operation, Vicinal, progressive, and fourfold.

Custom forbids the use of expressions so precise and technical; it demands brevity at the expense of completeness.

To understand the operation of industrial charm on education, it will be necessary to study the entire scheme of the associative mechanism, in which all incentives act by graduated impressions in different degrees. To calculate and determine all the branches of the social movement is an immense work, and its multitudinous details can only be explained successively. Before pronouncing on the truth of these details their combined operation as a whole must first be understood. I shall close my examination of the three orders of childhood by exhibiting an application of the principles of progressive and vicinal charm to the youngest order of children—to the nurslings.

The charm should be fourfold, namely,

Compound internal, created by the emulation of children of both sexes, taking part jointly in various branches of industry.

Compound external, created by the influence of two vicinal or contiguous ages—a superior, leading and admonishing; and an inferior, submitting to admonition and guidance.

TSO, II, pp. 131–54

HIGHER EDUCATION

Thus far I have explained the plan of education mainly in reference to the development of the body. The details will be more interesting when we come to consider its application to a period of life in which the culture of the moral nature is to take precedence over the physical. We are now to call into action generous sentiments, giving rise to noble acts of friendship, honor and patriotism—virtues which should reign with full power over the young in the combined order, and which at present are unknown even to adults.

The impulse to great endeavors is to be communicated by the older children—by the choirs of lyceans, gymnasians and juveniles. The example of these choirs is to act attractively upon the three choirs of younger children and induce imitation. I was, of course, obliged to defer the consideration of incentives of a moral character, since these could be imparted only by the example of older children. In considering the first two phases, I found it necessary to treat simply of physical education, of the means of attaining compound wealth—that is, health and industrial skill—the first end toward which the education of the young should be directed, since it is the first focus of attraction.

The child of the combined order will have reached this point by its ninth year; it will have secured vigor of body, with a high degree of dexterity; it will, moreover, possess a sure guarantee of wealth in the skill acquired in the various occupations of the industrial series.

It will then remain to develop the SOUL AND INTELLECT to the same perfection, to enable it to excel in social virtues, and in useful studies.

This is the program of the higher phases of education, which is to apply to the choirs of *lyceans, gymnasians* and *juveniles,* aged from nine to twenty.

A single circumstance will prevent the culture of the mind from being far advanced before the fifteenth or sixteenth year— children can not be instructed in the general system of nature, and the beautiful emblems of physical analogy which pervade it. The choir of juveniles alone can be initiated into such studies; the two choirs of lyceans and gymnasians are necessarily excluded from them; it would be requisite to give them instruction in the details of sexual influences and relations, which, at their age, they would be incompetent to understand; it must, therefore, be deferred.

It will be impossible, then, to explain to children twelve years of age the system of nature, whatever may be their precocity. They will nonetheless, however, enjoy all the instruction they now receive, combined in addition with practice; of this they are deprived in civilization, in which teachers possess but a quarter of the means of instruction provided in the combined order. They lack the theory of universal analogy, of unity of system in nature, which is one-half of education; and with the other half which they possess, they can not combine the practice of industry and its theoretic rules.

In the civilized order, education, then, is limited to the employment of a fourth of its natural resources; and this is a proper reply to those theorists who would make an intellectual prodigy of a child of twelve years, stimulate its precocity to the utmost, and force the growth of the mental powers instead of gradually developing them.

The combined order, avoiding this error, will follow a progressive method of development. It will cultivate—

> The corporeal functions in the first phase;
> The industrial capacities in the second phase;
> The affections of the soul in the third phase;
> The faculties of the mind in the fourth phase.

In accordance with this method, it will not endeavor to engage the child prematurely in the study of the sciences, because premature progress in this direction would render it necessary to disclose before the proper time that system of universal analogy which should be concealed from it until the age of puberty. Let us consider the purpose of the Creator in imposing this limitation upon the intellect of the young.

The Deity must have provided counterpoises against the excesses of each of the passions, particularly those of love, at the period of puberty, when it is so apt to preoccupy the imagination.

In the present state of society, there exists for youth no real counterpoise to the passion of love. The Creator has provided many for the youth of the combined order, among others the cultivation of the intellect by *compound studies*. Such studies will not be entered upon before the passion begins to be felt, and will be hardly less attractive than the passion itself.

At that age, love opens to youth a new passional world; and at that period also, the science of analogy will disclose to it a new scientific world, adapted to the new phase on which it enters, emblems of which will be unfolded by the new science. Other counterpoises, still more powerful, will be brought to bear and will counterbalance the impetuosity of the passion; they will modify, without repressing it, and will give it a salutary direction, consistent with the requirements of honor and social unity.

The effect of these controlling influences will be understood when the theory of the passion of love in all its degrees and that of universal analogy, or the unity of system in nature, are unfolded.

The combined order will not desire precocity in one set of faculties at the expense of another; in the intellectual sphere it will aim simply to cultivate the memory and judgment of the child.

Its memory will be sufficiently disciplined by the multitude of functions in which it will be engaged from attraction, by examining petty details, and by comparing the varieties of the fruits and vegetables it cultivates and their qualities, thus combining with practice theoretical studies.

Its judgment will be trained to accuracy, and continually

disciplined by the test of experience; this result will be attained by connecting its mental exercises with its industrial labors, or reflection with practice.

The child, possessed of these two mental qualifications—a *disciplined memory* and a *methodical judgment*—as well as the two physical advantages—vigor of body and industrial dexterity—will have satisfied the precept of Horace, "a healthy mind in a healthy body"; that is, compound perfection of the mind and compound perfection of the body. These are the four pivots of the *integral* precocity which will be possessed by youth in the combined order.

There will remain one other condition to be fulfilled which is still more important, and which is unknown to the system of education in the civilized order; and that is the development of the *soul of the child,* the moulding of it to the practice of the social virtues, to the sentiments of honor and friendship, to the sacrifice of the individual to the collective interest, to devotion to the cause of God and humanity, or the cause of social unity.

To attain this end will be the object of the corporate bodies whose functions and regulations I am about to describe. To these bodies I will give the name of the JUVENILE LEGION, and the JUVENILE BAND.

Upon these two corporations depends the important work of educating the soul—a work entirely unknown to our civilized methods, which seek only to give an artificial training to the mind, and that at the expense of the bodily health, and very often at the expense of the soul, which present social influences impel to selfishness and deceit, and to pretensions to virtue without the practice.

I always feel an aversion to use the words God and humanity, when addressing an age which has done so much to desecrate them, which has made them a convenient mask for selfishness and hypocrisy—a result inevitable in civilization, which is increasing in open or hidden corruption as it advances from phase to phase, and which will continue to do so until an issue or escape from it is discovered.

TSO, II, pp. 205–8

THE "LITTLE BANDS"

THIRD PHASE OF EDUCATION—THE JUVENILE LEGION

Young souls, hearts that are fresh, exhibit in the exercise of the social virtues, such as friendship, philanthropy and devotion to the collective good, a degree of ardor and disinterestedness which is rarely found in adults, whose training in the world leads them to make at every step compromises with truth and justice.

The combined order will turn to account this tendency in children to generous and devoted deeds; it will know how to employ them in labors from which adults would shrink—labors of an uncleanly and repulsive character.

The disgust which uncleanly and offensive labors excite in the present order is overcome by the incentive of pay; but in an order in which attraction is to be the essential lever of industry, means must be found to secure the execution of such labors from attractive and honorable incentives.

The whole system of industrial attraction would fall to the ground if means were not discovered to connect powerful inducements with the performance of all disgusting and repulsive works, now executed by poor hirelings, who are driven to the task by want. But if the performance of uncleanly and despised works can be secured by inducements sufficiently strong to render their execution voluntary, the performance of those which are difficult and irksome only, without being disgusting, will be all the more easily executed from the same motives.

To attain this end, to secure the execution of uncleanly works, a body or corporation of youthful Decii,[2] who will assume the performance of all uncleanly offices, and render them honorable, must be created. This will by contrast reflect honor on all

[2] A name in harmony for the little horde with historical allusion to a group noted for bravery.—Ed.

services in regard to which attraction is in a measure inoperative.

What tone of manners will exist among this brotherhood of children, devoted from enthusiasm, from the religious and unitary spirit, to the most repulsive employments, such as the removal of filth and the cleaning of sewers? Shall they have those delicate manners of our young fashionables? Certainly not. Their tone and language must comport with the work they have to perform, at least while engaged in it. Hence this youthful fraternity will have its cant terms and brusk manners.

In the education of the combined order, there is a much more important task to be performed than to make learned prodigies of children; the combined order will make them heroes in social virtues, devoted to the support of social unity. Of what avail is it to educate the intellect before training the soul, to initiate children into science before forming them to those habits and customs that fit them for a social order which shall secure the happiness of the entire human race.

The principal support of social unity, the *palladium* of passional harmony will be found in a corporation of industrial Decii, composed of children between the ages of nine and fifteen.

I will explain the organization of this corporation, which I will call the juvenile legion; it will execute a class of labors that will relieve adults from the necessity of engaging in uncleanly and disgusting occupations, and avoid any disgrace being connected with their performance. In the present and following chapters, I shall describe this corporation, and also another forming a contrast to it, to which I will give the name of the juvenile band, whose members will be of about the same age.

These corporations will not, like our present ones, be subject to statutes arbitrarily enacted according to the whims of a founder; they will be governed by laws dictated by attraction, and will have a definite function to perform in maintaining passional harmony and social unity. . . .

Among children under the age of puberty two-thirds of the boys make a sport of rough and uncleanly occupations. They love to wade in the mire, and take a special delight in playing in the dirt. They are self-willed, rude and daring, fond of gross language, and of assuming imperious airs.

Such children, in the orders of lyceans and gymnasians, are to be enrolled in the juvenile legion, whose function it will be to perform, from a sense of honor and a love of daring, every species of filthy and repulsive labor. This corporate body is to be a sort of semi-savage legion, contrasting in its bearing with the refined elegance of the combined order; but in manners alone, however, and not in its sentiments, for it will be animated with the most ardent devotion to the cause of collective friendship and social unity.

The legions will be made up, two-thirds of boys, one-third girls.

The bands, two-thirds of girls, one-third boys.

Each of these two corporations is to be subdivided into three classes, having special functions to perform, and distinguished by special names. For the legions, three rough names are to be chosen; for the bands, as many of a romantic character!

The first class of the legion will take upon itself the performance of all uncleanly and repulsive functions; the second, those of a dangerous or difficult character, such as the pursuit of reptiles, and other services which require dexterity. The third class will participate in the least difficult of both functions.

The female members of the legion will perform such functions as cleaning and preparing for the cooks the lesser animals; also the repulsive services in the kitchens, sleeping apartments and washrooms. . . .

The juvenile legions are devoted and ever ready to serve; they affect an abruptness and a tone of superiority quite unlike the mincing and affected manners with which the education of civilization would imbue children. In contrast with this, we shall find an extreme degree of politeness and refinement characterizing the juvenile bands. . . .

This body of youth is one which is to control the power that rules the world, namely, the power of money. In the devotion of the legions will be found an antidote to cupidity; they will put an end to all discords on questions of interest and secure the preponderance of disinterestedness and unity in all discussions regarding the distribution of profits, which of all others are the most dangerous; because every passion will create discord, if self-interest be not first subdued to order and harmony.

The juvenile legion will combat against cupidity and the power of gold, and compel them to yield to a civic and religious virtue—CHARITY. The philosophers will smile at this assertion. They judge of the resources of the combined order, and measure its means, by their own limited capacities. Doubtless gold would remain master of the field, if that order could oppose to it only their theories. But association will oppose cupidity with substantial virtues. For why should the Creator have inspired us with admiration for virtue, if he had provided no means to insure its development in human society and to secure its ultimate triumph.

CIVIC FUNCTIONS OF THE JUVENILE LEGIONS

The post of the legions is always at that point where any industrial difficulty and repulsion exist; they are a *corps d'élite* in the industrial operations of an association; they concentrate their strength on those points where *industrial attraction* is likely to be wanting.

If aversion to any branch of industry should bring it into disrepute, the series engaged in it would fall into disgrace, and its members would become a class of *pariahs*. Such a result would derange the whole working of the social order—friendship must be general among all the members of association, in order that the most refined and wealthy may have no aversion to share in the labors of the different series. Attraction should, then, extend to all branches of industry, and prevent any from falling into contempt or even declining in general estimation.

Yet there are some which cannot be rendered attractive; for example, the cleaning of privies and sewers. Means must be devised for overcoming an obstacle like this, and in default of *direct* attraction, *indirect* must be sought and applied to all functions, even the meanest.

It may be answered that, according to the law of exceptions the seven-eighths represent the whole, it will suffice that these seven-eighths shall be attractive, and that the one-eighth, which is repulsive, shall be provided for by an increase of pay. That is a principle which may be applied to incomplete associations; but if, in a perfected organization, attraction were inoperative in an eighth of all labors, such a deficiency would bring all menial services into disrepute, and as a consequence domestic labor generally—destroying that friendship, that tie of affection, which should exist between the members, between the served and those who serve.

We must, then, render the performance of the most menial functions—those which excite a *direct* repugnance—an exercise of religious philanthropy; we must counterbalance this repugnance by an *indirect and compound* attraction. To accomplish this will be the aim and function of the juvenile legions.

The first guaranty of attraction in the performance of their labors will be found in the shortness of the periods of their occupation; like those of every other series, their labors will be of short duration, hardly exceeding an hour and a half. . . .

When their work is ended, they go to their ablutions and toilet; then dispersing through the gardens and work-shops till eight o'clock, they return in triumph to breakfast with their colleagues. Each of the legions here receives a crown of oak or thorns, which is affixed to the banner; and after breakfast, they mount on horseback and return to their respective associations.

Among their duties the legions attend to the repair of the highways, that is, they give daily attention to keeping them in proper condition. The highways in the combined order are regarded as *courts of unity;* and, as a consequence, the juvenile legions, as devotees of unitary charity, make it their business to see that the roads are kept neat, and are properly ornamented.

The combined order will be beholden to the pride of the legions to have the roads which traverse the whole country more elegant than the walks of our lawns. They will be adorned with trees and shrubbery, and even with flowers, and the footwalks sprinkled.

If a road shall be in the least injured by any accident, notice will be immediately given, and the legions will proceed at once to make repairs, hoisting a signal flag that passers may not charge the association with having a negligent legion. The association would be liable to a similar charge if any loathsome or venomous reptile were found on its domain, or if the croaking of frogs were to be heard near the highways.

Although the labor of the legions will be more repulsive than any other, on account of the absence of *direct* attraction, the reward they will receive will be less than that of any other series. They would receive nothing, if it were considered honorable in association to receive no remuneration; as it is, they take the smallest dividend allowable; but this does not prevent their members from receiving the highest pay in other branches of labor, if they merit it; but as a body devoted to unitary philanthropy, they make it a rule to hold riches in *indirect* contempt, and to engage with zeal in repulsive functions from a point of honor.

A devotion like this, which will appear to us of little consequence, is the palladium of social unity, as we shall see when we come to treat of the equilibrium of friendship as a social power; this could not be maintained without the assistance of such a corporation.

Preservers of social concord and unity, defenders of the nobility of industry, they are to bruise the serpent's head in a material and a moral sense; and while ridding the fields of reptiles, they will purge society of a poison worse than that of the viper. By their disinterested labors, their self-sacrifice, they will annihilate every germ of cupidity which might disturb the general harmony; and by assuming the burden of uncleanly and repulsive functions, they will extinguish that pride which, by bringing into disrepute any branch of industry, would reestablish the spirit of caste, and destroy general friendship. They know how to employ for the welfare of society that self-denial which is inculcated by Christianity, and that contempt of riches inculcated by philosophy. In fine, they are the promoters of all the social virtues, both in a civil and religious sense.

They are rewarded in return by unbounded honors; the legions will constitute the noblest chivalry of the globe; they will take precedence over all other industrial series, and the highest authorities owe them the first salute. They are everywhere received with regal respect, and at their approach, they are greeted by the dipping of banners and other marks of honor. When in uniform, they are addressed with the greatest courtesy; in the temple, their place is near the altar, and in ceremonies and pageants, they occupy the first rank. . . .

They are always up at three in the morning, cleaning the stables, attending to the domestic animals, and executing any of those uncleanly or repulsive functions to which their corporation is devoted.

They have the general guardianship of the animal kingdom; whoever shall abuse quadrupeds, birds, fish or insect, either by hard usage or by unnecessary cruelty, will be amenable to the tribunal of the legion; and whatever his age may be, he would be brought before this tribunal of children, and treated as inferior in moral sentiment to children themselves; for it will be a rule in the combined order, that whoever shall abuse poor creatures incapable of defending themselves, is to be considered more of a brute than the animal he injures.

Whence this passion for filth in children of this age? Is it a defect of education? Does it arise from a want of moral training? Certainly not, for the more they are lectured about it, the more they practice it. Is it depravity? If so, nature is then herself depraved, for she excites these inclinations in them. If the distribution of attraction is right in all its details, these propensities, considered vicious, must have a useful function, for they are very strong in the majority of children of ten to twelve.

We can not solve this enigma in civilization; but the explanation of it is this—the fondness for dirt and filth is an impulse necessary to induce children to join the juvenile legion, to aid them in bearing with cheerfulness the disgust incident to the performance of uncleanly functions, and to open to them in the discharge of such functions a vast field for unitary philanthropy and industrial glory.

Here, then, as everywhere else, the Creator and Distributor of attraction, in what He has done, has done well; and science would have come to the same conclusion, even before the solution of the problem, had she known how to look beyond the horizon of civilized habits and prejudices, and *had she not believed that nature, in social organization, is limited to means already known*, that is, to the social systems now existing on the earth. The human mind, as yet engrossed with theories and abstractions, or with the details of physical science, has not risen to an investigation of the principles of social science.

The inclination to filth, so common among children, is but an undeveloped germ; it is like a wild fruit; it must be refined by connecting its action with that of the *unitary religious sentiment* and *corporate pride*. Supported by these two impulses, repulsive employments will become attractive sports—the attraction will be INDIRECT and COMPOUND. This condition, explained in the preceding chapter, is secured by the two impulses just mentioned.

In the performance of noxious functions, by which the health of the working classes is not often seriously compromised, the children of the combined order will not expose their own, since they are always engaged for but a short period and are submitted to a purifying process before and after their labors. The legions will be on their feet at three o'clock in the morning, even in mid-winter; but the scene of their labors being a palace, with its covered galleries and corridors, they go to and fro without exposure. They will pass from the main edifice to the stables by underground passages; they will not, then, be exposed to the inclemency of the weather in performing their morning duties. Retiring to rest at eight o'clock in the evening, they will have ample time for sleep; in their labors they will be compelled to violate none of the laws of health.

CORPORATION OF THE JUVENILE BAND; ITS ORGANIZATION

Among children as among adults, nature establishes contrasts of character. Without the principle of contrast, there would be no function for the passion I have termed the EMULATIVE or DISSIDENT, nor for the passional series, which can be organized only by dissidences and rivalries, the germ of which lies in contrasts of tastes.

We are now to study tastes and inclinations, the opposite of those of the juvenile legions described in the preceding chapters. There would be neither regularity nor perfection in the development of a passion if no scope were allowed for the action of its *contrast or counterpoise*.

Thus, however useful the functions of the juvenile legions, their emulation would double in intensity if counterbalanced by the contrasts which nature has provided for it. These contrasts may easily be discovered; let us proceed to the inquiry.

If the majority of boys incline to noise and dirt, the majority of young girls, on the other hand, incline to elegance and refinement. Here is a marked germ of rivalry; we must show how it can be developed and usefully employed.

According to the love of contrast, if boys constitute two-thirds of the legions, girls should constitute two-thirds in the juvenile bands, and the remaining third should be made up of young boys; the latter would be either those young precocious geniuses, like Pascal, that in infancy manifest a decided capacity for study; or those little effeminate fellows, that at nine years of age are already inclined to a life of delicacy and ease.

These two classes of boys will refuse to enter the ranks of the legions, and will join the rival corps, in which girls are in the majority; a corps which is doubtless highly useful, but which does not fulfill a cardinal function in passional equilibrium.

Though the juvenile bands are composed of children between nine and fifteen years of age, they will be so polite and refined in their manners that the boys belonging to them will defer to the lead of the girls, either because the girls will be in a majority of two to one, or because the dominant taste and law of the corporation will be extreme politeness—a tone of manners directly the reverse of that of the legions; the latter will be surpassed by the bands in the arts and sciences and various branches of industry.

This rivalry will be sufficient to create in the little bands a tone of manners quite the opposite of that prevailing in the legions. The difference of manners between the two corps will resemble that existing at present between the military and civilians. The contrast between these will be even more striking.

In short, the juvenile bands will be a group of children as refined and polite as are in the present order the most brilliant circles of our great capitals; but with this refinement will be connected a more estimable quality, the desire to excel in the arts and sciences, especially in agriculture, which is the first of the arts.

In distributing characters, the Creator has observed a fundamental rule, classing them by *strong or major,* and by *mild or minor* shades; this distinction reigns throughout nature—in musical tones which vary from grave to sharp, in colors, from dark to light, and so throughout the entire system of creation.

This contrast which holds good in childhood as well as in other periods of life, will be sufficient to enroll half of the lyceans and gymnasians in the bands, whose services are much less arduous than those of the legions. . . .

If one of these corporations shines in the conquest of material obstacles, the other will excel in spiritual conquests. Thus the bands will excel in studies and in the exercise of the arts and of industry. They will be generally more industrious, except in certain functions, such as equestrian exercises, the management of horses and dogs, hunting and fishing, which are more particularly the employment of the legions; but those animals, the care of which demands skill and patience, such as the zebra and beaver among quadrupeds, and the bee and silk-worm among insects, will be assigned to the bands, who will pride themselves on industrial refinement.

As the female sex furnishes two-thirds of the members of the little bands, their predominating tastes will be feminine, among others that of dress; and this, too, is a passion which the series will turn to account, as it does that of uncleanliness.

We reproach women for their love of ribbons, laces and other finery; and little girls, for loving dolls more than work. This defect, if it be one, will be predominant among the little bands, who will be passionately fond of dress. It will be perceived that this passion for dress, which is often so pernicious in the civilized order, will become the germ of industrial emulation in the series when it is exercised *collectively* in attiring the whole corporation, both males and females.

"Of what use," I hear the moralists and utilitarians exclaim, "are these bodies of children, so elegantly attired, so expensively fitted out? What use all this dress and display? It will not make wheat grow; would it not be better to give children a practical and moral education, to mould them to the simple habits which sound morality inculcates?"

Thus reason the moralists and philosophers, who, with their utilitarian theories, succeed only in repressing or smothering the natural instincts of children, giving to the passions a false development, which in adult age engenders excesses and vices of every kind.

The love of dress among the children of the combined order will lead to corporate sympathies, that is, to sentiments of fraternity and equality. If the little bands are gaily attired, it will be at their own expense, and not at that of others. Now, the daughter of a wealthy father, is finely dressed at the expense of a hundred poor working men whom he has despoiled or oppressed; but in the combined order, she will dress from the fruit of her own industry; and if she makes use of a part of her dividends, accumulated by economy, it will only be to aid in dressing her companions, and in making them partakers of her own happiness. To censure practices so honorable, before knowing to what good results they may lead, is to condemn those virtues which are now so highly praised in theory. . . .

To conclude this subject of the functions of the two corporations we are describing, and the services which they will render to industry, let me say that the legions accomplish in a negative sense what the bands perform in a positive. The former remove the obstacles to harmony; they extinguish the germs of discord, and of that spirit of caste which might spring from repulsive labors. The latter create positive attractions by their ability to organize industrial emulation based on minute differences of quality. Both corporations are highly useful; there can be no equilibrium without the opposition of forces.

Hence the educational system of the combined order, in its third phase, finds means to establish equilibrium between opposite impulses—the taste for uncleanliness on the one hand, and for elegance and display on the other—both of which are condemned by received authorities in the art of education. Have these worthy authorities any knowledge on the subject of passional equilibrium? If they had, could they have failed to observe that every one of the passions in the civilized order is in a false position, working palpably against its own interests, like the charmed bird that flies headlong into the open mouth of the serpent?

God has created no passion without providing for it a counterpoise and a means of equilibrium. I have concisely stated the effect of such a counterpoise in the third phase of education by saying that,

> The legions attain the beautiful by means of the good;
> The bands attain the good by means of the beautiful.

This contrasted action is a universal law of nature. For throughout her whole system we find a balancing of forces by movements direct and inverse, by progression and retrogression, by refraction and reflection, by major and minor modes, by centripetal and centrifugal forces, etc. There is everywhere this direct and inverse action—a principle absolutely unknown in the institutions of civilization, which would train children according to simplistic methods, and yet mould them to different systems of morality, to conform to the prejudices of different castes and classes.

In place of this incongruous and simplistic method, the combined order adopts the contrasted or dualized system, and, in addition, a complete scale in the modes of instruction. It is of no consequence what method the child prefers, provided that at eighteen or twenty years of age, when the education of the combined order is completed, the youth of both sexes shall have been so cultured as to appreciate both the beautiful and the good, the useful and the agreeable—a result impossible to be attained by the present system of instruction. By subjecting the young to one simple and uniform system, it necessarily fails with that half to which it is unsuited, and, as a consequence with the other half which, destitute of the stimulus of competition, will only advance at a slow pace, compared with the progress it might make if aided by the natural method.

The reader will derive no small advantage from the comparison here sketched between the two juvenile corporations, if he has comprehended and can fix in his memory the following theorem—

That the education of the combined order or the equilibrated system, in order to be unitary, must be compound and bicompound in its action; that it must tend simultaneously to the GOOD *and the* BEAUTIFUL, *but by contrasted methods, concurrently employed, and left to the free choice of the child—to the demand of attraction.*

That every deviation from this principle produces in the child a violation and consequent smothering of some of its attractions; the result is that instead of attaining to compound good by a balanced development—direct and indirect—of its instincts, it falls into compound evil from non-development, or false development.

A very novel doctrine is this—one wholly incompatible with our present theories which, in education as in every branch of social art, are miserably incomplete or one-sided, and opposed to nature.

TSO, II, pp. 209–22 *passim*,
pp. 227–30 *passim*, pp. 237–39

SUGGESTIONS FOR FURTHER READING

IN ENGLISH

Frank E. Manuel, *Prophets of Paris* (New York: Harper, 1965).
    The chapter on Fourier is the best short introduction to his
    thought available.
Nicholas V. Riasanovsky, *The Teachings of Charles Fourier* (Berke-
    ley: University of California Press, 1969). The only full study
    of Fourier in English of a scholarly nature.
George Lichtheim, *The Origins of Socialism* (New York: Praeger,
    1969). Places Fourier in the history of socialist thought.

IN FRENCH

Hubert Bourgin, *Fourier* (Paris, 1905). Remains the most compre-
    hensive study of Fourier.
E. Poulat, *Les Cahiers manuscrits de Fourier* (Paris, 1957). A good
    summary of Fourierist scholarship.
M. Leroy, *Histoire des idées sociales en France* (Paris, 1962). Vol. 2.
    An excellent survey of early 19th century thought.
Charles Fourier, *Le Nouveau monde amoureux*. Intro. by S. Debout-
    Oleszkiewicz (Paris: Editions anthropos, 1967). To pursue read-
    ing on Fourier's idea of love.
E. Silberling, *Dictionnaire de sociologie phalanstérienne* (Paris,
    1911). For an extensive index to Fourier's writings.
R. Scherer, *Fourier* (Paris: Seghers, 1970). The best essay on
    Fourier.

Gian Mario Bravo, *Les socialistes avant Marx* (Paris: Maspero, 1970). 3 Vols. An anthology of the utopian socialists.

Michel Butor, *La Rose des Vents: 32 Rhumbs pour C. Fourier* (Paris: Gallemard, 1970.

INDEX